Project Management
the Agile Way

Making it Work in the Enterprise

SECOND EDITION

John C. Goodpasture, PMP

J.ROSS PUBLISHING

Copyright © 2016 by J. Ross Publishing

ISBN-13: 978-1-60427-115-7

Printed and bound in the U.S.A. Printed on acid-free paper.

10 9 8 7 6 5 4 3 2 1

Library of Congress Cataloging-in-Publication Data

Goodpasture, John C., 1943- author.
  Project management the agile way : making it work in the enterprise / by
John C. Goodpasture. — 2nd edition.
    pages cm
  Includes index.
  ISBN 978-1-60427-115-7 (hardcover : alk. paper) 1. Project management.
I. Title.
 HD69.P75G6655 2015
 658.4'04—dc23

                           2015024833

Direct all inquiries to J. Ross Publishing, Inc., 300 S. Pine Island Rd., Suite
305, Plantation, FL 33324.

Phone: (954) 727-9333
Fax: (561) 892-0700
Web: www.jrosspub.com

Dedication

To all my agile students whose commentary and challenges made me a better instructor.

Contents

Preface

An Introduction to the Book

This is a book about agile methodologies, as seen through the looking glass of project management

There are new and challenging ideas in project management, ideas especially suited for managing innovation and technology projects, particularly software projects—projects that put ever increasing complexity in the hands of users and consumers. *Agile* is the umbrella term for what we are talking about:

Agile Means...
• *Agile* means small teams, working collectively and collaboratively, with this mission: • To deliver frequent, incremental releases of innovative functions and features, prioritized for need and affordability; • Evolved iteratively from a vision according to user reflection and feedback; • And produced at the best possible value.[1]

Methodologies

The methodologies included under the agile umbrella go by many names:

- Scrum
- XP (Extreme Programming)
- The Crystal Family
- Kanban

There are others: a rapid application development (RAD) agile variant; Dynamic Systems Development Method; Disciplined Agile Delivery (DAD); Feature-driven Design; Adaptive Software Development; Lean Development; Team Software Process (TSP); and Personal Software Process (PSP).[2] And there are framework systems like SAFe (Scaled Agile Framework) and LeSS (Large Scale Scrum). Before these, there were others that have a longer legacy and had set the stage: Spiral, RUP, JAD, and RAD, to name a few.[3]

The industry did not arrive at agile methods overnight. Over many years the processes to address customer need have been refined—motivated by constant feedback implying that projects and project management methodologies were unreliable for meeting business need. Too many times the wrong thing was de- livered, the right thing was delivered wrongly, or nothing got delivered at all. *The right thing in the right way* seemed to be a minority of project stories.

All agile methods have one common denominator: each, in its own way, addresses the ever-present dilemma encountered when building complex intangible deliverables with user interfaces, to wit: what the customer says they need and want is constantly uncertain. Indeed, the solution often de- fines the requirements—*I'll know it when I see it.*

What agile methods do is empower teams to rapidly respond to a chang- ing requirements landscape and deliver customer value quickly—well within the longer cycles of business and markets. Agile teams work in small chunks of need that can be stabilized over relatively short periods, consulting cus- tomers and users as the solution emerges, releasing product increments fre- quently, and then inviting serious critique after every release.

Many solutions have been offered, and there has been improvement. Feedback and iteration were added to the waterfall,[4] maturity models were introduced to measure and motivate staff and organization, and there was ever-increasing emphasis to be thorough about requirements. Interviews and storyboards, affinity analysis, tracking databases, modeling systems, and a myriad of other tools and frameworks have been introduced to ensure that nothing got dropped along the way.

Now, as more and more projects have intangibles that interact in almost unimaginable combinations, it's all the harder to *get things right*. Much of the past emphasis on improving the art and science of project management has been placed on *doing things the right way*, building quality into project processes and work streams.

Agile Ideas

- Requirements are too important to be left to the beginning; they must be evolved with user interaction and interpretation as all the implications come into view
- Process emerges to fit the circumstances; control metrics are empirically de- termined, not defined by historical performance in the manner of Six Sigma[5]
- Planning is very important, but following the plan is not as important as satis- fying the customer

Do Agile Methods Work?

A motivation for this book was to address these two questions: (1) When faced with unspoken or unknown requirements, is agile the answer? (2) What confidence can a program manager have that good project results can be achieved with agile methods?

And, how applicable are agile methods to large-scale projects, projects with legacy investment to protect, projects saddled with low trust, and projects needing commitment certainty for investors and enterprise managers?

Perhaps there is some reassurance to be drawn from the fact that even Microsoft and IBM are using agile methods on some projects.

The quick-read bottom line on agile methods is that they can work, they do work, they do shorten the schedule, and they do provide a very high quality product.[6] But agile is not a silver bullet; agile methods are not appropriate in all situations, and they only work if the proper environment and management mind-set are committed to the project.

Agile May Be the Answer

Project managers should look seriously at what is happening here. The troublesome shortfalls in performance and customer value—made all the more acute by the rapid business cycles in the web era—motivated some industry innovators to look at the whole thing in an entirely different way. From the product development community, the software engineering community, and the system engineering community, truly imaginative and practical protocols have been devised and put into practice. Agile methods and practices not only apply project talent differently but also reorder the intuitive sequence of project events that has been the mainstay for generations. With the most recent drive to mainstream agile methods, a large number of project professionals are giving these ideas a good look.

The practices you will read about in this book provide new means to collaborate, assign work, and measure results. The customer takes on a different and more near-real-time role as product master; customer participation and accountability are more intertwined in project success. Satisfying the customer is more valued than following a plan prescriptively. Certainly, part of the appeal and recipe for success are attractive opportunities for early benefits and possibilities for self-pay projects. And, agile methods get a jump on customer satisfaction by rolling out value sooner than a traditional sequential method.

The ability to handle changing requirements and to handle them later in the project lifecycle is an advantage of these methodologies. Handling changes later at lower cost flattens the *risk vs. amount-at-stake* curve, and thereby, changes the dynamic for project governance.

	About agile
A project management tip	The agile methodologies described in this book depart in significant ways from traditional project protocols for managing scope, cost, and schedule. Agile is the method of choice when requirements are changing, unknown, or unknowable until seen. Agile methods are best when in situations of fewer than a handful of small teams, typically less than 50 developers. Agile methods work better in-house than through the constraint of a contract; they are not appropriate for firm-fixed price contracting. Agile works better with co-located teams than through the cultural translation and limited communications channel of a virtual team.

Framing the Discussion

For purposes of framing the discussion, four methodologies are featured in this book:

1. *Scrum*: because Scrum is a management framework in the main; it is not prescriptive of actual technical practices—although there are a set of Scrum rules. Scrum is the simplest of the methods and it is perhaps the most popular today.
2. *XP*: because it is a highly disciplined approach with definitive software practices specified. XP—more oriented toward engineering—is less directive about management practices than is Scrum.
3. *The Crystal Family*: because it is the most empathetic methodology, calling itself *people powered*. *Family* recognizes that methods must adapt to scale. The Crystal Family is XP without a strong emphasis on personal discipline and documentation is a little heavier to compensate for less reliance on personal communications.
4. *Kanban*: because it is a very practical and lean workflow management paradigm for software projects.

Who Should Read this Book?

A book for the professional in an enterprise context

This book is written by and for the professional. It is written for experienced project managers, architects, and systems analysts who are comfortable in the classical and traditional methods of project management and now find that they are about to embark on an uncertain journey. Managers, architects, and analysts who read this book will not only find succinct and practical explanations of new and different practices, but will also find tips and advice to integrate and harmonize agile methodologies with those that are more familiar and mainstream.

You should read this book if you are involved with technology projects and programs and you are:

- Seeking awareness of new and alternative methods that are results-oriented
- Looking to improve the value of project management
- Examining alternatives because there has been trouble with other project protocols
- Seeking knowledge because you are assigned to projects using agile methods

The Book by Chapters

The architecture of the book is an emulation of an agile project architecture

This book is similar to the first edition, except for chapters 4 and 12 which are new subjects that have become quite relevant since the original edition. Additionally, the architecture of the second edition has been made more agile-like so that the book somewhat "walks the talk." Think of each chapter as a framework for the backlog (the chapter content is the backlog per se) and, in this second edition, the chapters are divided into modules which are similar to sprints. Each module is self-contained, just like a sprint would be. Each module has a theme, learning objectives, content, and a summary. When you've finished a whole chapter with all its modules, you've executed a "release." That chapter passes into "DONE" status.

Chapter 1 is a quick read of the four methodologies and practices that will be addressed in the body of the book. Subsequent chapters address specific project management topics in the context of agile methods.

Chapter 2 is about the business case. Projects are instruments of strategy for the betterment of the business and its beneficiaries. The agile business case respects and encourages the meld of business-cycle goals with the urgency and importance of customer need. In this chapter, there is discussion about how to efficiently align business case practices with agile methods.

Chapter 3 addresses quality—perhaps one of the most important motivations for adopting agile methods. Quality is not just a matter of being error-free, but is a more holistic concept: fitness to fit, function, and form; commitment to the customer's time frame and fulfillment of their value proposition; fitness to economical use and maintenance; and commitment to stakeholder expectations for business performance.

Chapter 4 discusses the so-called hybrid agile, that is: agile and traditional methods in different work streams but in the same project. Agile hybrid is sometimes called *agile in the waterfall*, since traditional systems are also sometimes called *waterfall* methods.

Chapter 5 is about scope and the means to gather and organize requirements. It addresses the work breakdown structure for agile projects, the means to assess complexity, and the techniques recommended for allocating requirements to releases.

Chapter 6 is guidance about planning the cost and schedule. The place to start planning is the business case; but from that point, planning is about how teams will deliver all the features and functions demanded by the user. The main planning paradigm is the planning wave, divided into time-boxed development cycles.[7]

Chapter 7 is an explanation of estimating cost and schedule in numeric terms. Cost is a roll-up of all the team's efforts, but the total effort is dependent on schedule—how fast the requirements can be transformed to completed product. Cost and schedule depend on the throughput of agile teams. Velocity is the throughput metric commonly applied. Velocity measures the productivity of the project by measuring burn-down rate—the pace of completing product increments.[8]

Chapter 8 is about teams, the centerpiece of the agile method's organization model. Each methodology employs teams a bit differently, but the idea is the same: people working collaboratively in small teams to achieve synergy and collective results is a win-win for all concerned.

Chapter 9 takes up governance. Governance is a good thing if applied with common sense. It creates the opportunity for stakeholder buy-in to evolving scope and delivery timelines. Governance brings resource commitment and provides a stable basis for the project to proceed.

Chapter 10 describes accumulating value and actually managing outcomes. Accumulating value means satisfying the customer, recovering investment, and setting up the benefit stream. Value tracking need not bring a large overhead to the project manager or to the teams. In this chapter we will look at practices that are not only effective, but also efficient in their application.

Chapter 11 provides ideas for scaling-up and for allowing contracts and outsource agreements to become a wrapper for some of the project activities. The fact is that agile methods have been designed around small self-organizing teams. Scaling agile practices to the enterprise level is the challenge discussed in this chapter.

Chapter 12 is about transitioning to agile from a traditional setting. Some of the project management and business management issues are addressed. Also, the customer is often called upon to transition to a different participation protocol than they are normally accustomed to. This customer transition issue is also examined.

Appendix I contains details of four agile methodologies featured in the book. Appendix II is a glossary for terms with unique meanings.

Chapter Endnotes

1. In this book, product base, product, system, deliverable, and outcome are used interchangeably. They all refer to whatever it is that the user or customer owns or uses at the conclusion of the project. The projects applicable to agile methods are software intensive, but may have many, and complex, hardware components. Projects may produce only a software supported process, or they may produce a system or application for internal use, or a system or product for business or consumer. The project may be to make small or large changes to an installed base, called a legacy in this book.

2. TSP, Team Software Process, and PSP, Personal Software Process, are service marks of Carnegie Mellon University.

3. Acronyms in this list are RUP for Rational Unified Process, a product of IBM/Rational, RAD for rapid application development, JAD for joint application development.

4. Waterfall is the name given to a sequential project plan that roughly steps through gather requirements, design the solution, develop and test the solution, and then deliver the outcomes. It gets its name from the appearance on charts of a series of cascading steps. To improve the waterfall sequencing, iteration back to prior steps was added in the 1970s.

5. Six Sigma is a "defined control" methodology consisting of a multi-step problem identification practice and a defect control standard formally stated as requiring less than 3.4 defects outside control limits per million opportunities. The actual control limits are determined by analysis and by historical measurements.

6. For some metric information on the track record of agile projects, see Appendix E, Empirical Information in: Boehm, B. and Turner, R. *Balancing Agility and Discipline*, Addison-Wesley, Boston, 2004, Appendix E.

7. Time-box concepts will be addressed in detail in many parts of the book. However, in a word, a time-box is a preplanned duration for an activity within which time constraint everyone works. Work is either finished or not, at the end of the time-box period; there is no partial credit.

8. Agile methods use some new terms for old concepts. Velocity is the agile word for throughput. It's a measure of how much product the team produces in the period of one iteration.

About the Author

 John C. Goodpasture, PMP, is a program manager, instructor, author, and project consultant who specializes in technology projects.

For many years, he has been one of the instructors for an online distance learning course in agile project management. He was the project director of an E-Business application development unit at Lanier Professional Services, where his team delivered a number of successful projects using agile principles and practices.

He is the author and contributing author of four other technical books in project management, numerous magazine and web journal articles in the field of project management, and has been an invited speaker at many professional project management events.

After graduating with a master's degree in engineering, John was a system engineer and program manager in the U.S. Department of Defense, leading high technology programs. Subsequently, he managed numerous defense software programs while at Harris Corporation in Melbourne, FL., eventually finishing his corporate career as the operations vice president for a document imaging and storage company.

He has coached many technology teams in new product development and functional process improvement, both in the United States and abroad, in industries as diverse as semiconductor manufacturing and retail mortgages.

For more on the subject of project management and agile methods, check out these websites: John blogs at: johngoodpasture.com, and his work products are found in the library at: www.sqpegconsulting.com.

Many of his presentations on agile methods are found at www.slideshare.net/jgoodpas. John maintains a professional profile at www.linkedin.com/in/johngoodpasture.

Web
Added
Value™

This book has free material available for download from the
Web Added Value™ resource center at *www.jrosspub.com*

At J. Ross Publishing we are committed to providing today's professional with practical, hands-on tools that enhance the learning experience and give readers an opportunity to apply what they have learned. That is why we offer free ancillary materials available for download on this book and all participating Web Added Value™ publications. These online resources may include interactive versions of material that appears in the book or supplemental templates, worksheets, models, plans, case studies, proposals, spreadsheets and assessment tools, among other things. Whenever you see the WAV™ symbol in any of our publications, it means bonus materials accompany the book and are available from the Web Added Value Download Resource Center at www.jrosspub.com.

Downloads for *Project Management the Agile Way, 2nd Edition,* include a new discussion and instruction guide that can be customized to meet the needs of the individual trainers or instructors, essay-type answers to critical thinking questions raised in the book, and new white papers.

1

A Quick Read

Agile means getting effective project results even in the swirl of complex and uncertain project requirements, primarily by applying small teams—working collaboratively—to frequently deliver increments of business value with priority according to business effectiveness, importance, and urgency.

> "Almost any methodology can be made to work on some project. Any methodology can manage to fail on some project. Heavy processes can be successful. Light processes are more often successful, and more importantly, the people on those projects credit the success to the lightness of the methodology."
>
> *Alistair Cockburn*

This chapter is a quick read about management principles for agile projects—guidelines for actions and behaviors. Agile is about delivering business value quickly—quicker than needs change in business and market cycles—and about being adaptive and responsive to evolving customer needs and business circumstances.

Serious and compelling issues have motivated many thought leaders to invest their time, energy, and ingenuity toward developing agile values, principles, and practices. They have worked tirelessly to make them useful, and to promote them to project managers, architects, and developers. Perhaps stimulated by the increasing pace of business (especially since the advent of the Internet and all the allied electronic communication capabilities) and perhaps reacting to the frustration of unsatisfactory project results that seem a victim of misunderstood, unknown, or unknowable requirements, untraditional ideas about how to go about high-technology projects have taken root. All share one objective and that is: *To deliver high-quality results that are beneficial to business and customer, even if there is volatility and uncertainty about what the customer needs and wants.*[1]

An agenda for improving the value proposition for the customer is something that no project manager can ignore, and it is an agenda that every project manager can embrace. Partly, improvement comes with better practices made specific to the project; other improvements come from better application of management regimes.

In all agile methodologies, the voice of the customer—in effect, the voice of the value proposition—is heard more often and heard in close proximity to the work results. Since those who read this book are project and program managers, business analysts, and other functional managers, the discussion that follows will look through the lens of management—specifically project management.

This chapter presents these practices comparatively and provides the *Cliffs Notes* for managers to size up these ideas for potential application in their projects.

	Agile methodologies are a management agenda
A project management tip	• The story of agile methods is first a story about management approaches; it is an agenda for a different management framework on which to hang familiar implementation practices • Agile is an agenda that places great trust in individuals • It is an agenda that trades command and control processes and documentation for real-time face-to-face communication • Agile enables managers to direct the maximum portion of project energy and activity towards value-added outcomes, and allows users and end customers a near real-time voice in the specification of value

Module 1: History, Background, and the Manifesto

Seeking a more effective way to deliver on customer and sponsor expectations

Module 1 Objectives

- Familiarize the reader with the motivations that inform agile history
- Inform the reader with the thinking of early agile leaders that led to the Agile Manifesto and the Agile Principles
- Discuss and explain the Agile Manifesto as a call for a shift in dominance of methods and practices
- Discuss and explain the Agile Principles as a modification of the traditional allegiance to plans and process

A Short History Provides Context

The genesis of agile methods was in the product development industry, first in Japan in the 1980s, and more recently in the U.S. software industry. Beset by the confluence of new-to-the-world concepts, software components that were hard to imagine until you saw them, and project cycles that were often longer than business cycles, products were often not meeting expectations. In the face of some unsettling performance, some in the industry set out to think of doing software projects a different way.

Early Thinkers

Some early research into untraditional methods began with two Japanese business research academics who examined product development projects at Honda, as well as at Fuji-Xerox, Cannon, NEC, and Epson in the consumer electronics industry. Hirotaka Takeuchi and Ikujiro Nonaka described their findings in a 1986 *Harvard Business Review* article, "The New Product Development Game."[2]

In that article, they coined the term *Scrum* to describe the behaviors they observed in the businesses they studied. Scrum is a closely knit team formation in rugby that involves the whole team working as a collective. The objective is to move the ball using tactics that are improvised and self-directed by team members in real time. Although software was not Takeuchi-Nonaka's focus, much of what they wrote about is similar to what is now embedded in the software methodology known as Scrum.

From his work done in the early 1990s, Jeff Sutherland is credited in the United States with being the early thought leader behind Scrum. Ken Schwaber became a close associate of Sutherland, and together they drove Scrum forward.

Another thought leader with early experience is Dr. Alistair Cockburn. Cockburn, the inspiration behind the agile method known as the *Crystal Family*, and a prolific writer and thinker in the human and process aspects of software development, had occasion to work with IBM in the early 1990s and to observe the performance of many of IBM's software teams. He was struck by the fact that many of the most successful projects were rogues, in the process sense. The team participants deliberately avoided the approved IBM processes in favor of their own invention. Although not formalized with a named methodology at the time, one characteristic that was common was developers sitting close together and talking to each other about what they were developing. Moreover, he observed that many of the teams that were following the IBM process were continually unsuccessful.

An early agile experimenter was Kent Beck. In the late 1990s, Chrysler engaged Beck and his associates to help with a new software development for its payroll system. By the time Beck, Ward Cunningham, Ron Jefferies, and Martin Fowler arrived on the scene, the project was in trouble—in spite of trying to follow a formal development plan. Not liking what they found, Beck, et al., redid the project successfully—perhaps the first Extreme Programming (XP) project. As one of the earliest industrial projects to use XP, and, as reported in October 1998 in the publication *Distributed Computing*, the C3 Team was very complimentary about the favorable results.

Group of 17

Cockburn, Schawber, and Beck were among 17 who, in 2001, gathered in a resort setting in Snowbird, Utah, with a mission to find common ground among competing and untraditional methods.[3] Although not a close-knit group at the outset, they were able to put together something they were all seeking: a framework they named the *Agile Manifesto*, purposed to guide practitioners of various lightweight methods. At that meeting, they also agreed on the name *agile* as a better representation for what they were promoting. The drafting of the Agile Principles and the founding of the Agile Alliance followed.

Agile Manifesto and Agile Principles Set Up Agile Methods

The Agile Manifesto is a statement of values—of strongly held beliefs—expressed as preferences, not absolutes. Generally, all agile methodologies incorporate the manifesto into their value system, some more than others.

The most important strategic idea is this:

- The manifesto calls for a shift in dominance, priority, and importance from baseline traditional thinking to agile thinking, but not for an outright rejection of the constituents of the traditional methodologies

---

The Agile Manifesto

We are uncovering better ways of developing software by doing it and helping others do it. Through this work we have come to value:

- Individuals and interactions *over* processes and tools
- Working software *over* comprehensive documentation
- Customer collaboration *over* contract negotiation
- Responding to change *over* following a plan

That is, while there is value in the items on the right, **we value the items on the left more.**

Source: www.agilemanifesto.org

Individuals and interactions over processes and tools: This first preference is for personal communications—face-to-face where possible—and recognition of the uniqueness of each individual and the contributions they make, thus different from just staffing and then following a process. While defined processes certainly present a framework for activity, defined processes put situational awareness and responsiveness at risk.

On the other hand, depending on interpersonal communication is an obvious limitation on scope and complexity. There is only so much people can keep in their heads or on whiteboards, even if subdivided into multiple teams. It is self-evident that as the project scales up, documentation must be added to facilitate communications, record decisions and results, document performance, and provide audit trails.

Working software over comprehensive documentation: This value is perhaps better stated as *working product* rather than *working software* since the total product context needs to be considered. The main point is to apply effort where it really helps deliver value. A disproportionate effort applied to writing and updating documentation, rather than developing and updating the product, does not serve the sponsor well.

Customer collaboration over contract negotiation: Collaboration draws the customer into the development in an intimate way. But many customers will not be ready for their required responsibilities, and for many enterprises, close customer proximity will be counter-cultural. Contracts provide a little more distance, but contract negotiations are arm's-length, often adversarial, and difficult to make adaptive. Either way—close collaboration or within the framework of a contract—mentoring and coaching the customer's performance may become a significant project task.

Responding to change over following a plan: A clear point of departure with a plan-driven method is putting a higher priority on satisfying customers—that is, dynamically responding to needs that change with experience—than on following a project plan. *Responding to change* is reactive in tone, but aligns with the XP value to keep product design as simple as possible and not to develop hooks for future capabilities not asked for by customers.[4]

However, the caution is this: oversimplification can damage product cohesion; the forest will be lost in the zeal to focus on pruning trees. Some proactive, heads-up architecture is required to anticipate likely change. The promise of inexpensive opportunities to make changes late may be nullified if holistic system impacts are not considered early.

Agile Principles

Subsequent to the Agile Manifesto, a set of the Agile Principles was drafted. These principles (listed further on in this text) guide specific project implementations by organizations practicing agile methods.

Again, like the Manifesto, there is a strategic intent that informs these principles, to wit: to be agile, there must be a shift in allegiance from the traditional plans and specifications to the value needs and demands of sponsors and customers/users.

In effect, this is a shift in allegiance from input to output, from being measured by how much input is consumed to being measured by how effectively the outputs are produced.

These measurement shifts extend to the performance measures of all project participants, and for many in the project management domain, who are accustomed to being measured by how well consumption conforms to plan (cost, schedule, resources), adopting these principles leads directly to new or modified measurements.

The 12 Agile Principles
1. Our highest priority is to satisfy the customer through early and continuous delivery of valuable software.
2. Welcome changing requirements, even late in development. Agile processes harness change for the customer's competitive advantage.
3. Deliver working software frequently, from a couple of weeks to a couple of months, with a preference to the shorter timescale.
4. Business people and developers must work together daily throughout the project.
5. Build projects around motivated individuals. Give them the environment and support they need and trust them to get the job done.
6. The most efficient and effective method of conveying information to and within a development team is face-to-face conversation.
7. Working software is the primary measure of progress.
8. Agile processes promote sustainable development. The sponsors, developers, and users should be able to maintain a constant pace indefinitely.
9. Continuous attention to technical excellence and good design enhances agility.
10. Simplicity—the art of maximizing the amount of work not done—is essential.
11. The best architectures, requirements, and designs emerge from self-organizing teams.
12. At regular intervals, the team reflects on how to become more effective, then tunes and adjusts its behavior accordingly.

Commentary on the 12 Principles

We maintain that everywhere in the Principles when there is a reference to software, that *software* should be understood to be a surrogate for product or service.

In this book we take the point of view that there are clear limitations to Principle 11, a principle that tells us that the best architecture and design emerge, and that these emerge from self-organizing teams. We believe that, to scale up to complex projects and products, emergent architecture leaves too much to chance. Thus, we say that the architecture must be somewhat stationary, in accord with the strategic intent of the business plan. Of course, any protocol to manage architecture will leave room for details to emerge from one team or another, but strategically architecture is too important to the business case to be left to any one team.

Other Agile Principles

As if 12 principles are not enough, to the 12 Agile Principles we add these:

- Delivering *best-value*—defined as: *delivering the most scope possible—for the available resources—that most optimizes business effectiveness, importance, and responsiveness to urgency*—is always an agile goal
- Agile projects are to be strategically predictable, but tactically emergent and iterative
- Principle 1 is consistent with being simultaneously faithful to the strategic intent of the business case

Module 1—Discussion for Critical Thinking

How do you interpret the Agile Manifesto? Does it call for shifting the importance of one constituent over another, yet retaining all constituents in some proportion; or does it call for a total change in paradigm that all but abandons the traditional constituents?

Module 2: Traditional Lifecycle

Predictable outcomes arising from up-front plans and specifications enforced by change management

Module 2—Objectives

- Familiarize readers with the constituents of the traditional lifecycle

- Introduce the Royce model to show iteration mixed with sequential patterns

Plan-Driven Lifecycle

Most project development lifecycles (PDLCs) have a simple organizing principle: build and deliver the specified outcomes according to a master project plan, a plan that specifies and baselines the scope, quality, budget, and schedule. The lifecycle is usually summarized in a few sequential steps, as illustrated in Figure 1.1. The shorthand for this methodology is often referred to as a *waterfall*, but for reasons explained in the upcoming text, we prefer the label *traditional*.

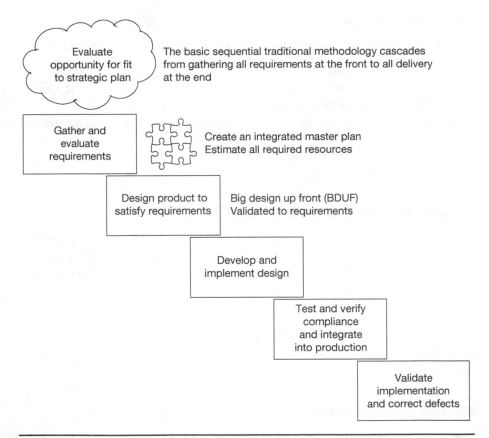

Figure 1.1　Basic traditional sequential methodology

PD-PDLC
• The traditional methodology is *plan-driven,* and our acronym is PD-PDLC.   • Most project managers centrally plan their sequential PDLC, so in this book we link the ideas of sequential waterfall and central planning and label the process the plan-driven PDLC, or PD-PDLC.   • Occasionally we will use other words for the PD-PDLC model, calling it the plan-centric model in order to emphasize the most salient point: *activities are planned and committed to well in advance, not just-in-time.*

Perhaps one of the earliest industry descriptions of the PD-PDLC methodology and the ceremony that surrounds it is found in a well-known paper authored by Winston Royce, originally published by the aerospace firm TRW and presented to the 1970 IEEE WESCON.[5] We refer to Royce's ideas as the *Royce model.* Royce envisioned a project plan of sequential steps, with prototypes and other risk reducing efforts as sidebars to the main project. Requirements are gathered by using structured analysis; feedback and iteration between steps provide checks and balances along the way, thus not really waiting to the end to see if the right thing is being developed the right way. The appendix at the end of this chapter has more information on the Royce model.

Achieving outcomes according to planned predictions and commitments are the motivations for driving the project by the plan. In this regard, the traditional PD-PDLC project is both strategically and tactically predictable and stationary: it doesn't matters when you look at such a project, both strategy and tactics are in constant alignment with the plan.

The idea of plan-driven methodologies is to imagine the needs and requirements at the outset, conduct sufficient analysis—sometimes called *structured analysis*—to flush out all the risks and dependencies, and only then commit to *product design and development.*

Changes to plans and requirements are resisted as a matter of policy and governance. Governance systems are employed to control the impacts of change that could put the whole plan at risk.

Business Opportunity

Plan-driven lifecycles begin with a business opportunity. If a new opportunity is a fit to the business and its strategic plan, sponsors may decide that a project to develop the opportunity's business potential is the next best step. The top-level and visionary requirements are gathered and approved by the business before any serious resources are expended. From the top-level requirements, a risk-adjusted forecast is made for the required resources, technology, environment, and a myriad of other commitments. Benefits are estimated and discounted for uncertainties.

Upon sponsor approval of the business case, the project begins its lifecycle. The integrated master plan for design, development, and test is written and approved up front. Many in the industry dub the plan-driven PDLC as the big design up front (BDUF)—we will call it the PD-PDLC.

Simple and Intuitive

The attractive thing about the sequential plan-driven PDLC is that it is an intuitively natural way of thinking about how to do something. And it fits any technology, industry, or engineering discipline. The plan-driven PDLC is deceptive in its simplicity:

- Start with a vision of what is wanted; then,
- Think of how that is to be done, step-by-step, in a chain of activities set down in a plan.

Each step is allotted resources; each step depends on the results of the prior step in the chain. Each step is done only once. Progress through the lifecycle happens sequentially in a straight line, linearly in system-speak. Timelines are well behaved—they don't spiral about in expanding circles, or double back with iteration.

The traditional has a track record of producing projects of amazing scope with spectacular success, and by stark contrast there is also a track record of many failures and partial successes that continues in the present time. It owes its longevity to its fit to projects of every size and complexity in almost every industry, from the smallest to the largest, and for its natural harmony with most managers' intuition—that complex endeavors must be carefully planned and sequenced.

The traditional acquires its name from the usual way it is presented in a picture as a cascade of steps in sequence, finish-to-start.[6] Look back at Figure 1.1 as a much-simplified view of the traditional.

Note in Figure 1.1 that the steps overlap, thereby relaxing a strict finish-to-start precedence that gates one task into the next. Strict adherence to a gated process is problematic because low priority and inconsequential tasks tend to lag behind. In more sophisticated renderings, feedback from a successor step is applied to the predecessor, allowing for some iteration of the predecessor to correct defects as early as possible.

In another refinement, some product is delivered early, on a fast track. However, even though sometimes incremental and iterative, evolution and emergence are missing. Evolution of the product after requirements are approved is not allowed unless a governance entity steps in and opens the design for change. Emergence of process and technique is also discouraged because emergent procedures are antithetical to maturity models that call for repeatable and predictable procedures.

High Ceremony

Many say about the PD-PDLC that it is a methodology of *high ceremony*, meaning a methodology steeped in process, metrics, and documentation— all formally defined and made into doctrine. The documentation becomes part of the handoff from one step to the next, provides a means to record approvals, and also serves as a record and a history of what happened at each step.

Thereafter, there are—or should be—more processes to maintain documentation with changes and modifications, so that content is always current with the state of the project. These ancillary processes, and others that affect the project, all defined and set down in standards, guides, and plans, are what we mean when we say high ceremony.

Methodologies with high ceremony depend on documentation as a key means to communicate. These projects often run for years, so there must be protection from staff turnover that might result in key information walking out the door. High ceremony discounts, to a degree, the contributions of people as individuals; jobs are defined with the expectation that any qualified person can step in and effectively do the job. Indeed, there need not be high trust when there is high ceremony. In fact, high ceremony is often accompanied by low trust.

High ceremony is intended to foster a predictable outcome, leading to more mature organizations in the sense that, under similar circumstances, nearly identical quality will be produced repeatedly with projects of nearly identical performance.

Role of the Customer in PD-PDLC

The customer is more at arm's length in the plan-driven methodologies, often separated by a contract from the development team. The customer is often quite distributed organizationally and spatially. The many disparate constituents are focused through an administrative channel that does the contracting.

Nevertheless, the customer will often do a lot of homework to prepare for the contract, eliciting requirements from many widespread users; many customers even develop their own prototypes and run their own simulations as pre-contract preparation. After award, it is reasonable to expect that the customer will provide functional guidance and will participate in product validation. Unfortunately, the arm's-length relationship is often adversarial and detractive to the project's purpose.

PD-PDLC *Advantages and Disadvantages*

Table 1.1 provides a summary of the advantages of the plan-centric method.

The downside of PD-PDLC is summarized in Table 1.2. Although the list is shorter than the advantages given in Table 1.1, the disadvantages are profound; in some cases, such as dynamic requirements, the issues are outright showstoppers.

Table 1.1 Plan-driven methodology advantages

• Fits large and very large projects, distributed and outsourced workflow, contracted projects done at a fixed price
• Has the potential for developing exceptional process capability maturity for repeatable and predictable outcomes
• Does not strongly depend on an exceptionally talented workforce
• Upfront structured analysis effectively supports high reliability and mission-critical safety-critical projects, e.g., space shuttle, medical instrumentation, precision robotics
• Easily supports prototyping and other risk reduction preliminary efforts to ascertain feasibility
• Supports bridging to legacy projects, maintenance of a large installed base, and products or systems where incremental capability is an oxymoron; e.g., space shuttle ascent control system
• Lots of tool support
• Large, trained base of practitioners, including contractors and consulting companies
• Supported by universities, certification organizations (e.g., PMI), standards and standards committees
• Enables history databases to support parametric estimating, job-book estimating
• Intuitively simple to understand finish-to-start precedence of easily imagined deliverables
• Handles dependencies among large workforce and many deliverables
• Rich with reporting, as usually implemented
• Supports specification verification and functional validation
• Supports certification and regulatory compliance with robust documentation and repeatable process

Table 1.2 Plan-driven methodology disadvantages

Disadvantages
• Inappropriate where requirements cannot be fixed, or where customer changes are frequent (inside the development or plan-driven cycle)[1]
• Inappropriate for small teams, with fewer than 25 developers, since the cost of process often exceeds the cost of the business deliverables
• Inappropriate where uncertain application overwhelms process discipline, causing continuous re-baselining and re-analysis of earned value forecasts
• Delivery of business value is late in the lifecycle; inappropriate where near-term value is paramount
• Values the plan, although the plan requires constant maintenance to maintain relevancy over long periods.
• Encourages discipline but discourages process inventiveness
• Changes coming late are very expensive to insert, much more costly than the value of the upgrade in many instances
• Heavy, expensive, process and documentation, prone to errors discovered at the end
• Requires high discipline and commitment to maintenance of artifacts of process to keep them relevant and current over a long project lifecycle
• Relies on and requires governance formality
• "Early stage" artifacts have to have a long life, else the end result is wrong

[1]Boehm, B. and Turner, R. *Balancing Agility and Discipline*, Addison-Wesley, Boston, 2004, pg 31: Boehm recommends that requirement changes after requirements baselining should be less than 1% for a successful PD-PDLC project.

Module 2—Discussion for Critical Thinking

With the introduction of the Royce model of structured analysis, prototyping, and feedback to prior steps of the traditional lifecycle, many criticisms of the *waterfall* were answered—yet agile has gained legitimacy, even so. What limitations or issues do you see with the Royce model that might lead you toward a different lifecycle?

Module 3: Agile Lifecycle

Strategically stable, but tactically emergent, iterative, and incremental

Module 3—Objectives

- Familiarize readers with the constituents of the agile lifecycle
- Link the agile manager's agenda with the features of the agile lifecycle

Agile Lifecycle

Agile methods are the antithesis of the PD-PDLC. The Agile PDLC (Ag-PDLC) is strategically aligned with the business case at all times, but the tactical implementation is emergent and sensitive to the demands and priorities as they become apparent throughout the project lifecycle. In this sense, we say:

The agile project is strategically stationary but tactically emergent throughout its lifecycle.

	Agile PDLC, Ag-PDLC
A project management tip	• Outcomes are incrementally planned and specified, built iteratively, and delivered in frequent releases. • Agile projects are governed by a top-level business plan that envisions a product goal, top-level requirements, business milestones, and investment funding pegged to affordability. • Scope and quality, the budget, and the schedule are framed by architecture at the top level in the business plan but the details emerge as the project progresses. • Value accumulates incrementally as outcomes are committed to production. • Customers are allowed to change their minds from one release to the next in order to keep the value proposition ever in alignment with business and market realities.

The Ag-PDLC has three distinguishing characteristics that set it apart from the PD-PDLC:

Emergent: The processes and procedures used by the implementation teams are informed by experience; by the enterprise culture; and by the need to be consistent with any certified protocols. Nonetheless, processes and procedures emerge from the team's analysis of the requirements and tasks. In effect, teams adapt. Process control is achieved empirically by observation and reaction, not by defined process control with error bounds, as in Six Sigma.[7]

Iterative and evolutionary: The Ag-PDLC is a string of development cycles called iterations or sprints. With each iteration, some part of the requirement backlog is put into production and then the backlog is revisited in subsequent iterations until exhausted. The design evolves from iteration to iteration driven by product experience and feedback from customers—the design is iteratively adapted and improved as the backlogs are worked off. Within the framework of the top-level architecture, the customer is allowed to reset priorities, add, delete, and change the backlog according to market and business need.

Incremental: The outcomes of iterations are packaged for release to production as an update to the product base.

To maintain alignment of deliveries with the value proposition in the business case, iterations are relatively short, from about two to three weeks in XP, 30 days in Scrum, to something longer according to circumstances in Crystal and Kanban. Releases are made as frequently as the business can absorb change, but typically no less frequently than a calendar quarter. There are no hard and fast rules; each project sets the agenda with the customer.

An Agile Manager's Agenda

Every PDLC has within it planning, managing, measuring, and accounting for results. In the Ag-PDLC, the project manager's agenda has a few featured elements. All of these elements are geared toward strategic fidelity to the business plan; all of these elements are complimentary to allowing tactical flexibility for handling changing and emergent requirements, demand, priorities, and urgent situations.

What Agile Managers Do

- *Customers:* Coach customers' and end-users' project participation that is near real time and nearly continuous. Many customers require help to be effective in this role and many organizations will have to make cultural adjustments for such customer intimacy.

- *Communications:* Encourage communications that are open, honest, and real time within and among teams. Manage the trade off between documentation and face-to-face discussion and interaction as a means to accurately communicate in a timely fashion.

- *Results:* Maintain a focus on results, not specifically on process and activity. In this respect, value is earned only when a product that serves the customer's need is put in production.

- *People:* Internalize the idea *things are managed; people are led,* a principle embraced by Rear Admiral Grace Hopper (1906-1992), a renowned computer scientist. Motivating and inspiring individuals are central to the success of high-performance teams that depend on individuals collaborating effectively, setting aside competitive secrecy, and attacking only problems.

- *Innovation and technical excellence:* Champion innovation and technical excellence as enablers for successful projects, discriminating products, and satisfied customers.[8] Be the champion for coherent architecture, unassailable quality, and system cohesion as marks of best practices.

Guiding Principles for Agile Managers:

Agile managers are guided by these principles:

Plans are adaptive: Agile projects are not driven from a single plan. There will be a broad-stroke plan in the business case, and there will be other detailed plans that are incremental, iterative, and just-in-time.

Value is the prerogative of customers: The value of requirements is ultimately a judgment by the business and the customer, envisioned in the business case and refined at each iteration.

Schedule and cost are derived: The business case frames the investment and major milestones, but actual costs and schedule are derived from the performance of teams deployed during the course of the project.

Change is embraced and encouraged: Change is not resisted. As a matter of policy and governance, agile practices encourage the end user to maintain the value proposition relevant to the state of the business and current to the market.

Documentation comes after personal interaction: Discourse and debate among individuals is recognized as a valid substitute for many formal documents. Documentation is still important, and acquires more importance with escalating project scale; documentation is just not as important as it is in the PD-PDLC.

Individuals are trusted: The concept of the high-performance team depends on trusting individuals to do the right thing the right way. In this context, doing the right thing means serving the interests of the customer, the project, and themselves while being committed and accountable for the results.

	Agile commitments
A project management tip	• Agile project managers commit to best-value for sponsors, customers, and users. • Total cost and resource consumption are dependent on value delivered, but are limited by investment funds and milestones given in the business plan. • The focus is on product quality in terms of form, fit, feature, and function as directed by customers and end-users. • Stakeholders and managers may have to give up the comfort of outcomes planned and forecast by central planning, but they do not have to give up an expectation for project outcomes consistent with vision, architecture, and the prospect of benefits.

Addressing the Major Risks

Agile methods address the major risks of the traditional methodology that are blamed for poor product quality and poor project performance.

Major Risks as Addressed by Agile

BDUF: Agile makes no attempt to do a big design up front that cannot sustain its relevance for the life of the project, nor is it assumed that complex systems can be fully imagineered by structured analysis at the beginning of the project lifecycle.

Unknown or unknowable requirements: Customers are allowed to add, delete, revise, and reprioritize requirements at the beginning of each iteration, but not during an iteration. This approach creates a piece-wise freeze to stabilize requirements for development.

Customers at arm's length: Customers are included on the development teams and coached for effective participation.

Testing and delivery is all at the end of the project cycle: In XP, test scripts are written as the first step in the development process. Test scripts are the means to document design requirements. Working product is delivered at multiple points in the project lifecycle. Only working product earns value, and only working product is integrated into the product base.

Documentation is not cost effective: Documentation is minimized insofar as instructions to guide development; documentation is replaced by daily collaboration and informal means to communicate: e-mail, instant messages, comments embedded in the product design, story cards, scorecards, and dashboards.

Module 3—Discussion for Critical Thinking

Unlike the PD-PDLC with its guiding plans and specifications, the agile paradigm gives managers considerable latitude to find the best path toward satisfaction of the strategic intent. Can you imagine, however, that some managers are very uncomfortable without the tether to up-front plans and specifications? What do you say to those with that issue?

Module 4: Scaling for Enterprise Agile

Hybrids and more; team network over linear team threads; complex over complicated

Module 4—Objectives

- Establish and explain that agile is scalable and not confined to small projects

- Discuss and explain the hybrid model as a business reality
- Discuss and explain team networks as a tool for scale

Scale: The Definition

Scale means enterprise breadth—functionally touching and impacting widely across the enterprise. Such may not necessarily require a huge code base; conversely, a large code base may not require much in the way of scale, if the enterprise touch is narrowly drawn. A small team working forever can produce a lot of code, but this is not necessarily large scale for our purposes.

Scale drives product architecture to a network of functional nodes from something less relational and more linearly interconnected. Scale introduces complexity, defined as: system performance and functionality not predictable from its constituent parts.

Agile-Traditional Hybrids

The fact is, any project of non-trivial scale is composed of multiple threads, swim lanes, or work breakdown structure activities that are supported by—or are supportive to—software being developed. These activities are most likely plan-driven and handled with traditional methods. With these, agile methods must coexist. The name given to these projects is *hybrid* or agile-traditional hybrid.

Of course, at first examination, having a plan-driven thread or swim lane be dependent upon an emergent or tactically planned development effort seems problematic at best—and simply incompatible and counterproductive at worst.

In fact, it can work if the project is first thought of as strategically stationary. That is, the project defined in the business case is the project being executed. It really doesn't matter when you look at it; strategically it's the same project. This is the essence of *stationary* in time.

That said, the project can be tactically emergent—in effect, agile—so long as it is architected as a number of objects or containers with defined interfaces—the functionality of which are determined first and made sacrosanct. Thus, by honoring interfaces, it is possible to develop the internals of the containers with a choice of methodologies—agile or traditional—and join the efforts like a network with the individual functionalities on the network nodes.

We'll develop this idea more fully in subsequent chapters. However, the principle of strategically stationary while allowing tactical agility is the key to successfully scaling to larger and more functionally complex projects, and to link such projects in a portfolio.

Scale as a Driver

Scale drives the product manager to become more than just one individual; scale may require a product committee or an organization. All manner of enterprise support is engaged. Remote, virtual, and contract practitioners may be drawn in. An existing product code base—if there is one—must be honored, thereby imposing constraints, introducing complexity, and perhaps diluting lean practices.

Scale drives the project team to be a greater-than-ordinary multi-disciplinary organization, involving functional, technical, managerial, and artistic constituents. And, scale drives multiple teams to form team networks to exchange information, maintain coordination, and pass partial product among them.

Module 4—Discussion for Critical Thinking

We assert that scale is a larger issue than just building more code or maintaining a larger code base. This module identified some of the issues and practices that are tools for scale. Can you think of others that are necessary for larger scale in the enterprise?

Module 5: Four Agile Methodologies

Management simplicity, process discipline, personal safety, and measurable progress

Module 5—Objectives

- Discuss and explain representative agile methodologies
- Familiarize readers with agile operations and practices

Representative Agile Methods

As stated in the introduction to the book, among all the agile methods, four methodologies are representative of the points of the compass:

1. Scrum because Scrum is a management framework in the main; it is not prescriptive of actual technical practices.
2. XP because it is a disciplined software engineering approach to agile practices and is less prescriptive than Scrum about management practices.

3. The Crystal Family because it is the most empathetic methodology, calling itself *people powered*. Crystal directly addresses the scalability issue, proposing a ladder of methods with colors as the moniker. Crystal Clear is the single-team program; Crystal Orange is a multi-team scaled-up version.
4. Kanban because it has a practical approach to managing the flow of work with little overhead and flexibility to handle emergent requirements.

All four agile methods share a common idea, which is the main point to grasp:

A common idea and the main point	Agile projects are a sequence of fixed-duration, variable-scope deliveries, each delivery guaranteed by its development team to add value and work as planned, but the planning starts anew after each delivery.

The image that comes to mind, as shown in Figure 1.2, is like a string of freight cars, each the same length, but the cars have varying capacity and functionality, each carload being important and useful to the customer.

Methodologies Compared

A good way to compare the methodologies is by looking at each from the point of view of people, process, and technology. People include stakeholders, sponsors, project managers, and team members that include the customer and end user. Process addresses management, communication, and measurement. Technology is really the technical practices that are main features of the methodology: estimating, developing, and closing.

Tables 1.3, 1.4, and 1.5 provide a comparison of the four agile methodologies from the perspectives of people, process, and technology. More

Each delivery of an agile project is an innovative and valuable feature or function

Figure 1.2   Agile simplified

Table 1.3   Comparison of agile methods—people

	Kanban	Scrum	XP	Crystal
Project management	Coach, coordinator, and facilitator	Scrum master[1]	Coach, coordinator, and facilitator	Project coordinator
Customer	Product master or experts	Product master	Embedded product manager	Business expert
Users	Other embedded functional users			Expert user close at hand and instantly available
Team leaders	From team members according to conventions of the project			
Team members	Highly talented and disposed to collaborative team work		"Whole Team" of all required technical skills[2]	Highly talented and disposed to collaborative team work
Team roles	Architect, lead designer, programmer, tester, writer, users and domain experts, technical experts, system Integrators, Infrastructure experts			
Others	Executives, sponsors, stakeholders			

[1]The three Scrum roles—Scrum master, product master, and the team—are explained in detail in: Schawber, K., *Agile Project Management with SCRUM,* Microsoft Press, Redmond, WA. 2004, Chapters 2, 5, and 8.

[2]Beck, K. with Andres, C. *Extreme Programming Explained—2nd Edition*, Addison-Wesley, Boston, 2005, Chapters 4 and 10.

information about methodology-specific terms, including their definitions, is found in Appendix I (Methodologies) and Appendix II (Glossary).

A Process of Cycles

All agile methodologies are about responsiveness, exercised iteratively. All methods embrace the concept of repeating nested cycles, although the terminology varies from one method to the next.

The building block is the standard day, ideally an eight-hour stint of value-added activity. Each day begins with a team review that is time-boxed—that is, limited to a prescribed time duration—followed by development activity, automated testing, and ideally ends with the day's outcome integrated into the preproduction product base.

Iterations are built up of days, lasting a few weeks at most. In Scrum, the iteration is called a sprint. An iteration is planned as a period during which the team develops a selected backlog of requirements. Once the selection is made, further changes to requirements are not allowed; for development purposes, the requirements are stable during the iteration. The finished deliverables, integrated into the product base at the end of the iteration, comprise a product increment.

Table 1.4 Comparison of agile methods—process

	Kanban	Scrum	XP	Crystal
Rules and doctrine	Agile Manifesto and principles	Agile Manifesto and principles — Scrum Rules[1]	XP values and principles[2] — XP practices[3]	Crystal principles[4] — Teams' rules
Communications	Face-to-face preferred, but allowances for scale — Reasonable documentation to fit scale	Face-to-face preferred, but allowances for scale — Minimum documentation except for user	Face-to-face preferred, but allowances for scale — Minimum documentation except for user	Osmotic Communications[5] — Documents as required to fit scale
Planning	Product vision and architecture Planning session for delivery cycle just-in-time	Product vision Product backlog Planning session for each sprint	Product vision Product backlog Planning session for delivery cycle just-in-time	Product vision and architecture Planning session for delivery cycle just-in-time
Estimating[6]	User stories and relative sizing; correct with experience and feedback		Velocity estimates Planning poker or equivalent	Use cases Delphi method Blitz planning
Delivery cycle	Multiple task cycles per delivery cycle Progress by KANBAN charts	30-day sprint — Releases potentially after every sprint — Progress by burn-down charts	2-3 week iterations — Releases potentially after every iteration but more likely 2-3 iterations per release — Progress by burn-up charts	Short iterations planned by teams — Releases potentially after every iteration but more likely 2-3 iterations per release — Progress by various charts

Measurements[9]	Various charts	Burn-down charts	Burn-up charts	Burn charts Other various charts

[1]Schawber, K. *Agile Project Management with SCRUM*, Microsoft Press, Redmond, WA, 2004, Appendix A.

[2]Beck, K. with Andres, C. *Extreme Programming Explained—2nd Edition*, Addison-Wesley, Boston, 2005, Chapters 4 and 5.

[3]Beck, K. with Andres, C (2005) op. cit. Chapter 7, 9

[4]Cockburn, A. *Crystal Clear—A human-powered methodology for small teams*, Addison-Wesley, Boston, 2005, pp. 19-34.

[5]Osmotic communications refers to communications by osmosis: absorbing information in your immediate vicinity, whether directly or indirectly intended for you. See: Cockburn, A. 2005 op. cit., p. 24.

[6]Several unique terms are used to explain estimating in agile methods. See Chapters 6 and 7, and Appendix I for definitions, explanations, and examples.

[7]Malotaux, N. *Evolutionary Project Management Methods*, Version 1.4b, 2007, retrieved from http://www.malotaux.nl/nrm/Evo/EvoEng.htm June 2009, p. 9.

[8]Malotaux, N. *Time line: getting and keeping control of your project*, Annual Pacific Northwest Software Quality Conference, Portland, OR, 2007 p. 2 and 6.

[9]Burn charts refer to earned value accounting wherein charts of planned and expended effort per deliverable object track progress toward accomplishing all the work. Burn up or burn down refers to working up or down a chart of required objects until the scope is complete.

Table 1.5 Comparison of agile methods—technology practices

	Kanban	Scrum	XP	Crystal
Developing	Work-in-process (WIP) cycles as short sequential cycles System architecture Frequent integration	Daily Scrum meeting 24-hour inspection Time-boxing Sprint backlog Refactoring Frequent integration	Daily stand-up meeting Daily build Time-boxing Test-driven design Pair programming Frequent releases	Crystal techniques and strategies[1] Methodology shaping Short cycles Walking skeleton UML use cases Refactoring Frequent integration
Test and integration	Automated tests Frequent integration Daily builds if possible		Test-driven design Automated tests Frequent integration Daily builds if possible	Automated tests Frequent integration Daily builds if possible
Closing	Reflection and lessons-learned — Frequent releases[2]			Reflection workshops — Frequent releases

[1]Cockburn, A. *Crystal Clear—A human-powered methodology for small teams* Addison-Wesley, Boston, 2005, pp. 46-105.

[2]Beck, K. and Fowler, M. *Planning Extreme Programming*, Addison-Wesley, Boston, 2001, Chapter 17.

One or more iterations build up into a release event. A release is one or more product increments going into production operations for internal or external use.

Releases are planned in waves. A wave is a planning horizon consisting of one or more releases. The planning horizon, typically not more than a few months, is the distance we can see ahead with reasonable vision of the evolving product.

Waves are synchronized with business cycles. The normal business cycles are quarterly, annually, and multi-annually to correspond to tactical results, yearly results, and strategic planning, respectively.

Figure 1.3 illustrates the agile cycles embedded in the longer business cycles of annual plans and strategic planning.

Advantages and Disadvantages of Agile Methods

Tables 1.6 and 1.7 summarize the material on agile methods. In many respects, these attributes are the mirror image of the PD-PDLC tables of advantages and disadvantages.

Agile project cycles are embedded in the longer business cycles of mid-year and annual plans, and the multi-year strategic planning

Many days make a time-boxed iteration
Repetitive iterations make one release
One or more releases are planned as a wave
One or more waves make a project

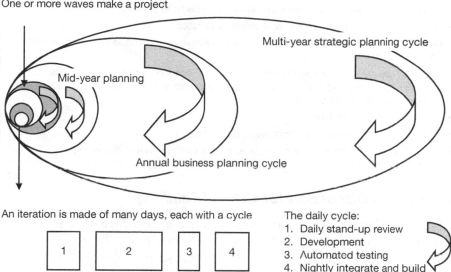

An iteration is made of many days, each with a cycle

| 1 | 2 | 3 | 4 |

The daily cycle:
1. Daily stand-up review
2. Development
3. Automated testing
4. Nightly integrate and build

Figure 1.3 Agile in the business cycle

Table 1.6 Advantages of agile methods

- Rapid and frequent deliveries to production get the benefit stream going early; there is potential for the project to be self-supporting financially.
- Relatively strong commitment to business milestones.
- Efficient adaption to changing customer priorities and requirements keeps the project current and relevant
- Very cost effective for teams of 25 or less developers
- Customers get an influential "seat at the table" to shape the value proposition of the project as it unfolds
- The innovative potential of small teams working collectively only on customer needs is unleashed
- A sense of accomplishment and a cause for celebration and reinforcement is offered at each successful iteration and release
- The project objective is customer-centric and not necessarily bound to a plan that goes out-of-date
- Validation of customer value is built-in and almost automatic by design
- Trust by stakeholder and customer is built with actual deeds

Table 1.7 Disadvantages of agile methods

- Weak commitment to overall scope in terms of tactical details
- Vulnerable to turnover in the team staffing
- Not architecture driven so there may be many dependencies discovered late
- Difficult to scale the small-team dynamics to an enterprise scope project
- Difficult to scale without commitment to documentation
- Difficult to contract the team work because requirements and scope are not known with adequate certainty
- Depends greatly on favorable logistics for team co-location, face-to-face communications, a pool of talented multi-disciplined staff, and instant access to knowledgeable and empowered customers or end users
- Testing is not independent
- Verification is by testing, not traceable to specifications
- High reliability and mission-critical requires strong verification that is missing

Module 5—Discussion for Critical Thinking

All agile methodologies embrace the idea that an effective software project cannot be planned up front for predictable outcomes. Thus, agile practitioners are led naturally to the conclusion that scope is not entirely predictable. What issues do you foresee internalizing this principle and applying it to your situation?

Some Terminology to Make the Reading Easier

In this book we will adopt specific definitions for some of the most important terms and concepts that will be used in the text. We've already used most of the terms already; these and others are defined in the working glossary in the Appendix to this chapter.

Summary and Takeaway Points

In this chapter we have been developing this theme: *Agile means getting effective project results even in the swirl of complex and uncertain project requirements, primarily by applying small teams working collaboratively to deliver increments of business value, with priority according to business effectiveness, importance, and urgency.*

In Module 1, we learn the short history version of agile, which consists of the key organizing meeting in 2001 wherein the Agile Manifesto was drafted. Also from Module 1, we learn not only that there was a manifesto, but that 12 principles were drafted to give operating substance to the manifesto.

In Module 2, we learn that plan-driven methods have their place, particularly on projects of very high scale, safety-critical requirements, mission-critical objectives, and many contract situations. However, they are decidedly inappropriate in a dynamic requirements environment, inappropriate to fast and incremental delivery, and inefficient on smaller projects. The sweet spot for agile projects is teams of less than a few dozen developers where there is high value placed on rapid responsiveness to changing business imperatives, incremental product deliveries are practical and useful, and there is acceptance that responding to customers is more likely a winning strategy than following a plan that may have obsolesced.

In Module 3, we take away the fact that there is still a place for the project manager in agile, though other management roles exist in most of the agile methodologies.

From Module 4, we learn that agile can be scaled to larger projects, and also can exist in a hybrid form with other work streams that are traditionally managed.

In Module 5, we learn that there are many methodologies that subscribe to the Agile Manifesto and the Agile Principles. Each methodology's thought leaders had a particular point of view that set the tone of the method: Scrum is a management method; XP is a set of disciplined practices; Crystal is about making methods habitable by mostly ordinary people; and Kanban is a practical way to manage workflow incrementally.

All of these methodologies fit within a cycle of cycles: the daily cycle → the iteration → the release → the planning wave → the business cycle → the market.

At the end of the day, *agile* is small teams, working collectively and collaboratively, with this mission:

Agile mission	To deliver frequent, incremental releases of innovative functions and features—prioritized for business effectiveness, importance, and urgency—as evolved iteratively from a business case vision according to user reflection and feedback, and produced at the best possible value.

Chapter Appendix

Mr. Winston Royce

Winston Royce was a technologist in the aerospace and defense business in the 1970s. He wrote a seminal paper, entitled *Managing the Development of Large Software Systems*, on the PD-PDLC that ushered in the demise of true waterfall. Royce was actually reporting on his frustrations of delivering working software on time and within budget. While explaining the cascading sequence very clearly in a short ten-page paper, he actually made the case for doing the process differently.

Perhaps prescient of the agile methods to follow some two decades later, Royce starts from the premise that if the project is of a small scale and likely to be locally deployed and maintained, then the project methodology can be just two value-added steps:

1. Analyze the problem
2. Implement the solution

Obviously, such a simple approach is *low ceremony*, but it is also one of high trust and high value. By high value we mean that each step adds materially to the end product. By high trust, we mean that the project team need not provide extensive written proof of what is being done. There is little command and control exercised by project management, and there is little documentation preparation and approval.

If the project is to be of nontrivial scale—that is, not a two-stepper—then Royce perceives certain risks that must be mitigated. Years of experience by the project management community, since Royce made his observations, have not changed the risk picture very much. The principal risks of the traditional PD-PDLC, which are pretty much universally recognized by managers, are given in the following project management tip:

	The principal risks in the traditional PD-PDLC
A project management tip	• The requirements are never complete enough to forestall discovery late in the project lifecycle of latent, unknown, and unknowable requirements. • Documents written early in the lifecycle are always at the risk of being overcome by events and rendered obsolete. • Requirements discovered after baselines are set almost always impact unfavorably. • The testing comes at the end. Testing invariably turns up issues and exposes unsatisfied requirements that should have been addressed much earlier when the cost and impact to project success was more manageable. • Benefits come late and may not materialize because the business and the market have moved on, regardless of the project outcomes.

To combat these risks, Royce argued for more steps early in the process so that there are more opportunities to reveal hidden issues and requirements sooner. These steps came to be known as structured analysis. Royce also strongly advocated feedback and iteration; he also called for a parallel prototyping effort so that the customer would not receive version 1.0 in production. He advocated very elaborate controls and procedures to manage implementation—processes that came to be called governance. And he called for team discipline to abide by the control mechanisms as enforced by project management. Royce was quick to recognize that much of what he advocated would not be perceived as value-added, not by the end customer and perhaps not by the business stakeholders. Few would argue with him.

	Mitigating risks in the traditional methodology
A project management tip	• Iterate between sequential steps and between non-contiguous steps in different phases to feedback errors and omissions for correction. • Be thorough and complete with the gathering of requirements and analysis of system design before any detailed implementation begins. • Incorporate sufficient prototyping and preproduction models so that the customer does not receive the first model of the deliverable. • Develop and maintain robust documentation of everything designed and developed and tested on the project. • Emphasize testing to the point that testing consumes more project resources than any other single activity. • Involve the customer early and often.

Glossary

Table 1.8 Glossary of working terminology

Term	The working definition
Agile methods and practices	Methodologies that are more situational-driven, less centrally managed and more self-managed, with an emphasis on near-continuous responsiveness to customer need. The focus is on the quality of the result, even if the result is not very predictable at the outset and not according to plan. Example: XP (Extreme Programming)
Business	The organization or enterprise that hosts the project. The business may be a governmental unit, non-profit, or a business unit within a larger enterprise. Organization, enterprise, and business are used interchangeably
Customer	The people and organization that are the principal beneficiaries of the project End-users, or users, are customers with detailed functional knowledge Customers may be external or internal to the organization
Knowledge area	A body of knowledge about how to do tasks, or activities, that has a common association. Example: Risk management
Method or Practice	A means of doing a specific activity within a knowledge area. Generally speaking, there are inputs which drive actionable steps, thereby producing outcomes. Example: Monte Carlo simulation of schedule outcome
Methodology	Activities linked to produce an outcome, with the specific methods or practices of each activity identified. In effect, a methodology is a life-cycle of the project, a PDLC as we have described elsewhere. Example: Crystal Clear
Non-traditional methodologies	See agile methods
Practice standard	An agreed upon way of doing a task, where the agreement is managed by a standards body (organization) with credentials in the standards community. Example ISO/IEC 12207 practice standard for software engineering
Process	Like a methodology, activities linked to produce an outcome, although the methods may not be specified. Example: Project initiating process
Product	The intended outcome or deliverables of a project that is useful to a customer and fits the customer's idea of quality in the large sense: feature, function, effective in application, efficient to use, environmentally compatible, and economically operable and supportable throughout a useful lifespan. Product may be tangible or intangible, and it may be a process, system, application, or product for internal or external customers.

Stakeholder	Primarily a business unit or individual that is in the supply chain, or provides some resources to the project, but has no specific commitment to project success. In other words, involved but not committed.
Traditional methodologies	Methodologies that are planned-out at the outset and managed centrally according to the plan to produce outcomes. The emphasis is on predictable results according to the specifications of the plan, a PD-PDLC as we have described elsewhere Example: Waterfall.
User	See Customer

Chapter Endnotes

1. In this book, the words *business, organization,* and *enterprise* are used interchangeably. The words *customer* and *user* are also used interchangeably and refer to the target audience of the project results, whether internal or external.

2. Takeuchi and Nonaka, "The New Product Development Game."

3. Beck, K. with Andres, C. *Extreme Programming Explained—2nd Edition,* Addison-Wesley, Boston, 2005, Chapters 4 and 10.

4. Schawber, K. *Agile Project Management with SCRUM,* Microsoft Press, Redmond, WA, 2004, Appendix A.

5. IEEE WESCON is a western conference of the Institute of Electrical Electronic Engineers (IEEE). See WESCON Technical Papers, vol. 14, (1970), A/1-1 to A/1-9.

6. Finish-to-start is a scheduling precedence taken from the Precedence Diagramming Method (PDM). It means that the finishing activity of a task must be completed before the beginning activity of the successor task can start.

7. Six Sigma is defined in Appendix II (Glossary). Defined process control is a concept from manufacturing, promoted strongly by the work of W. Edwards Deming and others in the post-World War II era. It presumes definable error limits that are acceptable in the finished product, means to measure, and means to correct. See Schawber, K., *Agile Project Management with SCRUM,* 2-4.

8. Highsmith, *Agile Project Management: Creating Innovative Products,* 27.

2

The Agile Business Case

The point of an agile business is to meld business goals and strategy with the urgency and importance of customer need.

> *"Every individual endeavors to employ his capital so that its produce may be of greatest value."*
>
> Adam Smith, The Wealth of Nations

Module 1: The Business Case

Describing the strategic vision of the project; justifying resources; establishing expectations

Module 1—Objectives

- Explain the value-add of a business case as an agile tool
- Make the case for best-value as the optimum project objective

Adding Value with the Business Case

There is always a case to be made for developing a business case, even in the public and nonprofit sectors. The project objective may not be to make money in a business context, but every project envisions some expectation and every project requires resources. Thus there is always an opportunity choice: do this or do that. The choice is explained and justified in the business case.

These points are valid for any project—even the smallest agile project. And, there is a case to be made that the agile business case itself should be agile in spirit and fact. Agile methods do not make the business case unnecessary; indeed, the business case supports and justifies the project as a strategy step toward business goals.

Even if the project is simply to burn down a bug list, the project benefits by imagining and exploring the opportunity and its alternatives—collecting everyone's thoughts in an organized way. Some put process labels on the effort with names like the *Envision* and *Speculate* phases or the *Explore 360* strategy[1]—or, even simpler: *Scoping the project*, Beck and Fowler, *Planning Extreme Programming*, Chapter 9.[2]

The business case is a capture document. It is an interface mechanism between the project and the business and between the decision-maker sponsor, myriad stakeholders, and the project manager. The business case itself should be an example of lean and agile principles: simple, value adding, responsive, and evolutionary.

	Stakeholders focus on outcomes
A project management tip	• The agile-thinking stakeholder has a bias toward outcomes; input and process are a means to achieve goals. • Agile managers forecast the outcomes based on the iteration backlog that is a small, stabilized slice of the project backlog. • Each iteration or delivery cycle produces an increment of product as developed from the iteration backlog.

Three Levels of Business Case

To that end, we define three business-case levels corresponding to business impact:

- *Level 0:* A one-page form for small projects with one team working on the least intrusive projects. Level 0 is approved by a one-step workflow-managed approval process.
- *Level 1:* A simple template for more complex multi-team projects; it is approved in a two-step workflow.
- *Level 2:* For enterprise projects that have significant business implications; Level 2 requires executive approval.

Every project has an impact on the organization; these four sets of questions commonly arise in the business case:

1. Is a project the right approach to obtain what the business needs and wants? Is there an approach other than a project that should be considered?
2. Specifically, why is the proposed project the right project to undertake? Have alternative project choices been examined?
3. Can the project deliver the required business value for the resources available (e.g., time, money, people, and technology)?
4. What are the risks, and how will they be mitigated?

An Agile Business-Case Framework

The business case is a framework to hold content; the content is intended to be adaptable to many situations, and amenable to iteration and evolution as the solution solidifies. The business case begins with a high-level idea from the business, a vision of the expected outcomes, discriminating features, and needed functional capabilities.

At the top level, these intended outcomes are the project scope. The exact solution is value-driven by the end users or customers, rather than plan-driven by sponsors and project management. In Chapter 1, agile projects were characterized as evolutionary—meaning that details evolve over time as customers evaluate each increment delivered to the product base.

There is an anticipated investment and expected payback—financial and otherwise:

- The investment goal is the limit on available funding
- The payback is an anticipated benefit stream tied to the vision
- Investment and payback are linked to milestones
- Milestones establish a timeline and relate expected outcomes and benefits to the calendar as prioritized by value.

Take a look at the framework in Figure 2.1 for an example of the discussion so far. Each business element evolves during the project lifecycle.

Best-value Emerges Tactically, but Is Strategically Anchored

The value proposition of a project is always in the eye of the beholder—business leaders and customers alike—meaning that it's the beneficiaries that bestow value. Ideas about values as beliefs generally come from the top of the enterprise; ideas about value as an opportunity come from all points of the customer base, internal and external.

The framework provides boundaries and limitations to govern project implementation

Framework elements	Business case details (example)
Opportunity	To improve new-orders customer service in a manner that invites repeat business
Goals	Raise customer satisfaction metric by 50% Raise sales from existing customers by 25%
Strategy	Improve the business environment and tools Transfer some order entry functions to the customer
Project vision	An integrated, near-real-time order entry application useable by internal and external customers that reduces order entry time and improves the quality of the entry process
Scope functionality	Web-based application that validates product, price, and customer account Integrates with product catalog and price books
Milestones	M1: Internal order process or capability M2: External customer user capability M3: Automated sales credits
Investment	$1M total, M1: $500K, M2: $300K, M3: $200K
Beneficiaries	Order processors, sales team, billing and credit, external customers
Benefit pay-back	Recover investment with increased sales and reduced operating expenses within two business cycles

Figure 2.1   Business case framework

Best value	*Delivering the most scope possible—for the available resources— that informs business effectiveness, importance, and urgency.*

We hold that a best-value outcome is the optimum outcome for agile projects, and the optimum objective to achieve.

Why so? Especially since best-value may not be:

- The lowest cost (there may be a value-cost trade that favors higher cost for much greater value)
- It may not be the shortest schedule, again thinking of the most advantageous trade off
- It may not be the most scope-deliverable because some envisioned scope may not be economically feasible

It is because best-value is the most likely meld of beliefs, opportunity, capability, and capacity deliverable at an affordable price. Beliefs and business opportunity provide anchoring of the business case; capability and capacity are the means to take advantage of tactical opportunities that emerge.

Imagine a chain with links from the fuzzy front end of opportunity and visionary ideas, through goals, to strategy and operations. Think of opportunity as untapped value that is waiting to be captured and processed into business results. Tapping into opportunity provides the fuel to power projects.

Figure 2.2 illustrates the relationships in the chain from opportunity to goal satisfaction. The chain is shown in the familiar *V* form so that lateral alignments are more apparent. Most organizations pull all this together in a strategic plan.

Strategy and Goals

As commonly practiced, strategic planning sets goals and identifies the means to achieve those goals. The means of achievement is called *strategy*:

> *Strategy is a linked and ordered set of actionable steps that point unambiguously to a goal.*

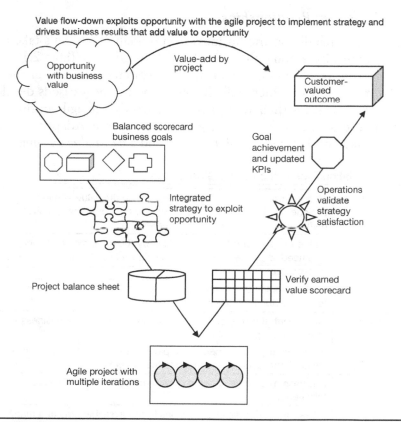

Figure 2.2 Value flow-down

Strategy is a plan for action set in the context of business culture, strengths and weaknesses, and threats and opportunities. The business makes projects part of the action, an element of strategy, and thereby an instrument to achieve goals.

	Projects are valued for their impact on strategy
A project management tip	• Opportunity is where the value is; a project becomes valuable if it can harvest and transform opportunity into business results. • A project's value proposition is derived from the strategy of which it is a part. • Best-value is the most scope that is affordable for the available investment, delivered in priority order, and consistent with the beliefs of the enterprise.

Planning Element Relationships

To get a better handle on the business plan fundamentals, let's take a look at the relationships among planning elements as given in Table 2.1. Notice that there is a lot of entanglement among planning elements in the agile business case, many of which will change as the business case is developed and customers express their wishes. In other words, the agile business case is expected to adapt as the project particulars emerge. Adaptive planning requires a trade off between a *point solution* and a *best-value outcome*.

Table 2.1   Relationships in the agile business case

Customer valued features and function	All the product capabilities that depend on the value and importance assigned by the customer, as evolved with operational experience incrementally over the lifecycle of the project
Scope	All the features and functions valued by the customer, and everything else needed by the project or the business even if there is no direct customer value
Resources	All the people, technology, and environment needed to produce value for the customer in the prescribed time
Investment and funds	Investment: the limit of affordability established by the business as the value of the opportunity Funds: All the money needed to pay for resources but constrained to the limits of affordability, according to the project
Schedule	Business milestones at which time features and functions are incrementally needed
Value	A best fit of features and functions to the available time and funds

The point solution is plan-centric; it has seemingly precise estimates and predictable outcomes, but the track record is often otherwise: estimates and outcomes wind up with distressingly low accuracy and wide variances. On the other hand, the best-value outcome emerges during the project as guided by the strategic direction given in the business case. Beginning with a product vision depicted in the business case, the best-value outcome progressively acquires definition and detail with each release—bound by commitment to customer-driven value and framed by architecture, the business case milestones, and available investment.

Both the business—including by extension, the customer—and the project have rights and responsibilities as they mutually engage in business project planning, as given in the project management tip that follows:

	Rights and responsibilities in the agile business case
A project management tip	• The business has a responsibility to provide a clear business vision. • The business has a right to a best-value response to the business need. • The agile project has a responsibility to be responsive to the value judgments of the business and provide a best-value solution. • The agile project has a responsibility to respect the limitations of funds and the business milestone identified by the business case.

Module 1—Discussion for Critical Thinking

- Some say that a business case is too much process for agile projects; that such an anchoring and documented case for the project is not necessary. Do you—the reader—agree, or not, and why?
- Best-value presumes the delivered scope emerges from the best meld of many business and project factors. Could you justify best-value even when it may not be the lowest cost, shortest schedule, or even the most complete scope?

Module 2: Business Value Models

Putting a context around the agile project to place it within the enterprise culture

Module 2—Objective

- Discuss and explain the applicability to the agile domain of popular business value models

Models for the Business Case

There are two business value models that set up the business cases for agile projects. One is the balanced scorecard that really engages the whole business with coordinated metrics. The other is the Treacy-Wiersema model that is more about describing the source of business value.

Each model, in its own way, helps to put a context around the agile project and to place it within the enterprise culture. In turn, these models then influence the selection of metrics in the agile project business case and their key performance indicator (KPI) quantification.[3]

Balanced Scorecard

The balanced scorecard is a tool invented by Robert Kaplan and David Norton. In the *Harvard Business Review* article entitled "The Balanced Scorecard—Measures that Drive Performance,"[4] Kaplan and Norton described four scoring areas for business value: financial performance, customer perspective, internal business perspective, and learning and innovation perspective.

1. *Financial performance:* This area is plan-driven and may not be agile in all respects. The financial plan has the ability to look forward while serving as a forecast, and to look backward while serving as a record of achievement. Historical data is valued by agile managers as a basis to calculate trends and evaluate risks for a look-forward forecast. The forecast is valued for its heads-up to all managers, to take corrective action to reduce variances and stay within the investment limitation of the agile business case. All projects regardless of methodology must respond to financial performance.

2. *Customer perspective:* Performance indicators in this area measure how well customers are satisfied. Agile projects score well in this space because the customer must be an active project participant. Customers readily contribute to decisions regarding business matters and make themselves readily available to interpret requirements.

3. *Internal business perspective:* In this area are measures of effectiveness and efficiency of internal programs—often referred to as the operational effectiveness (OE) perspective. Effectiveness is about impact—the degree to which a project makes a difference improv-

ing the lot of beneficiaries. OE is valued for bringing efficiencies and greater effectiveness to internal programs.

4. *The innovation and learning perspective:* The performance measures in this area not only gauge how the business is updating its products and services, but also how well the business is developing its human resources. This perspective is valued for the competitive edge it gives the enterprise.

	Balancing the scorecard for agile projects
A project management tip	• Every agile project has the potential to touch all four perspectives of the balanced scorecard. • Customer satisfaction is the primary motivator of agile projects. The Agile Manifesto favors delivering customer value over following a plan. • Financial measures and operational KPIs can be flowed directly into the business case, but plan-driven KPIs will have to be adjusted for agile performance.

Agile and the Balanced Scorecard

In the agile project space, project measures have a different priority and emphasis compared to the traditional project plan. Agile priorities require some adjustment in thinking about what success is and how it is to be measured. From the financial perspective, it is already established that cost and benefits are dependent on the evolutionary value-driven outcomes.

Obviously, there is a big change here; hitting a planned budget gives way to delivering as much scope as the available investment permits. The cost-recovery benefit stream becomes dependent on the choices made by the business and the customer during the course of the project—choices conditioned, in part, on how those chosen outcomes contribute to benefits.

Agile in the Financial Perspective

Every project requires investment. Evaluating an investment opportunity for its funding requirements touches on affordability, payback, and risk. Since there is no point solution to evaluate for cost, agile projects fall back to two parameters:

1. Affordability for the product envisioned in the business case: Affordability—the capacity and willingness to pay—limits the total project expenditures.

2. The likely payback if the imagined product is fully deployed and accepted: Risk colors business confidence about funding requirements.
   Confidence, capacity to pay, and tolerance for uncertainty drive a
   company's willingness to invest. Willingness is an election, a choice
   among affordable and beneficial alternatives.

Payback drives the go/no-go decision. Payback first recovers the investment,
then generates a return on the investment. Ordinarily, the decision policy
is to choose projects according to which provides the best performance
against the balanced scorecard, including investment payback. Without a
payback, no project goes forward. Risk discounts the payback and thereby,
affects willingness. However, in the agile space, early incremental deliveries
reduce risk and increase the value of benefits.

Figure 2.3 diagrams the investment and payback relationships discussed
thus far.

Agile in the Internal Operations Perspective

In the internal perspective, KPIs focus on reducing the friction of internal
processes. Used in this context, friction means the impediments to a smooth
and timely workflow that are not value-added or that detract from efficiency.

Agile teams are self-organizing, require minimum supervision, and communicate in near real time to avoid surprises to managers and sponsors. Operational effectiveness—measured as the ratio cost of value-added work to
the total work—is maximized by minimizing management overhead and

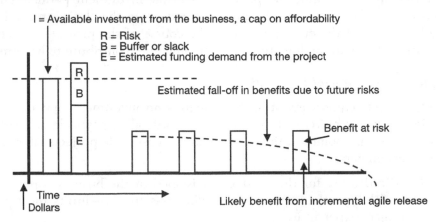

Figure 2.3   Investment and funding

other tasks not directly linked with producing product. Most noticeable is the absence of formal documentation of the kind recommended in IEEE 12207, as discussed in Chapter 1.

Agile in the Customer Perspective

The agile customer relationship is a strong suit. In Scrum, the product master is embedded in the development team. In all agile methods, the customer is available and committed to team participation—to set priorities, interpret requirements, test product, and provide feedback and evaluation. In the short run, this is all directed toward getting the most effective product development; in the longer run, this builds customer investment in the product, which should improve loyalty and satisfaction.

Agile in the Learning and Innovation Perspective

The learning and innovation perspective is target-rich for agile projects. The small teams and multidisciplinary assignments foster learning. Small teams are typically more nimble and more innovative—less risk averse and more likely to pursue unconventional ideas. KPIs to reinforce these behaviors include new feature and function inventions, time-to-market metrics, new product market-share capture rates, and responsiveness to new vision and direction.

Tables 2.2 and 2.3 illustrate the measurement regime of the balanced scorecard as applied to agile projects.

Treacy-Wiersema Model

Michael Treacy and Fred Wiersema described an interesting model of business value in their study, "Customer Intimacy and Other Value Disciplines,"[5]

Table 2.2 Balanced scorecard and agile projects—financial and customer

Perspective	Balanced scorecard values	Agile project measurements
Financial perspective	Earnings after tax on ordinary operations	Incremental deliveries may affect depreciation schedules for capital funds
	Risk-adjusted financial measures net present value (NPV) and economic value added (EVA) for cash flows	Cash flow benefits from early and frequent releases that are less discounted
Customer perspective	Loyalty and satisfaction measures	Customer participation on agile teams should favorably affect adoption rate and trouble and warranty actions post-project
	Revenues by product line and product	Customer participation on agile teams should favorably affect purchasing decisions on the project product

Table 2.3   Balanced scorecard and agile projects—internal and innovation-learning

Perspective	Balanced scorecard values	Agile project measurements
Internal perspective	Operating efficiency measured as throughput/resource unit	Agile teams are benchmarked for throughput
	Operating effectiveness measured as deployment and internalization of quality improvements	Operating effectiveness measured as process improvements driven by feedback, iteration, and reflection on lessons learned after each agile iteration
Innovation-learning	New feature and function added to the product line	New feature and function added to the product line as valued by the customer
	Quality of staff measured as skill diversity and skill achievement	Quality of staff measured as skill diversity and skill achievement on agile teams

which they expanded further in their book, *The Discipline of Market Leaders*.[6] Closely aligned with the balanced scorecard, the Treacy-Wiersema model has three focus areas, each of which are relevant to the agile way of thinking:

1. Customer intimacy—meaning to have insight and understanding, but also to have business-to-business relationships that create efficiencies on both sides
2. Product leadership—meaning product excellence, leading-edge innovation, and discriminators that draw customers
3. Operational excellence—meaning exceptional efficiency and effective processes and procedures that produce business results at the least possible cost

Treacy and Wiersema posit that an enterprise can truly excel in one of these three, developing the culture, mindset, and operating incentives to be the best—but usually this happens at the expense of being ordinary in the others.

	Customer intimacy and other value disciplines
A project management tip	• Project managers can easily adopt agile practices to organizations that share any of the value models described by Michael Treacy and Fred Wiersema.

Organizations that put relationship management foremost as a business value also practice customer intimacy. Companies that are strong in relationship management understand each customer and user individually, but also in context with their larger community. Understanding is translated into nearly instant familiarity when a customer or user calls, logs in, or otherwise comes in contact.

Some organizations make their mark with product excellence and superiority. They have a vision that their products will always be the benchmark. They design with an expectation of an *ah-hah!* reaction from those who appreciate quality in all its dimensions. Obviously, such demand usually supports a price premium, and returns a generous margin.

The third area is operational excellence. Internal processes, methods, and procedures are made as frictionless as possible. Lean thinking prevails. Low expense is the mantra and usually this is passed along to customers as low prices. Every resource is directed toward only the value for which customers are willing to pay.

Tables 2.4, 2.5, and 2.6 provide comparisons of agile values with the value models proposed by Michael Treacy and Fred Wiersema.

Table 2.4 Comparison of agile and Treacy-Wiersema—operational excellence

Value proposition	Agile projects
Focus ruthlessly on operational efficiency	Small, co-located teams that engage face-to-face with little overhead and minimum internal friction
Make easy and convenient for customers to participate in the business	Customers and end users embedded in small teams to state and interpret the business need
Remove barriers to flow—frictionless	Trust the team participants. Reduce the ceremony and formal procedures, including the supporting documentation.
Make processes work across functional and organizational boundaries	Include multi-disciplined members on teams that can address cross functional issues
Minimize overhead costs and pass savings to customers	Trust the team participants. Reduce the ceremony and formal procedures, including the supporting documentation required to measure, control, and track progress
Internally disciplined	Best represented by the XP methodology; assume high discipline as part of trust

Table 2.5   Comparison of agile and Treacy-Wiersema—customer intimacy

Value proposition	Agile projects
Products tailored to individual customers	Customers and end users embedded in small teams to state and interpret the business need
High value placed on customer loyalty—customer for life—and loyalty programs to tailor service	

Table 2.6   Comparison of agile and Treacy-Wiersema—product leadership

Value proposition	Agile projects
Product innovation with leading-edge feature and function	Small, co-located teams that engage face-to-face discussing and experimenting new ideas
Place high value on new ideas no matter the source	
Move ideas through product development to customer very rapidly	Rapid, frequent releases, typically spaced as rapidly as customers, users, and markets can absorb change
Self-cannibalize their own products for something new	Constantly address backlog and reflection for new ideas for innovation and improvement

Module 2—Discussion for Critical Thinking

- If balanced-scorecard thinking informs your project's business case, how might you respond as project manager when planning your project?
- The Treacy-Wiersema model asserts you can't be all things to all people. Assuming your organization subscribes to such a philosophy, how would you see that impacting an agile project where change is accepted—even provoked?

Module 3: Project Balance Sheet

Forming the relationship between business model value, and project model risk and capability

Module 3—Objectives

- Introduce, discuss, and explain the project balance sheet as an agile project tool

- Discuss and explain the value-risk-capability connection between the business case and the project charter

Communicating with the Project Balance Sheet Tool

To move the dialogue from the business value models to a project model, we need common ground. Here is the operating premise: project sponsors and business executives who charter projects are really investors. As investors, they are betting a stake on success. The business case serves a purpose much like a prospectus—forecasting outcomes, estimating inputs, and warning of uncertainties.

Like all investors, sponsors and executives understand that investment benefits come with some risk—and like all investors, they have an attitude about risk that is both institutional and personal. It is summarized in something called *risk tolerance*. Risk tolerance simply means that beyond a point, one more dollar at-risk has a perceived impact to the business equal to many times its face value. If the perceived impact is too large, investment is truncated.

Decision makers with an agile mind-set know that the project proposition is multi-valued. One value set comes from the business leadership who want to transform a perceived opportunity into real strategic value. Alignment with strategy imputes a longer cycle of change. Another value set, less definitive and fuzzier, comes from customers and end users—a phenomenon we call *customer-driven value*. Customer-driven value has these characteristics:

- All within the community may not fully share a common product vision
- Values are more diverse, reflecting the larger population of participants; the voice of the customer is vulnerable to being captured by the most vocal and urgent messenger
- Needs and wants are subject to a more rapid change than the business—and are even self-conflicting among customer groups

The project is successful only if both business and customer community constituents are satisfied. To that end, the project and the business seek alignment of business purpose and project performance. But even in the best of cases, there may be challenges. An alignment gap may remain between project capability and capacity on the one hand, and the value imperatives of the business and the customers on the other.

What to do? The answer is: *take a risk*. How much risk? Only as much risk as is necessary to balance business needs with project abilities.

And who takes this risk? It's the project manager—the ultimate risk manager.[7]

	Balancing business need with project capability
A project management tip	• The project manager is the ultimate risk manager of any imbalance between customer-driven value, business expectations, and project capability, capacity, and feasibility. • The project manager's mission is to manage project resources to deliver a best-value solution—taking measured risks to do so. • In the best of circumstances, the business case provides authority and operational latitude for a best-value solution.

A Framework for Value, Risk, and Capability: Project Balance Sheet

The value models just discussed provide a means for relating a business metric to a project metric. But, they do not directly address how well expectations from the business side align with capacity, capability, and feasibility on the project side. For this task, we can use the *project balance sheet*.[8]

	The project balance sheet is a framework for value, risk, and capability and capacity. Similar to the accounting version, the project balance sheet is a double-entry, two-sided device with three elements that form a balance:
The project balance sheet	1. Value: Business requirements or outcomes, and resources linked to milestones—the left side. 2. Capabilities and capacity: That which is needed to meet the strategic business intent as given in the business case with the allowable resources—the right side. 3. Risk: The risk required to close the gap between value and capability and capacity.

	Measurements reinforce performance
A project management tip	• Measurements are stimulating—in effect a competition to exceed expectations. • The project balance sheet provides the opportunity and means to measure achievement in a framework of expectation and challenge.

Project Balance Sheet as an Agile Management Tool

The project balance sheet implements the balance equation, shown in three forms.

The balance sheet equation	• Everything in the business column *can be mapped to a balancing* entry in the project column. • Everything in the business column *is the driver* for everything in the project column. • Everything in the business column *places limitations and expectations* on everything in the project column.

The balancing equation can now be written:

Balancing expectations	All the customer-driven value and business expectations *are balanced by*: • The project capability and capacity to be responsive to business needs within a set of iterations and releases
Balancing opportunity	All the strategic business vision about the value of an opportunity *is balanced by*: • The project's ability to evolve a product that captures the value envisioned by the business

Figure 2.4 is a pictorial of the project balance sheet. The business is conventionally shown in the left column; the project and balancing risk are shown in the right column. The balance sheet is shown in a way that puts the business in a top-down position and the project in a bottom-up correspondence. Top-down is usually a more qualitative view driven by concept and imagination; bottom-up is more fact based, quantitative, and risk averse— meaning risk attitude reflects actual experience. Fred P. Brooks summed it up nicely when he wrote: "Good judgment comes from experience, and experience comes from bad judgment."

Planning with the Project Balance Sheet

The sponsor's view on the left side is conceptual and value oriented, sometimes oblivious to implementation practicalities, as the project manager understands those. Often the sponsor has no specific understanding of project management, cost and schedule estimating, or risk management and

The project manager accepts risk to balance *resource-scope-schedule-quality* estimates with business expectations.

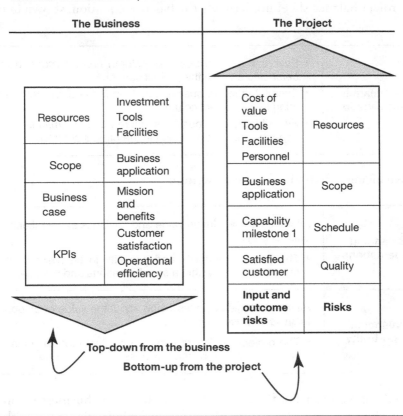

Figure 2.4   The project balance sheet

statistical analysis. The project sponsor sees the project simply as a black box with every detail encapsulated within the project boundaries.

The project manager has the facts and estimates about the project, even if they are only rough estimates in the context of the business case. However, the project manager does not have the sponsor's expert knowledge about the business and markets. A bridge is needed to unambiguously couple the sponsor's imperatives, constraints, and understanding of the project with those of the project manager, so that the business and the project manager are not talking past each other. That bridge is a common vision of scope and a mutual understanding of investment and benefits. Establishing the bridge is a key objective of the business case and the project balance sheet.

Module 3—Discussion for Critical Thinking

- The project balance sheet is a way to illustrate the constant and dynamic tension between the business and the project. In your experience, how might such tension impact the project management office as a primary arbiter of this tension in an agile project?

Module 4: Building the Business Case by Levels

Fitting the tool to the circumstances

Module 4—Objectives

- Discuss and explain that business case detail should be tailored according to potential impact to the business

Building by Levels

The nature of requirements	• Foundational and strategic requirements come from the strategic plan and the balanced scorecard • Situational, customer-driven requirements are only revealed in the course of the project, and are therefore fuzzy for planning purposes

Getting Started on the Business Case

To get started on the right path, answer these framing questions succinctly:
- What is it that brings us all to the table to discuss a new project?
- What is envisioned as the project's mission and scope?
- How will the enterprise and the customer constituencies be better off if the project is successful?
- How will the end state be changed or what goal will be reached?

Add some detail where necessary for understanding and context:

- *Background and context:* Describe what has led up to the opportunity at hand. A review of relevant historical performance is a helpful background. Current operating results are always welcome—examples: functional performance and process metrics, end-user evaluations and other voice-of-the-customer input, warranty or trouble reports, audit reports from across the balanced scorecard, supply chain metrics, and lessons learned from the relevant history of other projects.

- *The project proposal:* Lay out both sides of the project balance sheet. Present the business description of the whole value proposition: outcomes, expected benefits, quality fit, available investment, milestones with business importance, and customer needs. Describe the balance sheet project at a high level: scope, quality, cost, and schedule. The solution need not be too prescriptive but it has to be just enough to be credible. Identify any gaps necessary to balance the left side—include mitigations, if known.
- *Operational results:* Propose a *concept of operations* to describe who does what, day-to-day, in post-project operations with the deliverables. If there are KPIs, list and explain them.
- *Business preparation:* Address business preparation needs that lead up to operations. Any reasonably sized project will require proactive change management and executive buy in; training for users, support staff, and maintainers; sales and marketing plans; rollout and market adoption strategy; beta trials; legacy retirement; and supply chain readiness, among other readiness needs.
- *Ask for approval:* Last, and perhaps most important, ask for an approval decision. An approved case is the project charter and authority to proceed.

Level 0, 1, and 2 Business Case

The business case hierarchy is a three-level pyramid as shown pictorially in Figure 2.5—stacked, not by accuracy of the estimates, but by their impact to the enterprise.

Level 0 attributes:

- The Level 0 business case is driven by a backlog of requirements developed either by the end user, customers, or system operators and maintainers. The backlog requires prioritization by a Level 0 governance process and must fit within a Level 0 funding limitation.
- Items from the backlog need not be just bug fixes, warranty repairs, or other trouble fixes. Requirements could represent new features and functions, but at Level 0, their scope is limited in this way: new functionality or features approved at Level 0 do not materially alter the relationship with the supply chain, customer or user constituents, or other commitments and certifications that may have the force of contracts, compliance, and regulations.

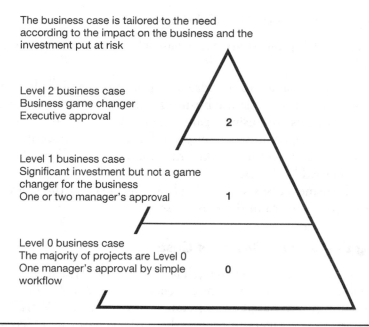

The business case is tailored to the need according to the impact on the business and the investment put at risk

Level 2 business case
Business game changer
Executive approval

2

Level 1 business case
Significant investment but not a game changer for the business
One or two manager's approval

1

Level 0 business case
The majority of projects are Level 0
One manager's approval by simple workflow

0

Figure 2.5 Business case pyramid

- Level 0 is typically approved by simple workflow at a first or second level of management. Level 0 requirements fit within the context of existing systems, processes, and business models.

Level 1 attributes:

- The Level 1 business case is a step-up in complexity; not only of the solution, but also of the impact to the organization, its end users and customers, and perhaps to its regulators, suppliers, and other third party associates.
- There may be, and usually is, more than one business unit involved, thereby complicating the workflow for approval.
- There may have to be approvals from outside auditors, regulators, and certification authorities; supply chain units may need to consult. Technical feasibility may be in doubt. Business-to-business testing and certification of both process and technology may be required.

Opportunities at Level 1 fit these limitations:

- They are not bet-the-business in scope.
- They do not materially alter the business model or the business values.

- They do not cannibalize other business units.

In effect, at Level 1, projects are not a game-changer for the business.
Level 2 attributes:

- The Level 2 business case addresses opportunities of such scope that a project might threaten the business's survival if it is not successful— Level 2 projects are business game changers.
- At Level 2, opportunities may go so far as to introduce a new business model, alter culture in some material way, and affect relationships across a broad landscape.
- Level 2 business cases are nearly always approved at the C level or by the governing board of the enterprise.

Building the Level 0 Business Case

Level 0 is a fill-in-the-form exercise. The information typically provided is given in Table 2.8 and is taken from the checklist in Table 2.7. In the best of cases, the form is web-based and operates with a database. Workflow provides a means for managers to review the business case, attach comments, and render an approval. Sometimes only one approval is required.

Building the Level 1 Business Case

Level 1 is a step up in impact from Level 0. Level 1 usually commands more resources, both in funds and in staff, but also perhaps in tools, environment, and support. The simple form for Level 0 is expanded to encompass Level 1 complexities. These may include impacts on the supply chain, customer or user constituents, or other commitments and certifications that may have the force of contracts, compliance, and regulation. These matters are consequential and require serious consideration and commitment by responsible managers.

Level 1 may affect variable compensation plans, profit and loss (P&L) commitments, and have balance sheet impacts that affect the capital structure of the business. Such impacts may draw in human resources and capital managers.

Table 2.9 is an extension of Table 2.8.

Building the Level 2 Business Case

The Level 2 business case handles all the situations that are not within the scope and authority of Level 0 and Level 1. The protocol for approval invariably involves the executive staff.

Table 2.7 Checklist of business case content

The opportunity and the window of opportunity	The value proposition in business terms, and the optimum timeline to take advantage of the opportunity
The background	What led up to this point?
The solution and the product master	What is proposed to address the opportunity? Who speaks for the solution? Who are the community of product users?
The sponsor	Who is the project sponsor?
Project manager and team	Who are the key participants needed for the project? Project manager, architect, lead designer, lead tester
The benefits from the balanced scorecard	What is the nature of the benefit proposition and how will it be measured? In effect, what is the payback to the project investors?
The beneficiaries	The customers: who is responsible for the value proposition? The stakeholders: who stands to benefit from the organization taking advantage of the opportunity? Who is the community of beneficiaries?
Benefit realization	To whom is the flag passed at project conclusion to follow through on benefit realization?
Limits of affordability	What is the maximum amount available for investment as capital funding and expense funding? To what extent is the project to be self-funding from an early benefit stream? Provide the estimated cash flow requirements and risk discounts. What is the limit of the downside before the project might be canceled to limit losses?
The investment profile	What is the investment over time needed to complete the project?
The known and knowable risks to success	What may impede success? How feasible is the solution?
Business readiness	Who will drive change for the organization? What other organizations are involved: sales, marketing, supply, manufacturing, distribution, warranty support, etc?

Level 2 projects are projects of scale—one small team rarely executes them. Large scale does not rule out agile methods; however, scale complicates all management and technical parameters, disproportionately adding risk. Chapter 11 addresses how to scale agile methods.

Table 2.10 is an extension of Table 2.9.

Module 4—Discussion for Critical Thinking

Can you imagine doing a project funded by other people's money without first stabilizing the conceptual objective and value proposition in a business

Table 2.8 Level 0 business case

Date submitted	Date usually assigned by the system when the form is submitted
Functional or system code	An identifier to place the project in context with the business overall
Description of need	The product vision A narrative of the outcomes and deliverables as functions and features
Estimated benefit and benefit period	Measures from the balanced scorecard or the KPIs of the affected functional users, and the timeline over which the benefits will occur
Reference to backlog or other requirements deck	Typically, a requirements database holds all the bug reports, warranty claims, unsatisfied requirements from prior efforts, and other according to some identifier
Source of need or primary beneficiary	Who makes the case for the need? This person may not be a member of the enterprise. Who is the primary beneficiary?
Requesting authority or sponsor	Who is actually requesting the need? In some organizations, users or external customers cannot submit a business case, so an internal requesting authority is needed.
Reason for a project solution	Why does this need require a project; is there an alternative to address the need by means of routine operations?
Project manager Product master Architect Others	Who are the primary project participants? In effect, the project community or primary team members.
Available funds	Investment available for the project; to be considered a cap on affordability Investment is a dollar-based value judgment by the business about the requested functions and features
Estimated complexity	To be provided by the project as a value judgment
Milestones	Business judgment on the timing of needed functions and features
Related or dependent projects, work orders, or other assumptions	Dependencies that will affect outcomes and assumed conditions that are necessary and sufficient
Training need	An assessment of business readiness requirements to receive and employ outcomes
Certifications, compliance to regulation, or other standards	Identification of constraints on the solution not under the control of the business

Table 2.9   Level 1 business case—additions to level 0

Capital funds needed?	• Capital is used to fund items whose value depreciates with use. In some instances, labor to develop an asset of the organization can be capitalized as part of the cost of acquiring the asset. • Capital funding either for leases or purchases have multi-year impacts on cash flow and P&L expenses. • Beyond some limit, significant capital requirements materially affect the capital structure of the organization, which in turn could affect credit worthiness and borrowing costs.
NPV or EVA calculation required?	• NPV and EVA are a measure of cost and benefit. All the cost and benefit flows are put into a common time period by a calculation technique called "discounting". • Discounting accounts for the value risk in the cash flows of both cost and benefit. • Discounting is usually managed by the organization's finance and accounting office. • Many companies impose a NPV or EVA calculation as a threshold for project approval. • Benefits should exceed costs, or the project should not be approved, at least on financial measures.
Cross-functional business units involved?	• The intra-dependencies among business units may become critical success factors and may affect the critical path of the project[1] • What are the assumptions about behavior and commitment of the involved units? • Does a customer or user team need to be formed?
Contractual changes required with the supply chain?	• Suppliers, dealers, distributors, and others with a relationship to the organization may be affected by a Level 1 project. • Modifying these relationships may be problematic and may be a risk to be identified on the right side of the project balance sheet.
KPI impact to P&Ls of affected business units?	• Many managers have P&L responsibility with a KPI attached. The KPI may affect compensation, promotion, or other success measures in the business. • In some cases, the project outcomes are designed to have beneficial impact to the P&L. KPIs for the affected P&Ls would then be changed.
Compensation changes recommended?	• Compensation is often used to motivate and incent performance on and about the project. • Team members who are drawn from the business to participate in the project and who are commissioned or variably compensated will require some compensation adjustments during their project service.
External threats to success	• Risks not under the control of the enterprise that could impact success. • Typically environmental, regulatory, financing, and certification authorities fit this category.

Upside opportunity not in scope	• Opportunity for upside that is not presently within the scope but is conceivably within grasp given a project's success.
	• Caution: opportunity not within the investment cap and not included in the product vision may violate the agile principle of "simplicity".
Market and sales assumptions	• For products and services for sale, what are the market and sales assumptions that go into the benefit calculation?

[1]The critical path is the longest connected path through a schedule network. Any slip of an activity on the critical path will cause the whole project to slip. Activities on the critical path are not necessarily the most important tasks in the project, but they are the most critical for controlling the project schedule.

Table 2.10   Level 2 business case—addition to level 1

Proposed changes in business model	Changes to the balanced scorecard or the Treacy-Wiersema model
Critical success factors requiring due diligence	Analysis to support major conclusions of the opportunity assessment, benefit stream, and attendant risks
Outside regulators, certifying authorities, and creditors	Identification of authorities who may have a say in the project's success not under the control of the enterprise

case—no matter how informal the presentation of the business case to sponsors?

Summary and Takeaway Points

In this chapter, the main point is: *The agile business case respects and encourages the meld of business cycle goals and strategy with the urgency and importance of customer need.*

From Module 1, we find that the business case adds value to the project narrative; the business case is the top-level linkage between the decision-maker sponsor, stakeholders, executives, and the project manager. It provides just enough information to win approval, and point the direction to the project manager.

The bridge between the business and the project is a common vision of scope and a mutual understanding of investment and benefits. Best value emerges tactically, but within the business case framework of strategic intent.

Keeping score by one means or another is the takeaway in Module 2. Two main scoring models are described: balanced scorecard and the Treacy-Wiersema model.

From Module 3, we learn that the project balance sheet compares the goals and strategy from the business with the project risks and capabilities that provide customers with important value in a timely fashion. The business case is simply the documentation of these facts and estimates, augmented with other information as the circumstances require.

As described in Module 4, the agile business case is designed to be consistent with Agile Principles: it is simple, timely, responsive to business and project need, and is open to adjustment as the value proposition evolves.

In its simplest form, the Level 0 business case is a one-page form that documents the envisioned product, the metrics from the balanced scorecard, and the project estimates. Level 0 is usually approved by a single decision maker.

Level 1 and 2 business cases are more robust, reflecting the greater impact on the business.

In the end, the business case is the setup for an agile response to customer need: a project responsive to an evolving need, early to production with beneficial product increments, and overall a best-value mix of cost and benefits.

Chapter Endnotes

1. Envision and Speculate are the first two of five phases proposed by Jim Highsmith. The remaining three are Explore (to develop), Adapt (to reflect on feedback), and Close. See: Highsmith, *Agile Project Management*, 81-82; Explore 360 is a strategy proposed by Alistair Cockburn in Crystal Clear. See Cockburn, *Crystal Clear*, 46.

2. Beck and Fowler, *Planning Extreme Programming*, Chapter 9.

3. Key performance indicator (KPI) is a metric used by organizations to measure the performance of business units and individuals against certain benchmarks. Compensation is often based on achievement of the KPI results.

4. Kaplan and Norton, *The Balanced Scorecard*, 71-80.

5. Treacy and Wiersema, *Customer Intimacy and Other Value Disciplines*, 84-93.

6. Treacy and Wiersema, *The Discipline of Market Leaders*.

7. Goodpasture, *Managing Projects for Value*, 31, 46.

8. Ibid., 40-45.

This book has free material available for download from the
Web Added Value™ resource center at *www.jrosspub.com*

3

Quality in the Agile Space

Quality is a nonnegotiable value. Quality is about making the customer ever more successful and about delivering more business benefits than the invested commitment.

> Quality is never an accident; it is always the result of high intention, sincere effort, intelligent direction, and skillful execution; it represents the wise choice of many alternatives.

> William A. Foster

In this chapter, we address quality as an influence on the outcomes of agile projects. Many quality movements have come along over the years, but none have actually disappeared entirely. The best ideas have adapted and conformed to modern practice.

When we think of enterprise projects and quality, we are immediately drawn to a myriad of quality models: scientific management, total quality management, zero defects, the Juran Trilogy, continuous improvement, quality function deployment, quality circles, defined process control, Six Sigma, plan-do-check-act, and others.

The question for us as we consider *agile* is this: are these enterprise models of use in the agile project? Actually, the answer is yes, for this simple reason: *customers and markets are very much in command of the quality agenda*, and those models address customer and market quality expectations. Quality control (an early quality idea) morphed into quality assurance—and quality assurance has morphed into market-driven and customer-driven quality expectations. This is where we find ourselves today.

Module 1: Quality Values and Principles

Best value is deeply satisfying

Module 1—Objectives

- Explain and discuss quality as both a value and an objective
- Explain and discuss the dominance of quality over cost and schedule

Quality: Values, Principles, and Practices

To begin, quality is a value; values are ideas we believe in and care about. Things of value are things for which we are willing to work and pay. Indeed, in another chapter, we will address the cost-of-value as a synonym for budget. And so it is with quality—it is that which we are willing to pay and invest to achieve and obtain. Though quality is a relentless goal of agile projects, most agree that quality is hard to define—indeed, for many, quality is one of those things that we know when we see it.

Quality makes its appearance to customers with project outcomes; thus, we think of quality as an outcome objective. As such, quality as an outcome objective is quite different from cost, schedule, and other resources, the control of which are input objectives. Following the paradigm of the Agile Manifesto, agile practitioners put more weight on achieving quality outcomes than adhering to an input resource plan—cost and schedule, etc. In this sense, agile projects are dominated by the shift of allegiance from *the input plan* to *making good on quality promises*.

Quality is inextricably linked with price through value. When quality, as perceived by the customer or sponsor, meets or exceeds the price to be paid, the product certainly has economic value—hence, "I got my money's worth." If there is no better opportunity, such economic value may be a *best value*.

Other chapters address best value in more detail; but, suffice it to say that when customers draw deep satisfaction with the quality of the product, they also believe they have received the best value for their investment. And, the term *customer* is meant in the broad sense: executives, sponsors, users, and those who pay—whether internal or external. Throughout the text, we will build on the quality values given in Table 3.1.

Every methodology includes principles labeled *quality principles*. Principles are the domain-specific guidelines that point the way and set boundaries for behavior and action. Principles support values, but principles bring the action. Every project dashboard should advertise the principles that

Table 3.1 Quality values

- Quality of communications: A respect for courtesy, timeliness, and accuracy of communications
- Product quality: A commitment to a product that is fit for use—reliable, maintainable, available, and conforms to standards and conventions; fit to form and function, and fit to its environment, both societal and globally
- Quality practices: A commitment to standards of practice: it can be taken on faith by the customer that the product meets all required certifications and standards of practice
- Resource conservation: A respect for resources, especially timeliness, and a pledge of integrity in all matters financial
- Quality of performance: A commitment to personal and collective performance that is lawful, moral, and trustful
- Quality of relationships: A respect for each individual as an individual; in effect, a commitment to a safe and enriching environment that values each member's contribution

---

guide their specific project and reflect upon their organization. The list in Table 3.2 can be a part of every agile project.

Within every project and every methodology there are quality practices that put principles to work. Quality practices are the things that are actually done to deliver and improve quality. Practices are implementations of principles. There are many more than the most important few listed in Table 3.3. Each of the quality dimensions—fitness to use, fitness to standard, fitness to cost, fitness to societal and global environment, and others—are achieved most easily when fully internalized by all the project participants.

Quality Values and Principles Are Planned into Agile Methods

The discussion so far is the setup for actionable quality practices in agile projects. Values and principles such as respect for courtesy, timeliness, and accuracy of communications, are guidance for day-to-day activities. Tools and techniques such as customer-driven value and plan-do-check-act come from the legacy of Taylor, Deming, Juran, and Crosby, among others. It now remains to apply this quality inventory to agile projects.

Planning and Deployment

Planning for quality is much like planning for the project itself:

- Establish goals,
- Conceive a strategy,
- Adopt principles to guide action, and
- Define practices.

Table 3.2 Universal quality principles for agile methods

- Everyone will be respectful of time
- Everyone will be respectful of other points of view; diversity is honored
- Problems are attacked, not people; a safe and trustful environment is everyone's concern
- Team members have a responsibility to add value to their team
- Learning and self-improvement is everyone's job, personally and to the mutual benefit of the team
- Every team member works to benefit the team and the project, eschewing self-optimization
- Every object delivered to the customer will have met its quality measures
- Every object is the simplest possible for the task, although the simplest object may be quite complex
- Every object will have sufficient redundancy to ensure availability of feature and function to satisfy customer need
- No iteration is complete until its lessons are learned
- Economy of effort and maximization of throughput is everyone's goal

Table 3.3 Quality practices

- Communications will be answered promptly and courteously within a time frame that is reasonable and customary
- Time-boxes will be enforced and respected for their specific time limits
- Daily stand-up meetings will be planned to allow every team member a chance to speak in a safe environment
- Users have a right to influence the functional design, but users have a responsibility to work for the best value to the enterprise
- Work assignments will reflect a reasonable adjustment for risk and uncertainty
- Performance will be honored by incentives or other recognition, and will be targeted and timely to the event
- Every object will be proven for fitness to use and standard with a unit test, followed by a user functional test and an system integration test
- Defects will be fixed when first discovered, provided there is economic justification
- All implementations will comport with the certified standards of the organization
- Object designs will honor system architecture
- Object design will honor the user's evaluation of feature and function according to a best-value standard

Ideally, the project's quality goals and principles will:

- Align with the quality elements of the balanced scorecard
- Reflect the values and principles of the organization as given in Tables 3.1 and 3.2
- Reflect the principles of quality practices in projects as given in Table 3.3

- Respect the values and principles of the specific methodology followed

Suggested quality goals are given in Table 3.4.

Deployment of a quality regime is first and foremost a communications task to inform, train, and educate—and also to document principles, standards, benchmarks, and practices. Deployment drives internalization. What is meant by deployment and internalization is that while it is necessary to inform and educate, it is imperative for each project member to take matters to heart, in order to have an effective program, to treat the *project* principles as *personal* principles, and to make quality practices natural and routine.

Quality program deployment steps for agile projects are listed in Table 3.5.

Scorecards for Quality

In physical systems, quantitative quality metrics are numerical measures compared to a benchmark or control limit. This, we know, is *defined process control*. Among many similar objects, the actual measurements—usually

Table 3.4 Quality goals

Goal	Measurement	Commentary
Customers will be satisfied with the value obtained in the product feature and functions	Subjective measures: not satisfied, satisfied, very satisfied	Agile projects value customer satisfaction over following a plan
Project sponsors will judge the project a best value fit to the business case	Subjective and quantitative measures of how well the vision is realized for the intended investment	The business case establishes milestones and funding affordability for the envisioned product
The business will feel that they are ready and able to accept and deploy the project outcomes effectively	Operational metrics, like training readiness, supply readiness, manufacturing process and procedures	Change management and business preparation adopt the product and drive benefits
Stakeholders on the balanced scorecard will judge the impact on key performance indicators (KPIs) and verify they are within the range of expectation	Balanced scorecard metrics	Sometimes stakeholders establish constraints rather than open doors, but still expect favorable impact on KPIs
Team members will feel that they had a fair and reasonable opportunity to provide a best value solution to the customer	Subjective evaluation of the team and project experience	Principles given in Table 3.3 are adhered to

Table 3.5 Deployment elements for agile projects

Deployment Task	Commentary
Publish values and principles of the project in a written form Make standards and benchmarks readily available	Think lean: make efficient to access the necessary information on a project dashboard
Establish scorecards for recording performance in the defect opportunity space	Use scorecard templates electronically accessible where possible for entry and update
Establish workflow for approving scorecards	Think lean: only as much approval authority as is required to maintain the integrity of the scoring
Hold team meetings or other forums to inform and educate on the quality program	Time-box the team meetings: be respectful of time and respectful of all ideas and discussion
Establish audit procedures for performance on key practices that drive quality	Inspect what you expect Caution: overly intrusive audit procedures may affect results[1]
Establish improvement goals	Use every iteration reflection and lessons-learned session as an opportunity to raise the performance bar for the next iteration
Use total quality management tools to identify problems and measure progress	Pareto Charts and Fishbone cause-effect diagrams are among the most used in agile projects

[1]The uncertainty principle: measuring actually changes that which is being measured

slightly different from one object to another—will largely cluster around the nominal value.

Acceptance limits are established to separate the good objects from the bad. Numerical measurements are recorded on a scorecard that is often called a control chart because the measurements are plotted between the control limits as shown in Figure 3.1.

With intangible outcomes, physical parameters such as size and weight are not usually measured; instead, functionality and performance are measured. Because many defects are unforeseen consequences of interactions among system elements, the system's latent chaos and entropy are unknown. Thus, the practical import is a near-real-time strategy to set quantitative defect limits empirically, meaning the quality standard is adapted to the observations of the actual situation. To gather empirical data, discriminating differences are observed and recorded.

At the unit test level, there are all manner of technical errors:[1] Syntax, spelling, definitions, and others. At the integration and functional level, us-

The defined-process control chart shows the range of acceptable outcomes according to process limits around an average value.

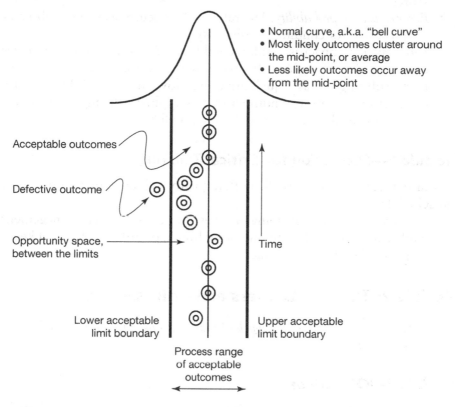

Figure 3.1 Example control chart

ers find errors of logic—such as retrieving only a last name instead of a first and last from a database—and errors of performance, such as too much time taken to populate a data field. And there are other defect categories such as defects of conformance to standards, and missing or inappropriate features and functions.

To develop a quality performance scorecard, design entries for:

- *Error condition*: The error condition is the unique problem observed, like retrieving only the last name rather than first and last.
- *Error condition frequency*: Occurrences of unique errors are scored as a 1 or 0—at each observation instance, the error either occurred or did

not occur. The total frequency count is simply the sum of the error scores.

- *Error condition probability*: The ratio of the occurrences to the observations is the error condition probability.
- *Error impact*: Impact is a judgmental factor about how much an error condition affects product effectiveness and customer satisfaction. Impact is often given as a qualitative (e.g., low, medium, or high) figure of merit, or sometimes a number scale is applied—the higher the number, the lower the customer satisfaction will be.

Module 1—Discussion for Critical Thinking

In your experience, is it more likely that quality will be dominant over cost and schedule, or not?

If your answer to the foregoing was yes, do you agree that management focus and priority has shifted to outcomes from a priority and focus of keeping to a planned cost and schedule?

Module 2: Thought Leaders and Agile Quality

Agile quality is built on the work of many of those that have thought much about quality

Module 2—Objectives

- Familiarize the reader with the most distinguished quality thought leaders
- Make the connection between quality ideas and agile objectives

In this module we examine the impact on agile of the thought leaders on quality. In this module, three different ideas of quality are presented, each represented by a different thought leader:

1. Business efficiency (think of lean);
2. Product excellence (think of a product with no bugs); and
3. Fitness for use (think of customer satisfaction).

F. W. Taylor's Lean Thinking

Fredrick Winslow Taylor, more popularly known as F. W. Taylor, was one of the first to study business systematically. Unwittingly, he was the lean thinker of his day. According to Taylor, managers must acknowledge and accept this principle:

> *Managers have responsibilities to design efficient and effective processes and procedures.*

Waste must be eliminated! It is not enough that the trains run effectively—they must run on time! Every action requires definition and a means to measure results.

Taylor came up with the original time and motion studies, perhaps one of the first attacks on non-value work. Peter Drucker, a management guru par excellence who coined the term *knowledge worker*, has ranked Taylor as one of the seminal thinkers of modern times.[2]

Taylor may have been the first lean thinker, but he was decidedly not agile-oriented regarding staff, which he thought of as interchangeable—according to job description, not individual talent. Taylor, more so than any of the other thinkers, was focused on business efficiency and not on making conditions right for innovation and customer influence.

Taylor believed that workers must be divided by skill and by role; quality is achieved by careful job design, handing off from one skillful person to another. Any residual errors are caught at the end by independent inspection. Taylor's ideas made mass production of process results possible:

- People, properly trained, were to be as interchangeable as standard mechanical parts
- Defined processes staffed with qualified people should be capable of consistently repeatable results

And Taylor ushered in quality control as an independent and external practice to catch anything the functional process did not detect and correct.

Kent Beck in *Extreme Programming Explained*[3] confronts the legacy of Taylor by noting that:

- Taylorism lies latent in our business culture and unconsciously affects day-to-day activity
- Taylor's idea that quality is a responsibility external to the mainstream work

The idea of quality outside the mainstream should be worrisome to all of us. As this chapter will present, quality is an equal partner with scope, resources, and schedule. Quality, as they say, is *built-in* and *job one*.

	F. W. Taylor's impact on agile projects
A project management tip	• Fredrick Taylor was the first lean thinker. • Taylor was the first to study and quantify non-value work and put emphasis on eliminating wasteful and time-consuming processes, procedures, and *environmental impediments.* • In a similar vein, Steve McConnell, respected author of *Code Complete,* states that "the general principle of software quality is that improving quality reduces development costs...." and that "the best way to improve productivity is to reduce the time reworking...."[4]

Lean Practices for Quality

Before World War I, Taylor was thinking lean. More recently, lean has come to mean a laser focus on making every practice value-added from the customer's perspective. Lean also means smoothing the flow from one step to another so that unproductive idle time is minimized, reducing or eliminating batch queues, substituting real-time processes, and minimizing overhead set up time. And *lean* means deferring production decisions until just-in-time to avoid inventory buildup and premature commitments.[5]

But perhaps most important for the customer-developer relationship, and also as a centerpiece of lean and agile methods, is the concept of *pull*. Pull means that features and functions are pulled into the product design as a consequence of customer request rather than being pushed out by a developer's whim.[6] Pull is the essence of the agile Kanban practices we discuss elsewhere in this book.

Pull and the concept of simplicity work in complementary ways. Simplicity is the avoidance of complex interactions, but it is also the avoidance of complexity caused by incorporating design before its time—before the customer states a need or sets a priority.

W. Edwards Deming and Defined Process Control

Deming introduced very practical ideas of process control as a means to limit variations in product quality. Today, it is called *defined process control.* Deming came at quality from the point of view of the product: make the product the same way each time and make it work within limits that are acceptable to the customer. The modern poster child for defined process control is Six Sigma. An explanation of Six Sigma is given in the Appendix at the end of this chapter.

Deming was influenced by the work of the process statistician Walter A. Shewhart, who is credited with identifying the fact that processes have two variables: *assignable cause* and *chance cause.*

Assignable cause is systemic and capable of being corrected and maintained to an economical minimum. Assignable cause is what agile teams address in the retrospective review after each review and each release.

Chance cause is randomly occurring in frequency and intensity, not always present in the process, and is mitigated by establishing performance limits for a given process. Agile handles chance cause two ways:

1. Only scheduling backlog for an iteration that is about 80% of the predictable throughput, thereby leaving "white space" for absorbing chance cause
2. Scheduling empty iterations as buffers to catch the overflow of debt that accumulates due to chance cause

A project management tip	W. Edwards Deming's impact on agile projects
	Deming focused on eliminating unsatisfactory results before they reached the customer. In agile parlance, every object must pass its unit, functional, and system test.

The modern version of Deming and Shewhart is Six Sigma. Suffice it to say, however, that defined process control is not what agile is about. Agile stresses empirical process control, meaning that circumstances in the moment are drivers for process design and control limits. That said, there are elements of Six Sigma that are adaptable to agile methods.

A project management tip	Six Sigma is supportive of agile
	• Six Sigma provides a very effective problem solving method (define, measure, analyze, improve, control [DMAIC]), which enhances the plan-do-check-act (PDCA) cycle. • The principles of DMAIC are usable without invoking other aspects of Six Sigma. • Six Sigma brings understanding of the defect opportunity space, and promotes the idea of setting limits at the boundaries of customer satisfaction. • Many defects will never be known and others are not economical to fix. All have the potential to contribute to the customer experience.

Joseph Juran Favors the Customer

More in line with agile thinking, Juran began the shift of the quality effort—away from Deming's *product* focus and toward a *customer* focus. He is known for his advocacy of the Juran trilogy: *quality improvement, planning,* and *control.*

Juran stressed the quality concept of *fitness to use.* He believed that meeting a specification is a necessary condition, but insufficient without fitness to use—that is, honoring the customer's idea of product value and utility. In other words, features are not valuable unless they are everyday useful.

Juran's ideas are what agile practitioners think of as favoring customer value over following a plan.

Juran defined five parameters that make up *fitness to use*:

1. Quality of design, a judgmental parameter with grades of goodness
2. Conformance to standards and customary expectations of the market
3. Availability, a consequence of frequency of breakdown and rapidity of repair
4. Safety in use
5. Usability in a customer's setting

Among tools, Juran popularized the Pareto chart, which he named after Italian economist Vilfredo Pareto who recognized the phenomenon of the 80-20 rule in his study of business activity.

The Pareto chart is a histogram arranged in descending order that shows distinct problems according to how frequently each occurs. One distinct problem might be a paper jam, and it might occur 100 times a quarter. The paper jam might be the most frequently occurring problem observed.

The 80-20 rule states that most histograms show that 80 percent of all problem occurrences are linked to only 20 percent of distinctly identified problems.

So, if by example, 1000 occurrences are reported, and there are 80 distinct problems among the 1000, by the 80-20 rule, 800 of every 1000 occurrences are forecast to be attributable to 16 of 80 distinct problems.

	Joseph Juran's impact on agile methods
A project management tip	• Juran shifted quality toward a concern for the customer and away from the goodness of the product. • The agile interpretation of Juran is to value customer satisfaction over following a plan. • The concept of fitness for use, a synonym for customer satisfaction, was promoted by Juran as a quality management concept. • The Pareto chart helps to focus agile teams on the most important features and functions.

Philip Crosby: Zero Defects and Free Quality

Philip Crosby came along a generation after Deming and Juran. Working in the aerospace and defense industry, Crosby became fixed on pushing Deming's ideas of assignable cause to the point of zero defects. He also authored the principle of *doing it right the first time*, known as *DRIFT*.

Crosby is best remembered for inventing the idea that *quality is free*! In his formulation, the cost of conformance is just the cost of doing business the right way. Thereby, the cost of quality is free; only the cost of nonconformance is an add-on.

	Crosby invents the idea that quality is free!
A project management tip	• Agile teams understand and practice the DRIFT principle. • Although zero defects is laudable, agile methods look to the customer to put a priority on fixing defects. Some defects are not economically repairable and will not be fixed.

Module 2—Discussion for Critical Thinking

In this module, three different ideas of quality are presented: business efficiency, product excellence, and fitness for use. This is similar to other business models that have a similar triangle. In the spirit of *triangulation*, which leg of the triangle would you make longer (dominant), and which gets the short end?

Module 3: Sampling for Quality Validation

You can't measure and validate everything; yet everything must have "quality"

Module 3—Objectives

- Make the connection between accepted methods to sample and the need for quality

Sampling is an advanced topic for readers who are interested in additional quantitative quality measures. Most experienced project managers and developers (whether traditional or agile) understand that it is impossible to validate every quality consideration—there are just too many conditions and combinations.

- Economic limitations
- Schedule constraints
- Undiscovered or unknowable defects hidden behind obscure functionality
- Operational flukes

Therefore, testing and verification is led naturally to sampling.

Sampling

Sampling shifts the mind-set from *descriptive statistics*, in which piles of data measurements describe actual conditions, to *inference statistics*. That is, a shift from *big data* that proves a condition or hypothesis, to an *inferred conclusion*, supported by much less than *big data*.

Thus, an inference is a conclusion that is *assumed to be true* based on observation and analysis of similar or closely related facts. Usually, an inference is accompanied by a statement of confidence about how certain the assumed conclusion is.

In project terms, drawing an inference is a pretty big shift from measuring every outcome. Drawing an inference introduces the idea of *trust me* into the validation results, thereby adding complication when communicating with executives and sponsors. Nonetheless, inference statistics are common:

- Opinion polls are an everyday example of inference statistics
- The opinions of only a few thousand seem to represent those of many millions within a reasonable margin of error—in other words, with relatively high confidence

In projects, the situation is much the same as in political polls. From a relatively small number of observations, validators infer those same results on a larger population that is too numerous to evaluate. For example, when testing database systems, there may only be the opportunity to validate a few thousand records out of tens of millions. But if the validation is designed correctly, then there can be confidence that the remaining data population will have the same quality.

In most practical situations, it is possible to actually quantify the confidence of the test results. Sampling is a big subject, but there are a number of simplifying assumptions and heuristics that make sampling a practical tool for day-to-day use, as shown in Table 3.6.

Picking the sample size and understanding the confidence limits is a subject for expert analysts. Suffice it to say that if the population is more than ten times that of the sample drawn from the population, and the error conditions are random occurrences distributed among all objects in the population, then many simplifications come into play to make sampling practical for projects.

Table 3.6 Simplifying ideas for sampling

The idea	Commentary
A population is a collection of objects having similar attributes	• The population need not be contiguous or uniformly populated • The population can have time-sensitive properties, such as time-of-day, or location properties, like elevation • It is possible to sample object A in order to infer performance in object B, as in a prototype vs. a production model
All members of the population do not need to be known before sampling begins	• A sampling "frame" defines the known elements of the population; the true size of the population may be unknown. • Example: the exact size of the voting population cannot be known before an election, but a "frame" of a likely set of voters can be known.
The best plan for picking samples from a population is really no plan at all	• Pick samples randomly for validation
The sample size need not be precisely sized in order to get good results	• The sample needs to be "large enough" but it can be quite small compared to the population size

Process Limits and Benchmarks

Quality gets translated by some means, procedure, and policy of the enterprise into some attribute that is measureable. Process limits, sampling, and quality are dots to be connected. You can also add work-in-process limits to the mix. Quality objectives connect the dots. Accepting that everything can't be economically or practically measured, samples are taken. But, what's the benchmark for acceptable quality to which the sample is compared?

A benchmark is typically not a point on some scale—it's a range defined by limits. The question is begged: when do the limits get defined? Traditionally, they are defined by analysis, and thus, become *up-front defined process limits*. But, up-front top-down constraints are not appealing to agile practitioners, so the idea of empirical limits has come into projects.

Defined limits are what are found on process control charts. Defined limits, or sometimes *defined process control* is the quality idea promoted by Deming and made famous in recent times by the Six Sigma practice. Defined limits presume advance knowledge of *how it's supposed to be* and what a defect is. Presumably the nature of a defect has been tested in some way with customers so that there's no question that a defect is unacceptable.

However, the agile issue is obvious: the product—at least during the project development period—is not tactically stationary, so the idea of fixed and predictable limits is an antithesis. Consequently, we are led to empirical limits.

Empirical limits have a *limits-on-the-fly* sort of flavor, and indeed that's the case. The quality limits are developed empirically as the requirements, stories, and use cases become project realities.

Quality Measures from Users

Since most of the project outcomes we have been discussing end up in a user community, it is common to ask, *"How do you like them?"* The answers often come back as *good-better-best*, and sometimes ranked on a scale of 1-10. Some caution, however, that in the absence of objective standards for numerical ranks, the ranking is often no better than good-better-best. Subjectivity, however, affords flexibility because all of the interpretation is driven strictly by the information given to us by our customers—another example of empirical analysis rather than fit to a defined standard.

Empirical analysis of subjective information benefits from something as simple as a histogram or Pareto chart. A Pareto chart is a ranking tool, as shown in Figure 3.2.

Quality is a consequence of both the number of error occurrences and their impact on the product as perceived by the customer

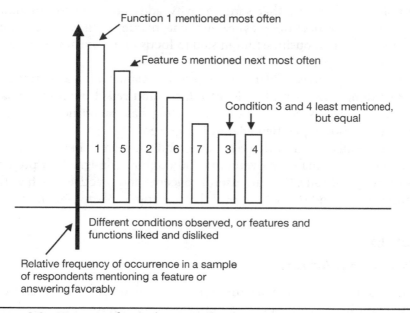

Figure 3.2 Histogram for quality measures

Module 3—Discussion for Critical Thinking

Sampling, rather than validating every outcome, is a risk. What if the customer receives that one defective unit, or stumbles onto that one bug left in the product? How does your organization approach such risk? Are you satisfied with empirical control limits, or does your organization demand defined process control like that of Six Sigma?

Summary and Takeaway Points

Our theme for this chapter is that *quality is a nonnegotiable value.* Quality is about making the customer ever more successful, and delivering more business benefits than the invested commitment.

From Module 1, take that there is no single definition of quality. Quality is expressed by its values, principles, and practices. Each of the agile methods has values, principles, and practices, but in this chapter, universal ideas are offered that are applicable in any methodology.

From Module 2, we learn that early leaders in business quality set up many of the practices that are still useful today. Taylor introduced lean thinking and the concept that some activity adds no value to outcomes. Deming told us to reflect upon every outcome, making defined process limits a common thing in business; Juran said to focus on the customer. Crosby declared: *quality is free!*

From Module 3, it is evident most projects cannot afford to test and verify everything. Thus sampling is introduced and relied upon to validate an inferred hypothesis or conclusion. Sampling has established itself as a proven practice, but a qualified analyst is required.

In the Appendix, we find that Six Sigma and the lean thinking paradigm are relatively recent quality movements. Although not designed for projects and software specifically, they are useful concepts and practices, such as the opportunity space and the idea of pull that are applicable to agile methods.

Appendix

Six Sigma Revolution

Six Sigma is a problem-solving methodology and defect control strategy with the purpose of identifying and mitigating error sources in defined process control. The control limits are established such that production yields *less than approximately 3.4 errors in one million opportunities* either above or below the control limits. This figure is derived from the error possibilities within six standard deviations of a bell-shaped curve, after allowing a 1.5 standard deviations drift of the long-term average defect rate.

The process derives its name from the Greek lowercase *s*, called *sigma* and denoted σ. σ is the symbol used by statisticians for standard deviation of the mean value of a risky or uncertain process—the lower the deviation, the lower the uncertainty in the process, and the fewer errors made beyond a process quality limit.

Ken Schwaber—a leading Scrum methodologist—objecting to defined process control, puts it this way:

> "[defined process control] is based on processes that work only because their degree of imprecision is acceptable.... When defined process control cannot be achieved because of the complexity of the intermediate activities; something called empirical process control has to be employed."[7]

In Schwaber's view, software is too complex to expect defects to be contained within predefined error limits. Empirical control is the answer;

empirical control is derived from observed facts, adapted to the situation, and not determined by preplanned limits from previous projects.

In spite of the fact that software projects offer little opportunity for statistical process control in the Six Sigma and Deming way, perhaps Deming's most noteworthy accomplishment from the perspective of project management and agile methodologies, is his famous PDCA cycle that he originally adopted from Walter Shewhart. PDCA envisions planning for what is to be done, then doing it—that is the *plan-do*. Next, measure the results—measuring is the *check* activity—and then *act* on the measurement results. To *act*, in the PDCA sense, means to reflect upon lessons learned and provide feedback for corrective actions to the next iteration of the plan.

Six Sigma was not designed for projects, software, or agile methods. Projects generally, and software specifically, do not remotely approach the error rates championed by Six Sigma. Six Sigma is not agile; its methods are supported by a myriad of documents, practices, and analysis. Six Sigma is the crown of the defined process control paradigm, eschewed by Schwaber and others. So why is Six Sigma in the discussion about quality for agile methods? Six Sigma has interesting practices that could be helpful to agile projects. Consider these two:

1. *Problem identification and solution design*: Six Sigma employs a problem identification and solving practice that builds off of Deming's PDCA. Six Sigma is said to *follow the defect*, which means to reflect on the product results and work back through root-cause analysis to identify defect sources. *Follow the defect* fits the agile mandate to always deliver a working product.[8] In Six Sigma-speak, the practice is referred to as DMAIC. DMAIC really implements the *check-act* component of PDCA in a more sophisticated manner.

2. *Opportunity space*: Six Sigma promotes the idea of an *opportunity space* where quality measurements are made. Opportunity results are partitioned between good and not good, acceptable and unacceptable, or non-defective and defective. The opportunity space for software systems is unique to the nature of software. In modern software (with few exceptions and certainly different from mechanical and electronic systems), program logic always works as designed, and works repeatedly the same way given the same initial conditions and operating data—there are no effects from wear and tear, age, environment, and material differences. But software does have defects:

	There are defects, a.k.a. errors, of many types
Software defects	• *Logic errors:* Defects from logic constructs that actually work, but not as wanted by the customer. • *Technical errors:* Defects that arise from technical issues such as incorrect language syntax, incorrect or inconsistent variable and data definitions, spelling errors, data out-of-range, or other similar construction problems.[9] • *Data errors:* Defects from data that does not conform to data definitions. • *Conformance errors:* Actual practices that do not conform to the quality standards.

Software complexity complicates the opportunity space. The opportunity space is populated by defects that are known, unknown-but-knowable, and unknowable. Known defects are those that are already discovered and in a backlog—they may or may not be fixed, according to priority and the cost of fixing. The unknown-but-knowable errors are a matter of discovery and testing, again subject to priority and economics. The unknowable defects are those that arise from unlikely conditions and conditions that only the user can recognize once the product is in an operational context; a developer, who is not an expert in the business, may not ever recognize certain defects for what they are.

The idea of continuous improvement is to make the best bet in partitioning the opportunity space, improving performance with every iteration. The opportunity space is sampled after iteration. All the counts are expected to change from one iteration to the next. Some defects will be deferred for a later fix, others will be ignored, but most will be fixed in the iteration in which they are discovered.

Because agile methods are iterative and the design is refactored, containment per se—a concept that seeks to prevent defect *creep* from one code base to the next—is not strongly enforced.

Chapter Endnotes

1. The terms *error* and *defect* are used interchangeably.
2. Wall Street Journal, "Frederick Taylor, Early Century Management Consultant," A1.
3. Beck with Andres, *Extreme Programming Explained*, 131-133.
4. McConnell, *Code Complete*, 567.

5. Poppendieck, *The Agile Customer's Tool Kit*, 4.

6. Womack and Jones, *Create Wealth in Your Corporation*, 67.

7. Schwaber, *Agile Project Management with SCRUM*, 2.

8. See Hallowell, "Software Development Convergence: Six Sigma-Lean-Agile."

9. Software as now designed is generally stationary in the statistical sense. That is, given the same initial conditions and the same data, the program will execute repeatedly in an identical fashion. Older practices that self-computed statements and variables, and thereby changed the program on the fly and created non-stationary effects that are not necessarily repeatable, are for the most part no longer followed.

4

Agile in the Waterfall

Embracing and respecting open and stationary qualities of architecture, functionality, and governance are the keys to a successful hybrid project context[1]

Module 1: First Principles and Requisite Conditions

Strategy, tactics, and environment

Module 1—Objectives

- Discuss and explain the principle of *strategically stationary*
- Discuss and explain *tactically iterative and emergent* as an overlay to strategy

Hybrid Operating Principle

Somewhat different from the agile principles we discussed in prior chapters, this operating principle is the foundation for a hybrid of agile and traditional methods that could co-exist in the same project.

Hybrid operating principle	Agile projects are simultaneously strategically stationary and tactically iterative and emergent

Strategically stationary means that:

- Whenever and wherever you look, the project has the same strategic intent and predictable business outlook—traditional methods require this, but business planners do also
- Strategic intent is what is expressed by the business for the opportunity and vision of the project
- A strategically predictable business outlook is the outcome that is expected of the project—typically expressed as the mission, but also found on the business scorecard

Tactically iterative and emergent means that:

- Flexibility is delegated to development teams to solve issues locally
- Teams are empowered to respond to the fine details of customer demand, while respecting strategic intent in all respects
- Teams are expected to evolve processes in order to be lean, efficient, and frictionless in development.

Business Case and Project Charter

As discussed in the chapter on the business case, the place you'll find the strategic intent documented and discussed is, in fact, the business case. The strategic business scorecard—the scorecard of the differentiated future—will reflect the impact of *mission complete* in the sense of the project's impact on the business.

Correspondingly, the business case is mapped to the project charter, which includes the project scorecard. The project scorecard, with a shorter timeline than the business scorecard, will nonetheless reflect the strategic intent in the form of project metrics.

Figure 4.1 illustrates these points. The business case always reflects the optimism of the business, though, at times, it is somewhat fuzzy or without definite boundaries. The business case expresses the mission, opportunity, vision, and narrative as we've discussed in prior chapters. Thence, a mapping occurs:

- From the business mission, the project discerns the project drivers
- From business opportunity, the key milestones are derived
- From the vision of the business leadership, we envision a responsive architecture
- From the narrative given by the business comes the myriad of functionalities of the outcomes

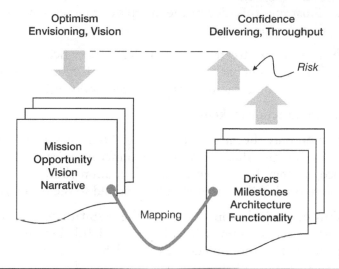

Strategic mapping from the business side on the left to the project side on the right establishes a cause-and-effect relationship between drivers and responses

Figure 4.1　Strategic mapping

Risk Response

We see in Figure 4.1 that the project charter always assumes some risk to project objectives, even if such risk is not explicit in the business case or runs counter to the optimism of the business case. So the question becomes: what is the arching risk response? Answer: be tactically emergent and iterative—which are exactly those qualities of agile methods that best address risk.

We define an environment that can provide those qualities as an environment with these attributes:

- Supportive of small teams with internal redundancy
- Locally manageable at the team level—perhaps even rotating the management among team members
- Supportive of proven protocols and lean practices
- Supportive of instinctive actions, lean principles, and frictionless interplay among team members

Overlay Strategy with Tactics

The upshot of a tactically emergent and iterative risk response is that we may find that actions in the moment are a seeming variance to the strategy—that is, the project plan. But, over time, we may take other actions that converge on the strategy. In effect, we overlay the strategy with tactical expediency at the moment.

Figure 4.2 illustrates this idea of the interplay of tactics with strategy. What are these actions?

- For the agile work stream, the most common tactical move is adjustment of the iteration backlog, the repository of *stories* or use cases that are the gist of requirements in the agile methodology.

And why are these actions taken?

- Most commonly, because the customer/user sees a better way to achieve a functionality; they see an unnecessary story that can be dropped; or they have been given information about a requirement, heretofore unidentified, that should be added to the backlog.

Another form of tactical maneuvering is the result of technical or functional debt—those small items which have been left behind on a *punch list* to be completed before the project ends. This debt may cause small changes which may seem to lead off the strategy, but more often they help to converge to the strategic intent.

Although this discussion is cast in the context of risk, the same applies as if we were talking about the dynamics of backlog management. No matter how one story or requirement might seem to lead us off course, in the long

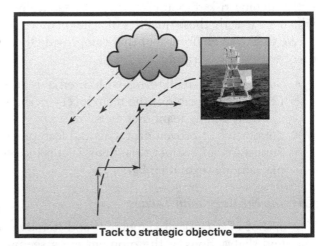

Overlay strategy with tactics to mitigate short-term conditions while maintaining strategic intent

- **Tactically responsive**
  to circumstances

- **Emergent**
  plan as conditions
  develop

- **Tactically respectful**
  of strategy as an overlay

Tack to strategic objective

Figure 4.2   Overlay of strategy with tactics

run, if we are faithful to the strategic intent, we will find our way back by subsequent adjustments in the backlog.

Module 1—Discussion for Critical Thinking

The two big ideas in this module are:

1. In the hybrid situation opposite ideas co-exist: to be stationary and to be emergent
2. No matter the strategy, there will always be tactical moves that are instinctive to the situation, as well as responsive to the customer demands on the backlog

What issues do you see in supporting these ideas as leader of the project office?

Module 2: The Black Box, Interfaces, and Connectivity

Yours, mine, and ours

Module 2—Objectives

- Discuss and explain the importance of open and stationary interfaces
- Discuss and explain how the black box can still be emergent
- Familiarize readers with extending these ideas to work stream and portfolios

The Black Box

The *black box* is a metaphor for encapsulation in which the internal structure and details of a unit of architecture are hidden and unknown to the outside world. The only way to employ a black box is to communicate through its interface.

Its generality is useful across a broad range of system design: black boxes for mechanical devices and structure; black boxes for software units; and even black boxes for whole work streams or projects.

Architecture is Mapped

The first use of the black box is to map or define the architecture of the project outcome—whether service or product—as a number of black boxes with some kind of relationship between them. In many cases coming up with a good mapping is more art than science, and strikingly the mapping often reflects the organizational biases of the enterprise.

Somewhat counter to the agile principle that suggests the best architecture emerges, we hold that the best architecture is the product of forethought. It is first an outcome of strategic intent; it is conceived top-down, only then to be refined with bottom-up mapping to a level of detail sufficient to put a project charter in place.

Strategic Architecture Is the Product of Forethought
• Partition by subsystems for near total isolation and independence (stand-alone model) • Partition by layers for efficient distribution of functions (Internet model) • Partition by application on a common foundation for application independence (smart phone model)

So, is the agile principle about good emergent architecture a nonstarter? No, indeed at a level lower than the strategic architecture, the tactical architecture can be expected to emerge and be responsive according to the fine detail of customer demand. Nonetheless, in the same way the point was made earlier, even tactical departures from the main architecture are made consistent with the larger architecture as respect for strategic intent.

Mapping continues from the business case to the project charter:

- Vision and narrative map to top-level architecture and functionality, respectively
- Architecture and functionality are allocated to work streams
- The labor of work streams is done according to a local choice of methodology

It's that latter idea that leads directly to a hybrid methodology to respond to the business case and project charter—provided the necessary conditions of our operating principle are in place, as we discussed.

Encapsulated Scope and Methodology

Encapsulation is a powerful idea that enables these possibilities for a hybrid agile-traditional enterprise project:

- Methodologies—agile and traditional—can be encapsulated and thus made noninterfering, but yet able to communicate through interfaces

- Work streams can be encapsulated, communicating with other work streams at certain milestones and interfaces
- Architecture components can be encapsulated to the interface level
- Projects can be encapsulated within a portfolio, communicating with other projects at certain milestones and interfaces.

Two big encapsulation ideas	1. Interfaces are all important for being able to communicate and interconnect from one encapsulated entity to another 2. Milestone planning is a necessary scheduling tool for ensuring the encapsulated functionality is ready for integration with other encapsulated entities

All of these encapsulation possibilities can be mapped to the black box paradigm given in Figure 4.3. The first thing noticed, and the most prominent visual, is that all details are hidden from the nonowners or teams not working in a specific box. With this seeming privacy, local decisions, local processes, and local issues are contained and known only to a small cadre of informed individuals.

In that regard, we see immediately that encapsulated black boxes can be a bit territorial:

- You have yours; I have mine
- We each have a piece of the architecture
- Although the internal details can vary and are largely my business and not yours, the open interface cannot change without engaging with change management

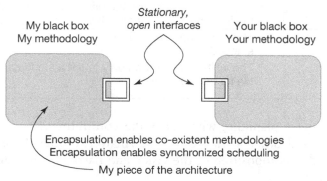

Encapsulated scope includes both "yours" and "mine"

Stationary,
My black box   *open* interfaces   Your black box
My methodology   Your methodology

Encapsulation enables co-existent methodologies
Encapsulation enables synchronized scheduling
My piece of the architecture

Figure 4.3 Encapsulated scope

- The open side of the interface must be stationary and supportive of strategic intent

Thus, each black box team is compelled to stand behind the open side of the interface. To not do so breaks a pledge to the rest of the project to remain faithful to strategic intent.

Tactical Emergence and Iteration

Other than holding the interface to the outside world open and stationary, the development team is otherwise free to design and develop the internal structure of the black box according to the backlog assigned to the black box.

First, let's be sure we understand that when the details of the black box are made known to the team working on that entity, we then have a *white box*. For those that see the black box transparently, they are working on the white box solution.

Second, the most important rule is given thus:

Rule for tactical emergence and iteration	The team is free to iterate and take advantage of an emergent backlog, and then refactor the white box solution, once the team has committed to the open and stationary interface.

Once the interface is defined, the team cannot then modify its functionality or attributes on the open side without coordination with every other black box team.

The white box	• For every black box, there is a white box • The white box is simply the description or specification of the internal structure and actions of the black box • The white box is the black box with the encapsulation stripped away • The white box is known only to the team that is responsible for the black box

From the project planning, when does the commitment to the interface functionality and other attributes occur? Answer: during the architecture definition and decomposition of the vision and narrative into functional architectural units.

So, given that the open side of the interfaces has been committed to by the various teams working on the black box, we turn to the idea that each interface of an active device, process, or component is itself active and is a function onto itself. Thus, in the context of integration of and communication between black boxes:

- Units communicate by addressing themselves to the interface
- Units pass parameter data or otherwise adhere to the interface structural demand
- Units expect to receive data in return, or to have the black box act in some functional manner

Network of Boxes

It remains, then, to consider how we go about communicating between and among the black boxes. There are three broad choices:

1. Dedicated point-to-point connections[2]
2. Shared connections over some type of network
3. Connections organized into, and governed by, rules of hierarchy

Certainly since the 1970s when layered protocols and the Ethernet topology came into general use, the network solution has been the topology of choice. By choosing a network as the means to communicate among black boxes, we must consider how to address ourselves to the interfaces. Essentially, we do these things:

- Create an open, active network as part of the product, service, or program architecture
- Apply layered protocols to achieve ubiquitous connectivity
- Arrange the black boxes as nodes on the network (function at node architecture)
- Apply application protocols, like file transfer protocols, as an overlay to the connectivity protocols

Network Attributes

There are several attributes of the network that connects all the black boxes into a system, as shown in Figure 4.4:

- Each node on the network is the interface to a black box, either a backbone bus topology[3] or somewhat like a mesh[4] of functionality and physical units
- The interface on the network side is open and stationary once the architecture has been set and agreed upon

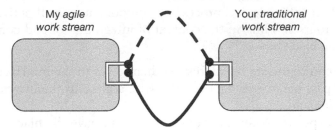

Network of boxes, representing work streams, illustrates interfaces between work streams

Network: Planning, physical, virtual (sneaker net), or combinations

Figure 4.4   Network of boxes

- Protocols on the network are open and stationary, and in accord with the strategic intent
- Connectivity is sufficiently responsive that the intended purpose of the black box is not compromised by an under-performing network
- The network is extendable to remote or virtual units

Network Operating System

If the network is active, and not a *sneaker net*, there is, somewhere in the foundation of the system, a network manager which executes a network operating system (NOS). As in all operating systems, many services could be provided that depend on the environment of the product, system, project program, or unit:

- Security services—to include authorization and authentication for the black box to be on the network, and to authenticate any agents that may operate on the network
- Management services—to include load balancing, address maintenance, and error control
- Reporting services—to include availability reports, error performance, user population and usage, and other management metrics

Network Extension

Now applying the encapsulation concepts discussed above, the network is extendable to both program entities—like work streams and projects—and to various objects, both hardware and software. The programmatic extensions can be local or remote, real or virtual, and can even involve *sneaker net* between the program units. For successful extension to program units, it is necessary to coordinate and synchronize milestone planning, a subject we will take up in the next module.

Of course, one programmatic network idea, which can also be embedded in the project outcome—that is, the project or service—is workflow. There are many workflow solutions, to include smart *service oriented architecture* solutions as one variant that involves middle-layer functionalities and applications.

The extension of the network among objects, both hardware and software, is a familiar concept to most project teams. There are a myriad of materials on layered protocols and networking ideas at the physical level, so we will not extend this discussion further.

Module 2—Discussion for Critical Thinking

If your project has a large hardware component such that integration of hardware and software is a major consideration, would you think the ideas in this section are still applicable, and efficiently applicable, as compared to other ways to go about integrating functionality?

Module 3: Governing

"... the people we are trying to govern are not carrying out orders, but are actively processing information.... In order to process effectively, they need to have effective but minimal boundaries (so they stay within the goals of the company) but maximum possible flexibility (so they can act in the best interests of the company and respond to variation in their environment)."[5] *—Jim Benson*

Module 3—Objectives

- Discuss and explain the governing issues surrounding a shift in allegiance and dominance
- Examine planning, monitoring, and control practices in the agile context
- Discuss and explain what *done* means to an agile project

Allegiance and Dominance

Jim Benson wrote the opening words of this module, effectively restating the operating principle we've been developing: successful projects will be stationary for their strategic intent (Benson: effective but minimal boundaries), while simultaneously tactically emergent and iterative (Benson: maximum possible flexibility).

Anchor Bias

For the past generation, the tension between traditional and agile has been about these traditional ideas:

- Traditional methods can confidently predict input and outcomes because between the input and output are proven processes that transform the former into the latter. Thus, a properly controlled input, applied to proven processes, will produce the predicted outcome.
- Management focus is naturally overbalanced toward input: cost, schedule, and scope according to plan dominate.
- There is an abiding faith in planning as the answer to risk. In turn, there is great support for structured analysis and requirements traceability as the best first step.

There are problems with that traditional thinking because of these factors:

1. There are irreducible uncertainties around the quality of the input estimates that are not resolved by the project processes—sometimes because the uncertainties are quite latent until discovered too late. Thus the effects of these uncertainties find their way into the character of the outcomes, creating a variance—sometimes quite large—between the plan and the reality.
2. A focus on inputs misses the effects of circumstance and environment that play against the effectiveness of processes—and misses the changes in the need and priority driven by the passing of time.
3. Planning is an answer to some risks—those that are known and for which there is some experience with mitigation—but planning is only the set-up; as the project unfolds, the value of the upfront planning diminishes rapidly, to be replaced by tactical plans and responses to the moment.

Those familiar with the work of cognitive psychologists Daniel Kahneman and Amos Tversky will recognize *anchor bias* in the ideas above.[6] The concept of anchor bias is that we get captured by an initial idea, estimate, or proposition in such a manner that we are reluctant to give it up or wander too far afield—to wit, we put ourselves on a short anchor line—thinking that perhaps the expert that set the anchor has, indeed, the best judgment on what is correct.

Taken into project management, anchor bias tends to cause these issues:

- Legitimizes estimates with more certainty than they deserve
- Gives unwarranted weight or credence to the first answer or offer
- Promotes plans to the level of direction rather than guidance
- Places the most important project metrics at the front where the plan is, rather than at the back where the results are
- Puts a faith in the eventuality of outcomes that is unwarranted by project circumstances

To continue the metaphor, the agile response to the traditional anchor is to set a different anchor entirely—promoting tactical emergence and iteration as two better ideas, as given in the operating principle at the beginning of this chapter. In this section we posit two important management mandates that are necessary to implement the operating principle, a *shift of dominance* and a *shift of allegiance*.

Agile management mandates	**1. Shift of dominance** **FROM**: dominated by consumption according to plan (cost, schedule, planned scope) Short-term scorecard values with a limited lifecycle **TO:** dominated by value-added throughput (output, customer) Strategic scorecard values that drive business success **2. Shift of allegiance** **FROM**: Faithful adherence to a plan Planning is good; but plans do not survive **TO:** Faithful response to customer need If customers are not more successful because of the project, what's the point of the project?

As between the two, the shift of allegiance is the most profound, affecting all manner of relationships from project plans to pay plans, but especially those bargains embedded in contracts. We'll address some of these issues in the sections that follow.

Agile Manifesto

One thing about the Agile Manifesto that stands out is that the manifesto posits the very shift in dominance we've been discussing, but not, as some have interpreted, an abandonment of all things traditional. So, in that spirit, this is a discussion about a shift in dominance from a process dominated culture—in which people are expected to conform to or look first to process for the rules and guidance—to a culture dominated by individuals working as teammates empirically solving problems. And, by the way, the solution thus arrived at may be: follow the process; it's known to work well.

Of course, as the Agile Manifesto encourages a shift away from process domination, we should pause to ask: why did businesses invent processes in the first place, as the modern business emerged from the cottage businesses that dominated the 19th century? The answer is twofold:

1. The need to substitute the intimacy of personal trust for the more anonymous rule-based processes (which don't require trust, just obedience—which is, itself, easy to measure) as businesses scaled up, even as the personal knowledge of others was impractical to scale up in parallel.
2. The need to institutionalize the knowledge base so that anyone could leave and the next person would pick up the process. This issue is a weakness of de-emphasizing process. Where do you store institutional knowledge?

Now, with agile, we are back—full circle:

- Regarding Point 1—personal intimacy re-emerges as we scale down the scope of relationships, and we can de-emphasize the process controls in favor of personal interactions
- Regarding Point 2—institutional knowledge gets stored in those elements of the product base that are reusable, and in those aspects of the architecture that are well documented

Nonetheless, when a key person leaves, something valuable always leaves with them.

Methods Similarity

Of course, in theory and more or less in practice, all agile methodologies embrace all elements of the manifesto and all 12 of the principles. Thus, in this respect, all share many common features, but of course, they apply different emphasis. That is, the *dominance shift* from traditional practices to agile practices is not uniformly the same in all of the methodologies we have read about in this lesson.

Nonetheless, all have made the shift in one way or another. So, the discussion is about how similar the shifts or degrees of emphasis are in the two methodologies that we are comparing.

In that regard, if you read through the descriptions given in Chapter 1 and the Appendix, you'll see that a common idea is rapid delivery of working software, though the emphasis varies, from every few months to as rapidly as possible, to the Dynamic Systems Development Method in the middle of these two.

The GRAND BARGAIN for Best Value

Somewhat as a transition-to-agile strategy and somewhat as an ongoing understanding, the shift in allegiance is often made easier to accept if there can be a grand bargain between the business and the project—really between the business sponsor and the project manager (PM).

The grand bargain for best value	In trade for the flexibility to be tactically emergent and iterative to the customer/user's needs according to priority and urgency, the project will deliver a best value outcome.
	Best value is the most scope and the most valuable scope attainable for the resources given in the business case, consistent with the strategic intent.

In effect, this grand bargain between the sponsor and the PM—with the customer's needs in the frame—fixes the investment to be made by the business, thus, establishing some predictability where the business scorecard is concerned. At the same time, this grand bargain gives the business the best shot at a strategic outcome that will best benefit the business. Wherein, for a fixed investment and usually a fixed time frame, the PM is charged with delivering the best value possible to fulfill the project narrative and business case.

Take note that the customer is present in the spirit of the grand bargain, but is largely a silent partner until the project gets going. Even then, the customer may not be entirely in the loop. Included in best value, but where the customer doesn't usually get a vote, are:

- The nonfunctional requirements, especially those required to maintain certifications (like Software Engineering Institute level or International Organization for Standardization)
- Compliance to certain regulations (particularly in safety)
- Some finance requirements, like adherence to Sarbanes-Oxley
- Certain internal standards for engineering or architecture best practices

Contracting Conundrum

The contracting process we know of today (including, but not limited to government and the public sector, of course) often shifts the dominance from output (what does the contracting agency want to get out of this project?) back to input:

- What will this contract cost? Or, the cost is firm and fixed.
- When will all the requirements be satisfied? Or, I assert that I know all the requirements upfront.
- Every requirement of the contract is binding on the contractor, and can only be relieved by formal change management.

For the contractor, this form of governance is in opposite alignment with agile, which is output dominated (working product, etc. from the Agile Principles). Dominance conflict is built in to any contracted arrangement, almost as a part of the contract DNA.

Is it possible to contract for the grand bargain? Perhaps. We'll take up the details of contracting in another chapter. But the contracting agency might respond, if the requirements passed to the contractor are verified to be complete, where's the dominance issue? Just build it.

Of course, that's the heart of the debate—traditionalists are confident of completeness and their verification procedures. The way traditionalists see it, a contract to transfer the requirements to the contractor is perfectly appropriate. Agile practitioners are equally confident that the requirements are not only always incomplete, but many are likely not needed or will go unused if built and delivered, or there are some requirements not yet imagined ("I'll know it if I see it by chance.")

All requirements fixed and known	To an agile practitioner, a fixed-set-of-requirements contract is unreasonable at best—ungovernable at worst.

Four Conditions

We wrap up our discussion of allegiance and dominance by drawing from the foregoing discussion that there are four conditions needed in order for a successful shift of dominance and allegiance.

1. Strategic intent must be held stationary so that the business remains confident that the project will meet business objectives and mission.
2. Scope must be allowed to be tactically emergent and iterative so that the customer remains confident that their needs will be satisfied.
3. Quality must be promoted to the superior position, thereby subordinating the control of inputs as the dominant control mechanism.
4. Milestone planning (as will be discussed next) is applied as a synchronizing tool between traditional and agile work streams.

Milestone Planning, Monitoring, and Controlling

Agile practitioners usually rebel at the words monitoring and controlling, but less so at the word planning. Larry Bossidy has written words to this effect:

> *"You cannot have an execution culture without robust dialogue—one that brings reality to the surface through openness, candor, and informality."*[7]

Certainly, agile is all about effective execution, so an execution culture is certainly no anathema. Thus, for the purposes of this discussion, we are going to focus on the idea of dialogue as the way to get at monitoring and controlling, rather than the big brother aspects of domineering management non-value-added overhead.

Monitoring and Controlling

A contributing practice for measuring progress so you know where you are in the work in process (WIP) is to actually monitor what is going on, and then apply control only where necessary to maintain faithfulness to the strategic intent.

Project monitoring (along with monitoring tools and systems) has these functionalities:

- Sense, measure, and gather metric data that can be used to take action to influence outcomes (progress). Corollary: don't sense and measure what you can't actually use. This seems like common sense, but often it's easy to sense, measure, and collect data—so we do it, only to store it for no real use.
- Interpret data and compare results to milestones, budget, and progress goals. The latter is more about outcomes, whereas the former two are more about input—though monitoring achievements at milestones is essential for any sense of "where are we?"
- Reflect on the results for lessons learned and means to improve.
- Report data (meetings, dashboards, reports), being cognizant that the quality of the report for agile purposes is not only a matter of accuracy and relevance, but also a matter of timeliness.

Project control has these functionalities:

- Impose or remove constraints to include authority; responsibilities and policies; standards; rules; and work flow that influence progress

- Allocate or de-allocate resources (money, staff, tools, elements of environment)
- Plan and execute responses to monitoring data (upon reflection, act on the monitoring)

Monitoring and controlling should form a closed loop:

- Plan *just enough* to guide execution
- Execute to meet strategic intent, while remaining open to tactical emergence and iteration
- Monitor the execution by sensing, measuring, and interpreting progress
- Apply *just enough* control to maintain faith with the business case.
- Monitor the effects of control

Thereafter, go around this loop—monitor-control-monitor—as many times as necessary.

Change Management, Risk Management

". . . but the software didn't work . . ." is, of course, the issue agile is designed to fix, where *work* is defined in the large sense of quality: fitness to use, fitness to support, fitness to environment, etc.

Many don't think of agile as a way to approach risk, but indeed agile is itself a risk response to the natural uncertainty of software requirements—the main issue being that there are often no real physical constraints to a software requirement, story, or use case. Thus, our imagination is the only real constraint.

But, of course, imagination is not linear or sequential—we can think of things in almost any order. Thus, the agile backlog we discuss in this book is itself *agile*, changing, and changeable.

Change Management

Any hybrid methodology enterprise project has to reconcile two change management paradigms that seemingly have to co-exist:

1. **Agile:** Change is to be provoked and encouraged so as to obtain maximum customer satisfaction within the parameters of *best value*.
2. **Traditional:** Change is to be resisted after plans are approved, so that the quality of predictability is not compromised and the outcomes of the project conform to the validated requirements in the plan.

Our approach to change management is encapsulation of methods and practices, just as described earlier in this chapter. At the interfaces, change is managed traditionally:

- Changes to open interfaces intended to be stationary are not provoked or encouraged
- Changes to open interfaces, when deemed necessary, are subject to change management protocols as governed by the change management authority of the project

Inside the black box, change management is a sibling of the methodology. Agile methods within the black box provoke change; traditional methods control change with an eye toward minimizing change.

Risk Management

Risk management is not so much a matter of encapsulating methods and practices. Most risk practices apply equally well to agile methods and traditional methods. The paradigm of identify-prioritize-assess-respond is so ubiquitous as to be universally effective.

The arching issues confronting risk managers are these:

- Will the risk to project objectives materially compromise the strategic intent?
- Can the risk be handled tactically, or is a more strategic response needed?

In general however, agile practitioners are more prone to just-in-time and just-enough risk management to stay on top of risks than are their traditional counterparts. Traditional practitioners put faith in rigorous planning as the first best step to risk management, writing risk management plans, and filling out risk registers as soon as the project begins.

However, the ideas of Nassim Taleb may be the most appropriate to software projects. In his book *Antifragile: Things That Gain from Disorder*,[8] one of Taleb's themes is that one of the best defenses against business risks is to put in capacity and capability to be able to sustain shocks without catastrophe to the business. And, as the book title suggests, the more mutually decoupled such capacity and capability is, the better to absorb shock. Mapped into projects, and especially agile projects, whether hybrid or not, are these antifragile points:

- **Always have redundant capabilities:** For the agile project, redundancy of skills on the agile team is the primary way the shock of losing a key person is mitigated

- **Always decouple effects when you can:** This is first an architecture consideration, but it fits the black box paradigm very well. A problem in one black box may be contained if functions are allocated to the black boxes with containment in mind.
- **Always diversify by not having too many functions in one black box:** In risk terms, this is the *square root of N* rule whereby the uncertainty of a risk event is reduced by the square root of the number of lesser events in which it can be divided.
- **Buffer every strategic milestone with schedule slack so that shocks in the activities leading to the milestone do not compromise the milestone:** This is a play on the idea of the *critical chain* method of planning, first described by Eliyahu Goldratt in his book *Critical Chain*.[9]

There are two ideas in agile that are directly responsive to the diversification rule:

1. Divide the long project schedule into N independent schedule units called iterations. The iterations need not all be the same length. Thus, WIP on a Kanban schedule qualifies.
2. Divide the scope into N independent backlogs, each backlog dedicated to an iteration. Of course, there is some interdependency between backlogs, due to sequencing constraints (A before B), foundation capabilities, debt that rolls from one backlog to another and the like. So the rule of N becomes the rule of approximately N.

Verification and Validation

Two of the conceptual conundrums of the hybrid methodology project are:

1. How do you verify that which is incomplete?
2. How do you validate the efficacy of that which is yet to be conceived?

Verification and validation (V&V) are traditionally held to be very important project practices that are difficult to map directly into the agile domain. Traditionally, V&V has these practices:

- **Validation:** Each requirement is validated for its business usefulness, in effect, its efficacy toward project objectives. Validation is usually not later than the last step in gathering and organizing requirements.
- **Verification:** When development is complete, and when integration of all requirements are complete, the roll is called to ensure that every validated requirement is present and accounted for.

Placed into an agile context, validation is applied both to the project back-log and to the iteration backlog, since changes are anticipated to occur. Validation is typically first applied at the story or use case level, validating with conversation among the interested and sponsoring parties that the functionality proposed is valid for the purpose. One can imagine validating against external rules and regulations, perhaps internal standards, and of course validating against the business case.

Verification is generally a practice at the iteration level, verifying that the iteration backlog matches the iteration outcomes, and logging any differences.

Depending on the project paradigm, V&V can be carried into integration tests and customer acceptance tests, again testing against various benchmarks and standards for validity, and verifying that everything delivered at the iteration level got integrated at the deliverable product level.

Are We Done?

There are many challenges facing an agile team—not the least of which is an uninformed business management team that is not conversant with the concepts of an agile project. And, if the project is a transition project, moving the enterprise from traditional to agile, the impressions of the business management will be all the more important to the adoption of agile throughout.

So, here's a challenge we address in this section:

> *How would you explain to the sponsor or other business management—presumably not experienced with agile—when the project will actually be done, given the variable scope?*

It's not so hard in the traditional project: *done* is typically when all the validated requirements have been verified as delivered to the product base. The basic question of *done* in agile is more complicated.

The Basic Question

Here's the set-up for our discussion—
Are we *done* when:

- Time or money runs out?
- The backlog is fully exhausted?
- The customer says it's done?
- The business management says it's done?
- The best possible value has been delivered?

The answer is: *yes*. Any of the scenarios are feasible for *done* in the agile context. It should come as no surprise that my personal favorite is the last one—best value delivered.

The least practical of the scenarios is *the backlog is fully exhausted*. Actually, the backlog is probably never exhausted. There is always something that can be done.

Zero Base

Agile is presumably *zero base* at every release, meaning that, at the conclusion of any release of working product to the product base, the project is *re-justified* for continuation to the next release. Consequently, if there is not sufficient justification, applying whichever of the criteria in the set-up is the preferred decision parameter, the project ends. It is *done*.

In the set-up we did not mention *capitulation*, which would only apply to a failed project with on-going WIP—but, it happens. Sometimes a project simply is not feasible and the time comes to shut it down—to capitulate to the circumstances. Capitulation is the harshest verdict and the most egregious metric for *done*.

	Other people's money (OPM)
A project management tip	• When you're doing a project with OPM—as contrasted with your own underwriting of your project—the people who have the money always have a vote on all strategic aspects of the project, including what is the meaning of *done*. • They not only have a vote on the meaning of *done*, but a vote on whether or not the project state has reached *done*.

Other Factors

Beyond the previous definitions given, there are a few other things to think about:

- **The business case:** The business case is the first place to look for and define *done*, especially *done* for the business, and even more especially if the project is public sector with *mission* built into the metric for *done*.
- **Other work streams:** No serious project has one work stream, so agile often only applies to the software development; the rest of the project often runs traditionally and according to plans with *done* defined by the satisfaction of validated requirements.

- **Strategy versus tactics:** In general, agile puts strategic responsibility with the sponsor as documented in the business case; tactical value judgments are made by the architect, system engineer, lead developer, and customer/user during backlog design at the beginning of each release cycle.
- **Sequencing:** Newtonian physics still apply—roof after walls—so some things the customer wants may have to be deferred to another project.
- **Quality, standards, and regulation:** The customer doesn't usually get a vote on business policies to adhere to standards, maintain accreditation, and conform to regulation. These take budget and thus, discretionary funds for customer needs/wants are thereby diminished, deferring some requirements to the next project.
- **Nonfunctional:** The customer usually doesn't have a say in nonfunctional requirements, and they figure heavily into *done*.

Value versus Cost

Here's an intriguing thought—value and cost are often not strongly dependent on each other. So, what's your answer to these two questions?

1. What's the *cost of value*, that is: the cost to create whatever value you perceive for the project?
2. How do you put a business value on the project outcome, especially if the outcome is *mission accomplished* in the public sector, or some *relief* given in the nonprofit sector?

It could be that best value is also the least cost, but not necessarily. We might spend a lot of money getting to best value. In other words, the value obtainable at a least cost may not be worth spending the money. This is the argument around *cheap* versus *inexpensive*. The former is not best value; the latter may be.

Thus, we are drawn to consider the *opportunity cost* version of value versus cost:

> *Among all the other things you could have done with the time, effort, and resources, is this project outcome (product) more beneficial or useful than any other alternate opportunity for the same time, effort, and resources?*

If the answer is *yes*, then the project has favorable opportunity cost (favorable means: project value minus the value of any other opportunity is greater than zero).

A project management tip	Best value and opportunity cost
	A best value project always has favorable opportunity cost. That is, for any other project of the same investment, less would be returned.

Module 3—Discussion for Critical Thinking

Resistance to the shift in dominance and allegiance are perhaps the most vexing management challenges in all of agile project management. How would you explain the advantages of shifting dominance and allegiance to a reluctant business manager?

Summary and Takeaway Points

The theme we developed in this chapter is that a successful hybrid methodology is only possible if there can be embracing and respecting of open and stationary qualities of architecture, functionality, and governance.

In Module 1, the important finding is that this operating principle is a necessary condition for a hybrid methodology:

> *Agile projects are simultaneously strategically stationary and tactically iterative and emergent*

At the end of the day, tactically iterative and emergent becomes an overlay to the strategic intent. Although there may be deviations of strategy along the way, at the project outcome, the deliverables converge to the strategic intent.

In Module 2, we learn that the hybrid methodology must reconcile two methodologies that produce intermediate results quite differently. This reconciliation is achieved in the following ways:

1. Encapsulation of requirements (architecture), method, and practices with black boxes that have open interfaces—which provides necessary isolation, yet an opportunity and capability for inter-functionality
2. Milestone planning—which provides the means to synchronize outcomes for customer deliverables

In Module 3, the takeaway is that governance practices promote two ideas:

1. There is a shift of dominance as to what to manage—the traditional dominance is toward the inputs (cost, schedule, scope), whereas the agile dominance is toward the outputs that satisfy customer demand
2. There is a shift of allegiance from traditional plans (maintain faith with the plan) to agile outcomes (maintain faith with customer need)

Consequently, there is an issue in the form of a question: if scope is flexible, when is the project *done?*

Our preferred answer is that the project is done when best value has been delivered. Our least favorite answer is that the project is done when the validated backlog is exhausted. Our contention: it's never exhausted; so it's never really done.

Chapter Endnotes

1. This chapter is based, in part, upon the author's presentation to the UX/Agile Conference, Melbourne, FL, April 21, 2015.

2. In the point-to-point situation, the numbers of connections grow exponentially, quickly overwhelming any reasonable system of scale.

3. One of the most common bus networks is the 802 Ethernet. Ethernet topology is a bus structure which supports delivery of data as packets as controlled and managed by a layered protocol. The Ethernet is managed by the NOS; black boxes each have a bus address. All data between black boxes flows over the bus.

4. A mesh is a network in which every node can reach every other node; if the *reach* is direct, then the network is *fully connected*. Fully connected networks are often internally redundant and not fragile to a failure within the network. However, nodes often have the functionality of a relay, thus obviating the need for full connectivity. It's beyond the purpose of this book to examine the tradeoffs between each topology for an agile-hybrid methodology.

5. Benson, J. "Your specific is highly general," moduscooperandi.com/blog/your-specific-is-highly-general/

6. Tversky, A. Kahneman, D. (1974). "Judgment under uncertainty: Heuristics and biases." Science 185 (4157): 1124-1131. doi:10.1126/science.185.4157.1124. PMID 17835457.

7. Bossidy, L. and Charan, R. "Execution: the discipline of getting things done," Crown Publishing Group, June, 2002.

8. Taleb, N., *Antifragile: Things That Gain from Disorder*, Random House, New York, 2012.

9. Goldratt, E., *Critical Chain: A Business Novel*, North River Press, 1997.

5

Developing the Scope and Requirements

Encourage requirements to change as often as necessary to ensure that the customer receives the best value for the resources committed.

> *A requirements paradox:*
>   *Requirements must be stable for predictable results.*
>   *However, the requirements always change*

Niels Malotaux

Agile methods trade on the concept of being adaptive to changing customer needs. The scope evolves as the customer is exposed to each product release, gives feedback, and thereby influences the next increment's design. Taken holistically, feedback, reflection, and next-iteration influences present unique challenges in scope definition and requirements management.

Actual outcomes are more dynamic over time than is a plan-driven project development lifecycle (PD-PDLC) point solution—that is, the natural volatility of requirements is felt with higher fidelity than is allowed by the requirements *freeze* imposed by a *big design up front*.

Module 1: Agile Scope
Scope is the variable among cost, schedule, quality, and scope

Module 1—Objectives

- Discuss and explain the agile idea of evolving, emerging, and adaptive scope
- Discuss and explain best value as the optimum outcome of agile projects

Evolving, Emerging, and Adaptive

In the agile context, scope changes; scope is the variable among cost, schedule, quality, and scope. Scope is constantly evolving, emerging, and adaptive to customer/user priorities. In this way, scope is profoundly different than the traditional project; this reality causes the most angst among business sponsors and project leaders accustomed to challenging change and volatility. For transition strategies, the idea of an ever-changing scope is perhaps the highest hurdle to overcome.

Volatility Is Managed

The most important point for readers is that volatility of evolving and emerging scope is managed. As we will discuss, the business case product vision is long-term *stationary*, meaning that at any time we view it, the vision is more or less invariant. However, within the framework of the vision, volatility is managed on a scale from *high and allowable*—for tactical planning changes leading up to development—to *stable enough for developers to work* during a specific development iteration.

The planning responses for scope and requirements are organized this way:

- The business case holds the product vision in a top-level framework, with rather less direction than customary about feature, function, and performance
- Scope is planned incrementally with evolution allowed and encouraged
- Planning occurs in shorter and more time-sensitive frameworks called rolling waves (a planning concept discussed elsewhere in this book)
- Development cycles—called iterations or sprints—are governed by a few rules that regulate requirements

Requirements governance is a lesser task for project managers, so long as fidelity is maintained to the spirit and strategic intent of the sponsor's vision. Indeed, successful agile project managers accommodate the different role central authority plays in evolutionary and adaptive methodologies.[1] The role becomes modulation and containment of exuberant and aggressive customers while allowing, encouraging, and facilitating innovative interactions—consistent with the business case framework—that arise from high performance customer-developer teams, a topic of another chapter in this book.

Emergent and Adaptive Methods

	Emergent and adaptive methods
A project management tip	Adaptive methods have the property of *emergence*, meaning the outcomes generally have more range and complexities than would be predicted by the simple combination and application of practices and project rules that govern development teams.

The range and complexity of emergent and adaptive methods arises from feedback, a form of reflection, which gives the process of transforming input into output the attributes of nonlinearity and circular dependency—output depends on input, but then input depends on including output effects, which requires the whole process to adapt to the mix of input and output in circulation.

This circular dependency with *adaption* forming a *closed-loop* system is markedly different from traditional closed-loop linear systems. The mission of linear systems is to accurately and predictably transform input to output with high fidelity; in effect to follow the plan.

This is not so with adaptive feedback systems. The mission of adaptive systems is to make outcomes satisfying to the system *agents*, who are all the active participants in the system processes. If the feedback is properly phased—that is, timed to arrive back at the input at a helpful moment—and if the interaction of all the participants is aimed at a common objective, systems with adaptive feedback can converge on high quality results.[2]

Moving the Scope Lever

Perhaps more so with agile methods than in any other methodologies, the hand of the customer moves the scope lever. The scope lever is one of four principle levers—the other three are schedule, budget, and quality. Schedule and budget are given in the business case; budget is simply the limit on funding, a cap on affordability, and a resource to be distributed among iterations as the value proposition evolves.

The business case milestones set the top-level schedule; milestones express business timing and set project value in the context of a calendar. Quality is a lever with little range of motion; quality is provided at a uniformly high standard; quality cannot be compromised without jeopardizing trust with the customer.

Scope as a Best Value

Agile projects value maximizing customer satisfaction over minimizing the variance to a plan. Putting scope-budget-schedule-quality together in a best-value formulation, scope is the most flexible, but with flexibility contained within limits of architecture, feasibility, and funding demand. To be sure, outcomes must make a worthwhile difference for the customer and put the enterprise in a better position, but within a budget cap. After all, someone has to pay for the project!

Best Value Defined

> The most scope possible—for the available resources—that most optimizes business effectiveness, importance, and responsiveness to urgency.

A best value outcome has the most optimum cost for what is delivered, even though what is delivered may not conform exactly as originally envisioned. Indeed, best value may actually be *more scope* than envisioned, but at exceptional and affordable investment.

A best value outcome is the most value-added outcome achievable for the available resources. *Most value-added* means the project is maximally lean about operating expenses and resource consumption. It also means that the difference between the value of ideas and opportunities pre-project, and the value of useful products and services post-project is maximized. Revisit Figure 2.2 for a pictorial of this discussion.

	Best value is the answer to scope
A project management tip	• Even though scope is flexible, stakeholder expectations are embodied in the project vision which is stationary.
	• The best answer for satisfying stakeholders is to always provide the most benefit for the investment made—to maximize the value returned.

Scope Defined

Scope is defined this way:

- *Scope is all the things we must do, all the things we want to do, and all the things we actually do*
- *Backlog is the scope parsed into work units, stories, use cases, tasks, and the like*
- *Architecture is the scope mapped into form and function*

There are some *must-dos* that influence scope—*must-dos* as a matter of governance and *must-dos* as a matter of custom and expectation. Projects must adhere to standards that have become generally accepted practices; processes and protocols must be applied in a manner that is consistent with certifications; and projects must meet the unspoken demands of the market that, over time, have become routinely expected—demands for reliability, availability, compatibility, responsiveness, and eco-friendliness, to name a few.

Module 1—Discussion for Critical Thinking

Accepting change, indeed; provoking change is perhaps the most fundamental idea in agile methods next to that of delivering small increments of useful functionality early and often. But, from your experience, how would you reassure a project sponsor that matters are under control and that resources will not be wasted chasing scope changes of little value?

Module 2: Envisioning

Envisioning a project outcome sometimes comes as an epiphany, but other times requires some method, even though you cannot legislate imagination

Module 2—Objectives

- Define envisioning in the agile context
- Explain the use of the Kano chart in the agile context
- Explain the *wicked problem* in the context of envisioning

Envisioning

In the same way you cannot legislate imagination, you cannot precisely mandate how to envision a product goal. Transforming visionary ideas into goals—real end-states that are achievable—is a work of art, a bit of process, and a dose of applied leadership. The story usually begins: "I had this idea one day...." However, imagination is but the first step.

Envisioning is an investment in ideas. The common understanding is that an unformed or immature idea is given richness and detail, conformed to the value system of the enterprise, and made actionable by a project team. A filled-in business case is the capture vehicle for envisioning.

Recall from Chapter 2 that in the business case, a high-level business story describes the need. A product vision is offered. A concept of operations, albeit at low fidelity, identifies the community of users and those who support them by roles and their needed features and functions. Value is given specificity by investment budget and milestones.

To envision beyond the business case, add depth and breadth to the business story. Consider these three steps:

1. *Assemble the agile team and interview the visionary.* Begin building executive and customer relationships. Involve everyone on the team to leverage multifunctional experiences. Get as much of a picture, in any and several forms, as possible—verbal, written, and the unspoken gesture. Take advantage of a person-to-person encounter to absorb the fullness of being present together—environment, responsiveness, and attitude; establish credibility with probing questions; be open to novel ideas and compelling motivations.[3]

   Search for the beginning. The *big idea* may have come as an epiphany, but more likely it evolved over time by means of many informal conversations, and then was shaped by influences from media, market, and friends. The opportunity may be the fortunate confluence of technology availability and market receptiveness. Perhaps the idea is a reaction to successful competitors, external threats, or some other *push*. It may be a consequence of public policy that unleashes opportunity and creativity. Or, there could be a great national imperative that demands innovation.

   In his book, *Winning at New Products*, Robert G. Cooper writes "the game is won in the first few plays.... The seeds of disaster [are] often sown in the early phases...[arising from] poor homework, lack of customer orientation, and poor quality of execution...."[4] Cooper goes on to list eleven ways to get and absorb good ideas, but the first three are the most helpful:

---

1. Identify a focal point to bring all the ideas, information, and interviews together.
2. List all the contributing sources that could add value to the idea formulation.
3. Engage the customer and users.

2. *Explore ideas* by spinning them about in a 360-degree view. What do they look like from the points of view of customer, user, supply chain, sales, marketing, and product support? Draw, diagram, or write down the ideas from each, and then look for affinity and common ground. One piece of advice: "If you can't draw it, you can't write it!"

3. *Do a Kano analysis of features and functions.*[5] Kano analysis is done on a Kano chart, a graphical tool for portraying product feature and function in relation to customer satisfaction.

Envision with Kano Charts

As shown in Figure 5.1, the chart is in four quadrants separated by horizontal and vertical axes. The horizontal is the product axis and the vertical is

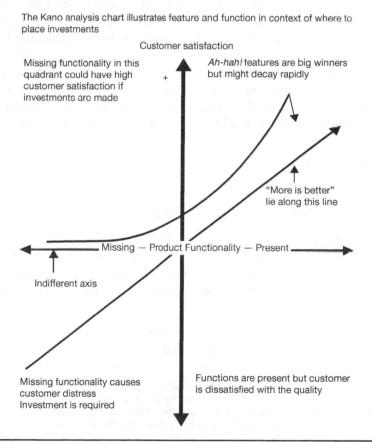

The Kano analysis chart illustrates feature and function in context of where to place investments

Customer satisfaction

Missing functionality in this quadrant could have high customer satisfaction if investments are made

Ah-hah! features are big winners but might decay rapidly

"More is better" lie along this line

Missing — Product Functionality — Present

Indifferent axis

Missing functionality causes customer distress Investment is required

Functions are present but customer is dissatisfied with the quality

Figure 5.1   Kano analysis chart

the customer axis. Features and functions that lie along the horizontal axis have no particular customer appeal. Customers are *indifferent* to these but they are nevertheless required by standards and conventions.

Opportunities and threats describe the four quadrants. The upper right quadrant is the a*h-hah!* space. In the upper right quadrant there is high customer satisfaction and unique product value. The lower left is just the opposite—it has missing product value and correspondingly poor customer satisfaction. The two remaining quadrants are the middle ground between customer and product value.

The Kano analysis provides insights like these:

- Features that lie along the horizontal axis require continuing investment but return little in customer loyalty; customers expect them in every product so they rarely provide any discriminating value.
- Features in the upper right quadrant are usually *high value—high investment* opportunities. But as competitors recognize the attractiveness and provide similar offerings, these features decay toward the horizontal axis over time.
- Any feature that is missing—as identified in the lower left quadrant— becomes a must-do investment, to catch up with evolving expectations of the market. Investment in this quadrant is *me-too* investing that simply levels the field for discriminators or disqualifiers.

Wicked Thinking

The wicked idea is this:

The requirements are not knowable until the solution is knowable.

Does that sound agile? It might; but unlike agile most of the time, it's certainly circular in logic. Wicked problems, issues, or needs arise when there are many interlocking issues and competing stakeholders for which there seems no obvious point of entry. All resolutions seem to conflict with something else. Thus, some methodologies of *wicked thinking* are required.

	Wicked thinking and agile
A project management tip	• Wicked problem solving has a natural affinity with agile methods because to solve a wicked problem, the analyst thinks iteratively rather than linearly, somewhat like a spiral, and generally begins with the end in mind. • Try to envision the desired end-state first, and then work back to what the requirements must be.

Problems like these also arise when constraints constantly change, thereby introducing new conflicts and dependencies that force the solution to change also. Wicked problems are a constant test of whether any specific outcome is ever really an answer. A sure sign of the wicked problem is constant spinning about on an issue. From a project perspective, as conventionally governed, such an idea is a really perverse feedback loop. Nonetheless, solutions to wicked problems can be envisioned.

In Excel terms, solving for a wicked problem is what the *resolver* does: it tries a solution on the source to see if it fits. That's pretty much the wicked situation. You talk about the requirements, then you talk about the solution, and then on the basis of yet another solution that might actually be doable, you back fit the requirements.

One of the source documents for this line of thinking is *Dilemmas in a General Theory of Planning*. Authors Rittel and Webber outline 10 *wicked issues*; among the more intriguing for agile projects are these:

Wicked Issues*
2. Wicked problems have no stopping rule.
3. Solutions to wicked problems are not true-or-false, but good-or-bad.
6. Wicked problems do not have an enumerable (or an exhaustively describable) set of potential solutions, nor is there a well-described set of permissible operations that may be incorporated into the plan.
10. The planner has no right to be wrong. Here the aim is not to find the truth, but to improve some characteristics of the world where people live. Planners are liable for the consequences of the actions they generate.
* Numbered according to the original source list.

Module 2—Discussion for Critical Thinking

Sometimes our vision comes to us as an epiphany, creating that *ah-hah* moment that maps to the Kano chart we discussed. But, sometimes we start with the *green field* and no firm idea of the project need. In that event, what process have you employed for developing the business case vision?

Module 3: Requirements
Shifting the process from structured analysis to conversations

Module 3—Objectives

- Introduce and explain the agile approach to and process for developing and analyzing requirements
- Discuss and explain stories, use cases, and models for agile requirements

Process for Requirements

The literature of projects is rich with guidance for developing detailed requirements, not only for software, but also for all manner of engineering disciplines. In plan-centric methods, some call the developing requirements structured analysis, some call it requirements engineering, some simply call it *the requirements process*, and others may not have any name at all for what they do. Taken altogether, there are literally dozens of practices hosted in one methodology or another.[6]

How to Write Requirements for Software

IEEE 830:[7]

The guidance for writing software requirements for a PD-PDLC, normally taken to be IEEE 830-1998 *Recommended Practice for Software Requirements*, is not usually applied to agile methods, primarily because 830-style requirements are product focused lists of functions and features—a return to Deming—rather than customer and user focused on why features and functions are needed—an embrace of Juran's trilogy.

There is danger in 830-style requirements because, in practice, they are more *push* than *pull* in the lean sense of the words. There is tendency to list many requirements that have marginal day-to-day usefulness, since there is minimal means for customers to express priorities in the traditional PD-PDLC.

Use Cases:

Use cases originated in the so-called Rational Unified Process. Use cases are supported by many tools and aides; the text style can be very lean and agile. Use cases are strongly recommended in the Crystal Family agile methods.

The main feature of use case is the scenario—a generally complete story of the user need. Scenarios are very applicable to agile methods, as discussed in Chapter 4.

It is easier to maintain coherence with architecture using a higher level and more complete description like a use case.

User Stories:

User stories are vignettes of scenarios.

User stories originated as an XP practice as a means to express vignettes of functional requirements.

User stories can be identified by decomposing use case scenarios.

Recommendation: In this book, we recommend use case scenarios and user story vignettes to document user functional requirements.

Agile methods go about requirements in more natural language, the language of themes, scenarios and stories. Much like the way this book is put together with major themes at each chapter heading, lesser themes to discriminate major sections, and then section topics, agile methodologists begin with the top-level theme—the business story—in the business case, and then build out use cases that are then dissected into user stories, ultimately to test-driven development (TDD) scripts.

Begin with a Framework

The steps described in Table 5.1 guide overall agile requirements processing. By tailoring and adaption, the steps in Table 5.1 are applicable at any level of the pyramid shown in Figure 5.2.[8]

The business case, vision of the solution, and customer partnership are the prerequisites for building-out requirements. There are six steps:

1. Adopt the business story and product vision as the pinnacle of a requirements framework.
2. Assemble summary-level, low-fidelity use case scenarios that identify the user community, user roles, operating conditions or states, user processes, and needed feature function, and performance. The summary scenarios become the project-level backlog.
3. Parse the project backlog into planning wave backlogs according to customer priority, technical feasibility, and sequencing governed by architecture. Planning waves are time horizons, each one more distant, to which scope is allocated; each scope allocation is progressively less detailed and more loosely defined the farther out in time you go. Planning waves are discussed elsewhere in this book.
4. At the time each wave comes up for planning in detail, parse the wave backlogs into iteration backlogs, again taking into account sequencing, feasibility, and business priorities.
5. During the iteration planning session, as discussed in Chapter 6, decompose the use case backlog into user stories, prioritize the stories, and implement those that fit the team's capacity for one iteration time-box. Those that don't fit are reallocated to the next backlog.
6. After each wave, release, and iteration, restack the requirements backlog according to priority. Apply governance to introduce new and materially changed requirements.

Figure 5.2 illustrates the discussion.

Table 5.1   Framework practices

Process Step	Commentary
Gather requirements	• Seek, identify, and gather requirements by interviewing stake-holders and accessing other relevant business and regulatory materials that range from the small details to the big picture.
	• Be conversational: Many requirements are latent, brought to the surface only by conversation and discussion.
	• Probe for requirements that are functional and non-functional to include performance, environmental, regulatory, quality, and other needs.
	• Select candidates for interviews from sales, marketing, users, service and maintenance, supply chain, and other infrastructure support, as well as ancillary groups such as training and human resources.
Organize according to attributes	• Organize requirements by affinity, by hierarchy, and possibly by categories such as high risk, interface, user, etc.
	• Set an initial priority among requirements. Since agile methods encourage requirements to change to meet demand, so will priorities.
	• Examine feasibility, affordability, and consistency with architecture and legacy demands.
	• Prototype and model, especially if approaching significant risks where a spiral front-end process is effective.
	• Estimate complexity as a figure or merit until detail estimates are made in the iteration.
Make a record of every requirement	• Commit requirements to a template managed by a database to be able to trace and track requirements to stories and vision.
	• If using the TDD from the Extreme Programming (XP) methodology, document requirements at the lowest level with a test procedure.
Verify and validate	• Verify completeness, compliance, accuracy, and testability of the solution by answering the question: "Are these the requirements to do the job right?"
	• Validate to answer the question: "Are these the requirements to do the right job?"
Manage changes	• Develop and employ a protocol to elicit changes, manage validation, and manage priorities.
	• Develop and employ a governance program as an integral part of the change management.

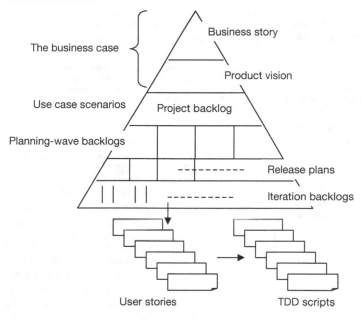

A pyramid for requirements is peaked by the business case that flows down to individual iterations

Figure 5.2   Requirements pyramid

Successful Interviews

Talking to executives, customers, sponsors, stakeholders, and users is the one best way to find out what is on everybody's mind. Sometimes a casual conversation works best, providing an opportunity to absorb the general atmosphere of the situation—something Alistair Cockburn calls communication by osmosis. Other times, it's more appropriate to structure an interview.

There are many helpful references for interviewing for needs and wants.[9] They can be distilled to a few common sense guidelines, as given in Table 5.2.

Stories, Models, and Prototypes

The detailed work on development requirements are done by teams. Development teams work at the last couple of layers illustrated beforehand in Figure 5.2. Analysis and examination of the backlog begins in a session called Iteration-0.

Table 5.2   Guidelines for interviewing for needs and wants

Action	Comment
Interview with a small team in a comfortable and familiar setting.	• Focus questions through one person, another helps with the conversation and observes non-verbal signs, and a third takes notes. • Adopt a familiar setting to remove distractions and thereby facilitate the focus on the topic.
Prepare in advance. Have an agenda or outline to guide the interview and do homework to be subject matter conversant.	• Share the agenda in advance, but also let the conversation flow naturally to points not anticipated or even out of order. • Bring a subject matter expert into the preparations, but minimize jargon that is not commonly understood.
Ask questions that cannot be answered with one word, but be cautious not to lead the interview to a foregone conclusion.	• Engage in conversation. Conversation is necessary to enrich the experience with detail and metaphor, fill out the value proposition, and find the limits of risk tolerance. • Capture the minutiae for fit later with the bigger concepts.
Follow-up on the corollary or the flip-side of the question.	• Ask questions from many points of view. The 360-perspective is always revealing and often useful for evaluating and setting priorities for items not on the critical path.[1] • Complete the circle of examination of the concept. What would the customer, competitor, or supplier say differently than an internal stakeholder?
Search for the minimum, but seek the horizon.	• Find the simplest thing to do. Agile methods stress not doing everything at once, rolling out sequentially until the limits are reached. • Get a sense of the minimum, anticipate a plan for a bit more, and probe for the limits of the opportunity.
Remember the project balance sheet! Test for risk tolerance.	• Probe for the down-side limitations, triggers that are made sensitive by attitude, and what eagerness there is for up-side opportunity.

[1]The critical path is a scheduling concept. It is the path from inception to completion that is the longest. A slip along this path causes the end date to slip.

Iteration-0

The team prepares the backlog in the first iteration, commonly called Iteration-0. The *zero* signifies that the iteration produces no product. The two prerequisites to Iteration-0 are:

1. The top-level theme and business story has been developed, following interview steps (as shown in Table 5.2). Some methodologists call the top level an *epic*.

2. The project-level backlog has been developed and parsed into planning wave backlogs as illustrated in Figure 5.2.

To execute Iteration-0, follow the steps in Table 5.3.

Use Cases, User Stories

Use cases, models, and prototypes are all tools to get a mind's-eye image of the requirement.

Use cases: Alistair Cockburn, the godfather of Crystal Methods, is a strong advocate for use cases. Use cases are ordinarily thought of as a model of the requirement presented in text, graphically, or pictorially. However, use cases also lend themselves to models supported by a modeling language commonly called UML, the Unified Modeling Language.

The Unified Modeling Language (UML)

UML is a tool that facilitates visualizing, specifying, constructing, and documenting system artifacts.[10]

UML provides a means to structure the case elements and also allows for scripted evaluation of the model for completeness, accuracy, redundancy, and efficiency.

UML has three building blocks: things, relationships, and diagrams.

1. Things are structural meaning nouns, behavioral meaning verbs, grouping meaning organizational parts, and notational meaning explanatory.
2. Relationships express associations and dependencies.
3. Diagrams are graphical presentations of the language.

A use case is a scenario; a scenario is a functional script with specific conditions. In the pecking order, use cases are more complex and involved than user story vignettes; several user stories are typically contained within a use case. The use case specification includes identification of human and system actors, the main scenario, and success criteria for the scenario.

Pre- and post-conditions on the system and actors are specified, somewhat like asserts; triggers that initiate action are identified. Alternate situations, called extensions, are described. There may be other use cases related to the use case under discussion, referred to as inclusions or extensions.[11] The main scenario is the normal course of action; alternatives and error or contingency responses included by extensions. "Inclusions" are like subroutines in the main scenario. Figure 5.3 depicts a typical use case.

User stories: Many agile methodologists write user stories on 3×5 cards and post them in a common area. Cards are decidedly low tech to be sure

Table 5.3   Iteration-0

Step	Commentary
Assemble the team	Ensure everyone, including the customer, participates
Organize information	• Organize all the information topically using white boards, sticky notes, or other means • Form affinity groups, typically by scenarios, that are themselves a collection of stories • Create hierarchies to organize little ideas under big topics; create relationships between affinity groups
Interview for completeness	Conduct more interviews to fill in the blanks and confirm relationships
Allocate requirements to iterations	• Allocate a set of requirements from the planning wave backlog to the iteration • Consider customer priorities, functional or technical sequencing, feasibility, and available technology
Create a story card	• If not using use cases and the UML, commit one testable requirement to a card or spreadsheet record. • Add amplifying or clarifying information
Estimate complexity	By group consensus, arrive at a figure of merit for the complexity and effort for each testable requirement
Create a burn-down list (SCRUM) or burn-up list (XP)	List all requirements with attributes for who, what sequence, how much effort, what status—hours to finish
TDD	If test-driven design is a team practice, commit the requirement to a test script

and certainly limited to small projects, but posting cards is effective for common access. To scale up, electronic facsimiles to include spreadsheets are used.

Obviously, the 3×5 card imposes a limitation on content and detail, and purposefully so. One or two sentences usually suffice for the story. The functional complexity is limited to that which can be developed in a matter of a few days. Amplifying detail is written on the back of the card or on companion cards. User story detail is enriched by conversation with the end user at the time a developer begins work. Subsequently, the developer documents design level detail with test scripts.

One suggestion for a simple story outline is: Actor *<name>* acting in role *<role label>* according to action *<action verb>* with attributes *<skills, security, time of day, etc>* has expectation *<result of action>* because *<motivation for action, or reason for storyline, or dependencies or triggers>*.[12]

Use case: Place a product order	
Business story	• An order placement clerk places an order for an item that is on a price list associated with an existing customer.
	• All customer account, sales credits, pricing, and product information fill the order automatically; the order is scheduled for fulfillment.
	• Acknowledgment is provided when the order is closed. Manual overrides are allowed.
Main actors	• Order placement clerk.
	• Order entry, pricing, and customer profile application.
Main scenario	• Order placement clerk selects *new order* to pull up a blank order entry screen and enters customer identification number.
	• Order header fills automatically from the customer's account profile.
	• Clerk enters product identifiers and quantities on an order line.
	• Product accessories and options are configured automatically.
	• Pricing and billing information is filled automatically.
	• Order is scheduled for fulfillment.
	• An order acknowledgment with confirmation is produced when the order is submitted.
	• Sales credits are posted automatically to account sales team.
Initial conditions	• Customer account is set up in the customer database.
	• Product is configured in the inventory system.
	• Price lists are configured for the customer-product combination.
Success criteria—minimum	• An order is confirmed.
Success criteria—nominal	• An order is confirmed, scheduled for delivery, and priced according to the customer's account.
Trigger	• Purchase order from customer.
Extensions	• If pricing is not available for the selected product, pricing application provides alert to screen.
	• Clerk is allowed to price the order on-the-fly.
	• Clerk is empowered to override pricing.
	• Clerk is empowered to override options and accessories.
	• Clerk is empowered to override sales credits to sales staff.

Figure 5.3 Use case example

User Story
An *order management associate* acting in the role of *order entry clerk* according to action *select customer* with attributes *order placement and pricing authority, customer account identifier, and customer profile* has an expectation that *order header will fill automatically* because *customer profile information is automatically linked to order header.*

Models and Prototypes

Models and prototypes are facsimiles of the end product. Models mean everything from a text description, UML diagram, and user interface screen mock-up to a formal mathematical model, structured diagram, or prototype code. Prototypes are commonly thought of as an actual working device albeit in a low-fidelity implementation, or an implementation using short cuts and temporary structures to support the demonstration. Some project managers resist prototypes as throwaway, but refactoring can salvage much of a prototype. Table 5.4 briefly describes the common models encountered.

Validation and Verification

Traditional Validation and Verification

Traditional projects rely on validation and verification (V&V) for end-to-end auditing of requirements:

- **Validation:** After structured analysis, and before any significant investment in design, the requirements *deck* is validated for completeness and accuracy. If there are priorities expressed within the deck, these priorities are validated since priorities are influenced by the dynamics of circumstance and context.
- **Verification:** After integration testing, the deck is verified to ensure that every validated requirement was developed and integrated into the deliverable baseline; or that changed/deleted requirements were handled as intended.

Agile Validation and Verification Defined

Agile projects are less amenable to the conventional V&V processes because of the dynamic and less stationary nature of requirements. Nonetheless, the spirit of V&V is a useful and effective concept, given the danger of misplacing or misstating:

Table 5.4 Requirements modeling tools

Model	Description
Entity relationship diagram	Identifies each logical entity in the system and documents the logical relationship among them
Data flow diagram	Shows the data flows, directionally, with triggers or stimulus between entities in the system
Quality function deployment	Provides a related set of matrices that trace requirements through a decomposition, showing some cause-and-effect relationship.
Class diagram	• Provides a template for a real object. • An object is a specific instance of a class according to the rules of the template. • A class diagram shows relationships between classes, listing the public and private procedures or operations of the class and data requirements of the class.
State transition diagram	Shows the before and after state of a system, and the triggering mechanisms to change state. Initial conditions and post conditions are shown.
Dialog map	• Shows the interaction of the user with the system and the possible navigation paths with triggers and controls. • A dialog map is a form of a state transition diagram that mimics the nonlinear method of problem solving that people actually use while conversing.
Data dictionary	• Holds the definitions of the data elements in the system. • It typically includes all the attributes like field size and field type, and also the business and system name and purpose of the data.

- Validation: After the business case is set, some structured analysis can occur on the top-level requirements. Typically, such analysis is an Iteration-0 activity. As in the traditional project, and before any significant investment in design, the requirements *deck* is validated for completeness and accuracy, insofar as the business case defines top-level requirements. If there are priorities expressed within these business case requirements, these priorities are also validated, since priorities are influenced by the dynamics of circumstance and context.

- Conversational requirements are also validated, typically after the project backlog or iteration backlog is updated. However, individual conversations often don't have sufficient context for effective validation. Thus, some judgment must be applied. Multiple conversations are aggregated into a larger scope scape and validated for completeness, accuracy, and priority.

- Verification: After integration testing, the deliverable functionality is verified to ensure that every validated conversation was developed and integrated into the deliverable baseline; or that changed/deleted conversations were handled as intended.

- During development, we can expect some consolidation of stories, and we can expect some use (or reuse) of common functionality. Thus, we are not suggesting that agile is to maintain a fully traceable identity from the time a conversation is moved into the design and development queue to the time integration testing is completed. However, the spirit of the conversation should be that there is some form. It's to those conversational forms that verification is directed.
- In some organizations, verification is seen as just a part of integration testing; the last thing you do before signing off on a completed test.

Module 3—Discussion for Critical Thinking

The essential matter to grasp about the requirements for agile projects is that they are conversational—less dependent on structured analysis than traditional methods. As such, there are more challenges for V&V. How would you suggest overcoming these challenges?

Module 4: Planning at a Distance

In spite of the immediacy of iteration planning, planning also requires perspective

Module 4—Objectives

- Discuss and explain the planning horizon in the context of agile needs
- Discuss and explain the reach of architecture over the horizon

The Planning Horizon

Even though the business case product vision, business story, and top-level architecture provide a working framework for deliverables, scope details emerge iteration-by-iteration, unplanned beyond the descriptions given in the project backlog. Scope detail is deferred until developers are ready to address a specific backlog.

Planning for scope is emergent, adaptive, and in alignment with the evolving solution. Central planning gives way to just-in-time planning. Project timelines give way to incremental timelines. Scope is allocated and adjusted according to customer priorities for each increment. The principal increments are defined by the project milestones from the business case; the planning horizon encompassing one or more releases; and the development iteration, one or more of which make up a release.

Detail specification is reserved for relatively short time segments, the longest of which is the planning horizon, which is a matter of a few months. Beyond the horizon are only fuzzy estimates, some would say guesses, anchored by the top-level architecture.

Over the Horizon with Architecture

We said at the beginning that architecture is the scope mapped by form and function. Architecture provides scope cohesion by carrying that mapping from one horizon to the next; as such, architecture should be largely invariant from one horizon to the next. Architecture serves as a framework to which many applications, functionalities, and user features can be fastened. Architecture describes the topology of the system, product, or process.[13]

Topology describes hierarchy, interconnectedness, and whether nodes are reached by point-to-point, hub-and-spoke, or some mesh circuitry. Architecture provides the protocols, that is, the rules by which elements of the system tie together.

Architecture gives form to requirements. It tells whether the product is built in layers, tiers, or subsystems. Architecture gives guidance on how loosely coupled components can be, and how cohesive they need to be for good maintenance and operability.

	Architecture brings out the best
A project management tip	• Architecture is the means to bring cohesiveness to disparate requirements. It provides form and shape and connectedness. • Coherence amplifies individual effects by harmonizing alignment. Coherency wrought by architecture can provide the *ah hah!* moment.

Architecture establishes boundaries, especially the boundaries between interconnected services, functions, and capabilities:

- Modular architecture with stand-alone black boxes, each with its own functionality, but mutually interconnected with an architectural framework
- Layered architecture, much like the familiar layer topology of the Internet, where services are provided in each layer, with protocols for moving among and between layers

- Application architecture, much like we see on mobile devices, where independent and somewhat stand-alone applications share a common set of services

The architecture of modern systems has introduced enormous security concerns into business and personal domains. Now there must be careful attention to the scope of authentication and authorization, encryption and disguise, solicitation and misrepresentation, intrusion into what used to be a sanctuary, and all manner of Trojan horses.

The Rolling Wave

All of these ideas for managing scope over multiple horizons collect under a concept called rolling-wave planning.[14] The metaphor is one planning period rolling into another—like waves rolling onto a beach—the next wave being planned as the current wave is completed. Each planning period is called a planning wave. The objective is to allow evolution and change to be rolled forward into the next wave where the changes can be incorporated into the product execution plan for that wave.

The wave length is different in each project. The usual planning wave encompasses more than one release. As a practical matter, the planning wave is a matter of months, about 3 to 6 total. The idea is that a 3- to 6-month horizon is about as far as anyone can see with the confidence necessary to do planning.

Requirement Priorities for Planning Waves

Setting priorities is really about managing impact. The effects of the really important things should be felt first. Stephen Covey writes in his acclaimed book, *7 Habits of Highly Effective People*, about importance and timeliness. He constructs four quadrants using importance and timeliness as the axes.[15]

Covey's idea is shown in Figure 5.4. In a stable project, problems in Quadrant I (most important-most urgent) should not come up often—but if they do, lower priority work is deferred, in order to free up resources to resolve those issues.

Covey's advice is to put real management effort toward Quadrant II (most important-not urgent), prioritizing away from Quadrant III and IV to the extent possible.

Of course, deciding what scope is important and urgent is often no small task. A good practice is to apply three priorities:

- **Priority I:** *Minimum must have* requirements that provide essential features and functions that benefit the customer but don't completely

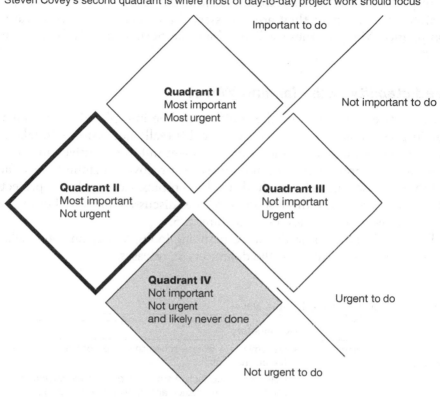

Figure 5.4 Covey's Four Quadrants

satisfy. Some of these may lie along the horizontal axis of the Kano chart; others may be in the upper right Kano quadrant.

- **Priority II:** *Useful and wanted* requirements that are the nominal center of what the customer has in mind, perhaps driving much of the benefits. Requirements in this priority are important for benefits, but perhaps not time-sensitive. Benefit realization drives these requirements to Priority II.
- **Priority III:** *Not essential to the baseline functionality*, but nonetheless are useful refinements, which add convenience, improve efficiency, add unique and discriminating features, but may only contribute to benefits at the margin. Importance is minimal and there is no time urgency. Some of these may fall into the lower left Kano quadrant: if missing they affect customer satisfaction, but if present they do not drive customer attraction.

Unimportant requirements are not prioritized. They will not be implemented except where they are necessary for regulatory and certification compliance. Many of these will lie along the horizontal axis of the Kano chart.

Predictability with Planning Waves

An objective of segmenting the project timeline into planning waves is to obtain predictable results, wave by wave. It's really not possible to take on larger projects that have significant investment unless executives and sponsors can be assured of benefits and investment recovery. Planning waves are a strategy for scaling agile methods to the complex scope of larger projects, and for addressing the three scope priorities discussed above. The steps to plan a predictable wave are listed in Table 5.5.

Figure 5.5 shows how the wave planning looks, laid against a timeline with customer milestones as the delimiters on releases.

Table 5.5　Planning a predictable wave

Planning Step	Commentary
Respect the customer's timeline	• Determine the release schedule based upon milestones in the business plan. • Releases to production are dependent on the customer's ability to absorb change and apply the deliverables. • Releases are made up of iterations. Iterations are typically time-boxed to a few weeks.
Allocate team capacity according to priority	• Allocate no more than about ⅔ of the iteration capacity to Scope Priority I, leaving ⅓ slack. • If the planning risk tolerance is more conservative, back off to ½ of the iteration capacity. • Allocate the remaining capacity to Priority II and III.
Fit requirements to available capacity	• Estimate the complexity of requirements. • Create a backlog based on available capacity to handle estimated complexity.
Plan a buffer between iterations	Assume some overrun will need to be absorbed in the buffer.
Plan a release from the iteration schedule	• Plan a release around the business case milestones. • Respect the customer's input on importance and urgency. • Take into account technical feasibility, functional sequencing, and dependencies with other teams and work streams.

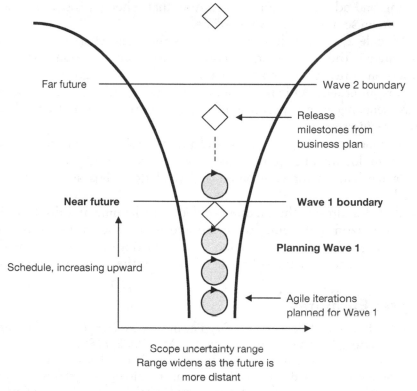

Wave planning laid against a timeline with customer milestones as the delimiters on releases

Figure 5.5   Wave planning

Module 4—Discussion for Critical Thinking

Planning horizons and rolling waves provide the middle-ground timelines between the stationary attribute of the business case vision and the immediacy of the iteration—as such planning horizons compare well with release schedules. If your project has unusually high volatility, what use would you make of planning horizons?

Summary and Takeaway Points

The theme of this chapter is that agile methods encourage requirements to change as often as necessary to ensure the customer receives the best value for the resources committed.

In Module 1, we learn that volatility can be managed, in spite of evolving, emerging, and adaptive requirements. And, that when all is said and done, the optimum scope is a best value scope.

In Module 2, we conclude that whereas the Kano chart is a good tool for separating the really unique requirements from the mundane—placing them in context with customer interest—it is not a good tool for the wicked requirement. Agile methods are actually a good approach to wicked requirements because experimentation may be the only way to break into circular requirements.

In Module 3, stories, use cases, and prototypes are all given as potential ways to document requirements. However, the hybrid project certainly needs a mechanism for verification and validation, thus an agile V&V is defined.

Module 4 addresses the unique problems of planning at a distance. The planning horizon and rolling wave are two tools that are useful for that planning need. In effect, the rolling wave provides agile methods with a means to inject some degree of predictability into the requirements process.

Chapter Endnotes

1. Ollhoff, J. and Walcheski, M., *Stepping in Wholes: Introduction to Complex Systems*, Sparrow Media Group, Eden Prairie, MN, 2002, p. 86.

2. Adaptive feedback systems, sometimes called complex adaptive systems, (CAS), have been studied extensively in social and biological systems. The term CAS was coined at the Santa Fe Institute by Dr. John Holland and colleagues, noted academics in the field.

CAS are nonlinear, meaning their outputs are not weighted sums of their independent elements as given in the classic linear equation: output $= a \times$ input $+ b$, where a is a weighting and b is an initial condition or bias.

Traditional use of feedback is to improve linearity and faithfully follow, transform, or reproduce inputs. Linear feedback systems are described in: Hellerstein, J. et al., *Feedback Control of Computing Systems*, IEEE Press, John Wiley & Sons, New York, p. 5.

CAS produce output based upon agents and agent processes interacting in seemingly unpredictable ways, adapting to circumstances, but bounded by rules set down by governance. Such output is often called *emergent*: the interaction of simple rules and parts creates very complex systems and responses. For an introduction to CAS, see: Ollhoff, J. and Walcheski, M. (2002) op. cit. Chapter 20, and Holland, J. *Emergence: from Chaos to Order*, Perseus Books, Reading, MA, 1998, Chapter 3.

3. An excellent reference for executive and customer visits is: McQuaririe, E., *Customer Visits: Building a Better Market Focus*, Sage Publications, Newbury Park, CA, 1993, pp. 21-24.

4. Cooper, R., *Winning at new products—2nd Edition*, Perseus Books, Reading, MA, 1993, p. 121.

5. Goodpasture, J., *Quantitative Methods in Project Management*, J. Ross Publishers, Ft. Lauderdale, 2004, ppg 8-13.

6. The major standards bodies for the international community, specifically ISO and IEC, and in the United States, EIA and IEEE, have numerous standards for requirements engineering in various disciplines. In software for example, 12207 is the ISO, IEEE/EIA, and DoD standard for software lifecycles. IEEE/EIA 830 addresses software requirements and is a compatible implementation standard for 12207 compliance. Other groups, like the Software Engineering Institute, have practice guides for requirements engineering. Similar standards extend to quality engineering, and all manner of engineering for networks, hardware, safety, environmental, and many others.

ISO: International Standards Organization

IEC: International Electro-Technical Convention

EIA: Electronics Industry Association

IEEE: Institute of Electrical and Electronics Engineers

DoD: U.S. Department of Defense

7. For more information on requirement methodology tradeoffs, Michael Cohn's text provides insight. Bear in mind Cohn is a proponent of user stories, not use cases or 830-style requirements. Cohn, M., *User Stories Applied for Software Development*, Addison-Wesley, Boston, 2004, Chapter 12.

8. For more information, the reader is referred to SEI at Carnegie-Mellon University, www.sei.cmu.edu, *Requirements Engineering; Wieger's Software Requirements*, op. cit. Chapter 3; and Sommerville, I. and Sawyer, P., *Requirements Engineering: A good practice guide*, John Wiley & Sons, New York, 1997, p. 11.

9. See: McQuarrie, E. (1993) op. cit., Chapter 4; Wiegers, K (1999) op. cit., Chapters 7 and 8; Kulak, D. and Guiney, E., *Use Cases: Requirements in Context*, Addison-Wesley, New York, 2000, Chapter 4.

10. Booch, Grady, Rumbaugh, and Jacobson, *The Unified Modeling Language User Guide*, Addison-Wesley, Reading, MA, 1999, pp. 14, 17-26.

11. Cockburn, A., *Writing Effective Use Cases*, Addison-Wesley, Boston, 2001, pp. 2-6.

12. Another similar outline for human users is given by Kelly Waters on his website www.agile-software-development.com in the form of: As a <user> I want to <goal> so I can <reason>.

13. In this book, a lot of words will be used interchangeably to represent the project outcomes: product, system, and deliverable. The outcome could be tangible, like a consumer product, or intangible, like a service. The project outcome could be a new process applied internally in the enterprise. Except in the

most trivial cases, most outcomes depend upon being part of a system, whether legacy or new-to-the-world. In this sense, consumer devices like telephones are systems.

14. Goodpasture, J. (2004) op cit., Chapter 7, and Goodpasture, J., *A Risk Perspective: Rolling Wave Planning Is a Bet*, Projects and Profits magazine, ICFAI University Press, Vol. VII Issue 12, December 2007, pp. 48-53.

15. Covey, S., *7 Habits of Highly Effective People*, Simon & Schuster Free Press, New York, 15th edition, 2004, pp. 150-183.

6

Planning and Scheduling

Adapting plans and estimates to changing customer needs and maximizing value at an affordable cost are the planning imperatives for agile projects.[1]

Planning is everything. Plans are nothing. No plan survives contact with [reality].

Field Marshall Helmuth Graf von Moltke

Module 1: Planning in the Enterprise Context

Where are we? And, what are we doing? No project is an island onto itself.

Module 1—Objectives

- Discuss and explain the need for agile planning, especially in the enterprise context
- Familiarize readers with planning drivers and the need to adapt

It's Agile! Why Plan? Why Schedule? Why Estimate?

Why plan, why schedule? Indeed, the question might even be: Why estimate? It's all going to change anyway.

The answer is quite clear:

> *If there are no plans, any outcome is acceptable; if there are no plans, there is nothing to estimate; without estimates, there is no reason to measure. Without measurements, there will be no benchmarks, no*

improvement, and no answer to the questions of where are we? And what are we doing? In fact, without a plan, anywhere and anything will do.

Planning Dominates Management

A few activities dominate almost every aspect of project management, whether for agile projects or others—planning and estimating on the one hand, communicating and executing on the other. Managed properly, the ideal project trajectory hits within reasonable error bounds of targeted cost and schedule while satisfying customers to the maximum extent possible. Taken together, planning, estimating, communicating, and executing are a big stage. This chapter concentrates on planning for cost and schedule.

Plans are not altogether objective, taking into account as they do values, conventions, and business imperatives of the enterprise. But even without complete objectivity, plans are an effective tool to provide the rationale and evidence that stakeholders require for committing resources. But to be credible, evidence needs backup in the form of estimates. Estimates we define as the objective results of analysis and melding of historical performance with judgment about future achievement. Estimates are the subject of another chapter in this book, where they are discussed in detail.

Are We Done?

So the team needs a plan, but a plan consistent with the role of the project manager to facilitate and motivate performance—not to direct the team's day-to-day activities.

But, just as we need plans to get started, we need a plan for when we are done. After all, one big theme of agile project management is to shift much—but certainly not all—of the management focus to outcomes, put rather less on managing inputs. The operative questions become:

Are we done? And, if so, what are the parameters of "done"?

Look back to Principle 5 of the Agile Principles given in Chapter 1.

Agile Principle 5	Build projects around motivated individuals. Give them the environment and support they need, and trust them to *get the job done.*

Trust them to *get the job done*. What job?

- It is the job described in the business plan and in subsequent project plans, albeit lean plans consistent with the Agile Manifesto
- It is the job estimated and scheduled
- It is the job as interpreted in near real-time by the functional user
- It is the job that evolves over several iterations and is adapted to the emergent value proposition

Trust them to *get the job done*. What is the definition of *done?*

- Is it done when time/money runs out?
- Is it done when the backlog is fully exhausted?
- Or, is it done when the customer says it's done, or someone else says it's done?

To the first point, *what job?* The job is to be strategically predictable according to the business case, but tactically opportunistic according to Agile Principles. In practical terms, tactically opportunistic is *best value*—the most scope, and the most valuable scope from a business/mission perspective, that is affordable.

We've addressed this idea before, but for emphasis the *job* is to be as responsive to customer need as is practical in a best value sense, given a project narrative (the strategic aspect) which must be honored, while optimizing tactical opportunities that have parameters like urgency, business priority, sequencing constraints, risk to project or business outcomes, investment and financial return impacts, etc. All else goes in V2.0.

To the second point: are we done? Certainly agile is done when the money runs out; it may be done if all the best value backlog is achieved before the money runs out (take note: better is the enemy of good, so release *good* now). But, if you say it's done when all the requirements are satisfied, you'll never finish, because all the requirements are never known.

Of course, *done* is not entirely in the hands of the customer. There are a myriad of requirements that are part of the project backlog that answer to others:

- **Nonfunctional:** The customer usually doesn't have a say about nonfunctional requirements, yet they figure heavily into *done*.
- **The release:** Theoretically, an agile project is *zero base* after every release and could be ended right then and there. A specific release could be the marker for *done*.
- **Technical and functional debt:** Debt is the myriad of *punch list* fixes and tuning that polish the deliverables for final delivery. Such debt could be small-scale tests that are incomplete, last minute look-and-feel changes, or small-scale functionality that needs to be tweaked.

- **Undelivered backlog:** There's always another project to absorb the undelivered backlog.

As the project goes along, note that the backlog may increase due to the accumulation of *technical debt* or added requirements, or we may abandon some of the backlog because we've come to understand, as things emerge, that they are no longer needed or necessary, thereby creating space and capacity.

Agile Planning Portfolio

The thing about planning agile projects is that there is not one plan, but many plans—and the plans change frequently. By doctrine, plans are simple in structure and amenable to updating. The planning is distributed over time and among teams as the need arises. Plans will often be just spreadsheet or database templates with certain information filled in. Scorecard templates and a dashboard are lean and useful means to convey the information and support team planning meetings.

The need to create points of coordination and integration among projects in a portfolio, among work streams in a project, and among development teams within a large-scale project is what distinguishes a portfolio of plans useful in an enterprise context and those more limited plans needed to support one project more or less in isolation.

At a scale that has impacts throughout the enterprise, plans are of necessity more structured, less elastic, and more formal. However, even in the enterprise context when the planning is close to the work—at the iteration level for instance—plans, schedules, and estimates are more in the character expected of agile: all but informal, elastic and adaptive, and structured only insofar as the team finds value in the structure.

Agile Plans Adapt

Empirical process control, emergent solutions, nonlinear methods, customer-driven value—with all of these unplannables, is it possible to make a useful plan? Yes, the agile team can be coached to converge on an acceptable solution within a reasonable range of possibilities. Some governance and project management are needed, just enough architecture is required, and a planning framework called *rolling wave planning* is necessary for adaptive plans.[2]

Agile projects are expected to adapt repeatedly in close proximity to the need. The working assumption is that the complexities of intangible requirements and systems preclude knowing enough to write a complete plan at the outset. Much like the wicked problem, the solution will ultimately define the need. Furthermore, the team is expected to modify practices appropriate to the evolving product, mentored by the project manager and other subject-matter experts.

Plans must adapt if for no other reason than because planning is the creative and innovative part of management. Planning is thinking; planning requires thoughtful consideration about an intended course of action. And planning is where many of the discriminating *ah-hahs* emerge. Planning creates a focus, forces creativity to be committed, and adds order to what might otherwise be chaos.

In plan-driven project development lifecycle (PD-PDLC) methods, planning absorbs many resources—it is hard to do in the first place, and once done, detailed plans are even more consuming to maintain so that they retain their relevance and value. In reaction to the experience of the PD-PDLC, the Agile Manifesto steers the other way. Discussion, debate, and conversation are valued over documentation, but documentation is not absent, only minimized to improve effectiveness.

A project management tip	Plan sufficiently
	Caution is advised—adopting too literal of an interpretation of the Agile Manifesto may lead to under-planning—insufficient to properly represent the project to the stakeholders and provide guidance to the teams.

Work-stream Plans

Master plans for each work stream are derived from the business plan; master plans are adapted horizon-by-horizon. The planning horizon is a time box of sorts applied to the release schedule. All planning conforms to the concept of rolling waves from one horizon to the next. As one horizon is achieved and the next appears, another set of plans are cast.

The project manager maps major business milestones to the work streams. Work-stream milestones are the most important release dates. They frame the planning horizons for a product going live to production. Recall Figure 5.7 (Wave planning) which is adapted to the work-stream planning horizons and shown in Figure 6.1. It is evident from Figure 6.1 that the uncertainty of each work stream is not the same; the product development work stream has the most far future uncertainty, reflecting the uncertain influence of customers on the scope of delivered features and functions.

Each work stream is planned for one planning horizon at a time, understanding that uncertainty increases in the far future, although the degree of uncertainty is different for each work stream

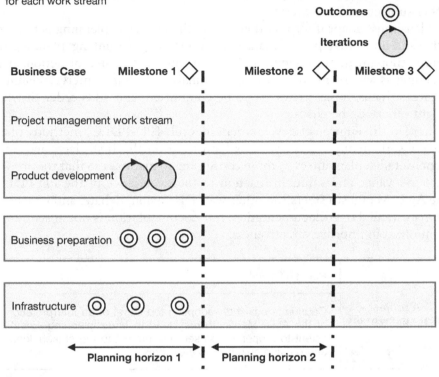

Figure 6.1   Business case milestone planning horizons

On the other hand, project management has relatively little uncertainty, reflecting that the work of project management is insensitive to variations in scope details.

A somewhat similar approach is followed to come up with a budget plan for each work stream. Developing the budget at the work-stream level is tantamount to developing the project balance sheet for each work stream. The left side of the balance sheet is developed first and is provided top-down by the business. Investment is usually allocated proportionately to the work streams according to a value judgment by the business.

As explained subsequently, other methods may also be appropriate. The right side of the balance sheet is usually built from estimates arrived at by looking at facts and forecasting future performance. Right–to–left side gaps are addressed between the project manager, team leads, and stakeholders.

	Plans for work streams and teams
A project management tip	• No project balance sheet, milestone plan, or budget is imposed on the project without consultation. • Management by Agile Principles requires conversation, iteration, collaboration, and negotiation to make allocations and identify gap mitigation.

Release Plans

Agile Principle 1 demands frequent delivery of working product to satisfy customer needs. This requires a process for releasing completed objects into production or go-live. Usually there are these process steps to be planned in a release planning session:

- From the project backlog, select backlog for the next release based on velocity predictions for throughput, priorities, and sequencing demands
- Allocate the release backlog among iterations or sprints, allowing buffer space for working off debt, ensuring a sustainable pace, and addressing unforeseen needs
- Plan a *release buffer* as an empty iteration to protect the release date and release process
- Establish the release protocol for sign-off, integration tests, user acceptance tests, and the go-live play book—the order and nature of scripts that run to put new objects into a production state

Leading into the release there may be useful information gathered at retrospective points as each iteration, sprint, or work-in-progress (WIP) grouping is completed. Such *lessons learned* and other input into the release plan evolves and emerges as the iterations proceed. Thus, a second round of release planning is appropriate to take these data into account.

Time-boxing Plans

Within work streams are teams, each working on iterations or sprints to develop and deliver some working scope to the product base. Time boxing is the main strategy for planning the schedule horizon-to-horizon instead of lower-level Gantt or network task and activity schedules.[3] So a plan consists of some number of teams executing within time boxes, each team operating at its own estimated velocity—throughput—and each team executing a portion of the business-case backlog as its scope.[4]

All things being otherwise fixed, the total duration of the work-stream timeline is the sum of the non-overlapping time-boxed iterations. By Agile Principle 4, every iteration ends with a working product that can be released to the product base. The project can end at the discretion of the sponsor and the project manager after almost any release.

Obviously, there must be points of coordination and reconciliation of team efforts. These points form a network with dependencies. The network can be simplified by having each team perform synchronously in time boxes of the same duration so that work products from one team are available to all teams when the next iteration cycle begins.[5]

Work-In-Progress Plans

WIP plans show the sequence and timing of WIP among all Kanban or pipeline processes. Not all methodologies apply time boxes, as we read in Chapter 1. For instance, Kanban is not a time-boxed practice, though it could be a practice embedded in a time box. Thus, some other working plan is needed, often using a planning tool or practice that is visual. Kanban charts, burn-down charts, or some combination of a Gantt chart and a milestone chart is used. Elsewhere in this book we address the Kanban chart and the burn-down chart.

Labor Plans Team-by-Team

Given a time-boxed duration and a velocity benchmark team-by-team, a labor plan can be derived for each team and iteration within a planning horizon. These team-iteration labor plans identify individuals, skills, and time commitments. When there is more than one team, key individuals may have to be shared. Multiply the labor plan commitments by the chargeback rate[6] for each resource to obtain the labor-cost plan.

When planning individual commitments, care must be exercised because each team's velocity is sensitive to its cross-functional makeup, its experience skill-by-skill, and its membership—not too few and not too many. The training and experience of the team as a self-organizing and collaborative body, as well as the environment and tools, also affects velocity.

Daily Plan

Each day begins by putting together a daily plan for the work to be done in the day ahead. Teams do this for themselves. The project manager provides facilitation. Each team member contributes a few simple sentences identifying what he or she will work on that day and what accomplishment he or she expects. The plan is reviewed at a morning daily stand-up meeting.

The meeting is time boxed to allow each member just a few minutes to talk about his or her personal plan. Every team member is expected to participate and to speak to his or her day's plan. Solutions are not discussed, but if there are needs for special-topic meetings, then these are arranged.

At the end of the day, the results of the day are checked into the product control system. The product base is rebuilt each day whenever practical.

On some teams, an end-of-day stand-up meeting is also held. It is similarly time boxed; it is not a solution meeting. Its purpose is to assess whether the daily plan was successful and to identify impediments and barriers for the project manager to address.

Summary of Planning Portfolio

Table 6.1 contains an abstract of the discussion.

Planning Drivers

A planning driver is a condition, circumstance, policy, or external influence that causes a plan to be written in the first place, or bears upon the scope and content of existing plans. Of course, this begs the questions: On whose

Table 6.1 Summary of plans

Plan	Commentary
Work-stream plan	• A *flow down of the business plan* milestones and budget limits to the work stream according to the WBS • Flow down is controlled by estimates made the project management staff and team leads • Planning detail is *rolling wave* in style, reevaluated at each planning horizon
Release plan	A plan for all the actions necessary to put into production, or go-live with the backlog capabilities selected for a specific release
Time-boxing plan	A plan of some number of teams executing within time boxes, each team operating at its own estimated velocity—throughput—and each team executing a portion of the business-case backlog as its scope
WIP plan	WIP plans show the sequence and timing of WIP among all Kanban or pipeline processes
Labor plan	A team-iteration work assignment plan to identify individuals, skills, and time commitments
Daily plan	The working plan for the day developed by each team member for their own activities

shoulders do these drivers fall? Is it different in an agile project than it might be in a traditional project?

Principle of Subsidiary Function

The first question, *on whose shoulders does planning drivers fall* is answered by the Principle of Subsidiary Functions. Agile methods follow this principle, which holds that no central authority should do what a subordinate entity can best do for itself; authority that is not specifically enumerated is delegated to subsidiary or subordinate units. And, to authority please add *responsibility*. Both march as a pair in the agile project domain.

There are rights and responsibilities that come with this principle. The central authority has a right to expect responsible behavior of its subordinate, but retains the right to verify performance—to trust, but with verification—and intervene to impose corrective action. The subordinate unit has a right to expect a degree of autonomy with reasonable inspection and verification, so long as the subordinate acts responsibly. The subordinate has a responsibility to act in its own interests and in the interests of the central authority, taking care to not over-optimize at a low level.

When the subsidiary function principle is extended to project planning, the first agile planning criteria is that it should not be unnecessarily obtrusive; an agile plan should not direct, prescribe, or otherwise limit maneuverability or activity beyond the establishment of acceptable norms and conventions. In other words, planning is to be done by the most competent and responsible decentralized project unit. As a practical matter, what it means is that the plans developed at different organizational levels, and shown in Table 6.1, are to be respected.

Cone of Uncertainty

Agile planning is not immune to business attitudes about risk; in part, risk shapes the funding and affordability limits of the project. Risk attitude, embedded in a concept called *utility*, affects both the topside-funding cap and the limits of financial support for unforeseen difficulty.

Agile planning estimates need not be too exact at the outset since the project body of knowledge is too uncertain to justify and support precise estimates. When we say uncertainty we mean risk without foreknowledge of risk events and mitigations; but as the project progresses, our knowledge changes—uncertainty morphs into knowable risks that, in turn, either materialize or are mitigated. Project managers who have studied risk and uncertainty are familiar with the concept that risk is opposite the amount at stake.

That is, before any real work is done, the amount at stake—the amount still available to the project manager—is at a maximum, but certainty about cost, schedule, and deliverables is at a minimum. As time unfolds, the backlog is burned down and the amount at stake shifts from uncommitted to committed; only then does uncertainty transform into point solutions, thereby reducing residual risk.

Only then are more exact estimates justified and meaningful. In fact, unjustified precision can be misleading to those who are unfamiliar with the so-called cone of uncertainty.[7] Figure 6.2 is a pictorial of the idea.

Dr. Barry Boehm is credited with conceiving the cone of uncertainty and with showing its applicability to complex systems—although he did not use the phrase *cone of uncertainty* in his texts.

Boehm presented his concept as cost-size uncertainty versus project phase in his book, *Software Cost Estimation with COCOMO II*. His data was shown symmetrically around a nominal cost-size; the data showed a maximum variation of four-to-one above and four-to-one below the nominal value.

In the representation shown in Figure 6.2, different from Boehm's approach, uncertainty is represented above and below a neutral axis. There is an opportunity to under-run the cost—the optimistic outlook—as well as to

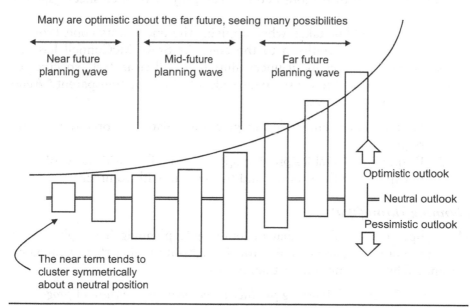

Figure 6.2   Cone of uncertainty

overrun—as in the pessimistic outlook. The asymmetry depicts the nature of project estimates—they are more often too optimistic about the distant future rather than too pessimistic. On the other hand, the picture changes as the distant future becomes near term.

Optimism transforms to pessimism as more detailed and precise knowledge of the immediate future is increased. So, it would be better to represent the optimistic under-run opportunity as less possible than would be the overrun opportunity. The changing attitude from optimism to pessimism is represented by the asymmetry above and below the planned value. Figure 6.2 shows an asymmetrical cone-like figure representing both a varying range of uncertainty and the idea that optimism and pessimism change over time.

An inspection of Figure 6.2 shows that in the very near term, there is enough information to prove that optimism and pessimism are overall more constrained and about equally distributed about a nominal attitude. As the horizon moves out, pessimism grows as the uncertainties set in, but then in the far future, there is a general optimistic feeling that solutions can be found.

For agile planners, Figure 6.2 is a heads-up: risk attitude changes over the lifecycle of the project. Plans reflect attitude; business plans will be optimistic; corresponding rolling wave plans will be more pessimistic, but then iteration plans will turn more neutral. The project balance-sheet gap will flux as the timeline matures.

Some care should be taken when applying the uncertainty cone. Projects do not automatically conform to the cone. As Steve McConnell has observed, there is nothing about uncertainty that will clear itself; specific actions must be invoked to cause opaque ideas to become transparent.[8] Agile projects respond in two ways:

1. Customers are embedded to give immediate interpretation to the requirements
2. Frequent deliverables provide opportunities for a wide array of users to experience the product and to weigh in with comments

Planning Throughput

Throughput is a big driver that bears on agile planning. Throughput is a measure of outcome, and planning for throughput requires that planning be dominated by outcomes rather than inputs.

Agile Principle 7: Working product is the primary measure of progress.

Unlike activity planning, which is the centerpiece of the PD-PDLC, outcome and throughput planning is the centerpiece of agile methods. In fact, there is an entire science around the concept of *throughput accounting* that focuses on the value difference—the value added—between project outcomes and pre-project ideas and opportunities.[9] There are two estimating parameters that are controlling, and each can be known only within a statistical certainty:

1. Complexity of the user stories in the backlog
2. Velocity of each team

Complexity is figure of merit—a dimensionless number that is used as a multiplier to make one complex object stand out from another. For example, we say Object A is two times as complex as Object B—the number 2 being the multiplier. Complexity multipliers are applied to units of scope. As a multiplier, complexity escalates the effort and time required to develop a unit more complex than the baseline unit.

Velocity is the throughput of the team measured in units per scheduled iteration. Units are increments of product developed and completed by a team in the calendar duration of one development iteration. Velocity depends on team size, member competencies, team cohesion, and environment effectiveness.

As an example of how these two parameters work together, assume a team has a throughput of 40 units of scope in four weeks. The production could be 40 individual baseline units, but in another situation, the production might be four units of complex scope, each with a complexity multiplier of 10 on the baseline unit.

To be prudent, each of the parameters should be weighted for risk. After all, the accuracy of the parameters is limited to a range of certainty. There are statistical rules of thumb to make risk adjustments that are useful and practical day-to-day. Some have already been discussed, to wit: the fact that most naturally occurring phenomena acquire symmetry around a mean value over the long term; the risk-weighted average converges to the center of a symmetric distribution of values.[10] In the short run, however, the likely distribution is decidedly asymmetrical, skewed either toward optimism or pessimism.

Risk Distribution as a Driver

The questions often arise thus:

- Should the project plan protect the team from the worst case?

- How important are the odd situations that are a project long shot?
- How should the distribution of risk possibilities be represented in the project?

The project rule of thumb is that distributions of very near-term estimates are usually symmetrical, so risk impacts on plans is all about the central and most probable outcome. But time works curiously on risk distributions. Typically, as we saw in the cone of uncertainty, risk plans are more pessimistic than optimistic for risks in the midterm, and more optimistic for far future risks.

Within one iteration, a confusing situation often arises: when asked if they can develop within a certain time limit, many developers will often answer yes—an optimistic response. But when asked if they can deliver earlier, the same developers will often say no to giving up any schedule—a pessimistic response. Statistically, this can only mean that distributions of outcomes would have a long tail toward pessimism, something like that illustrated in Figure 6.3.

Recall that the expected value of a distribution is a weighted average of all the possible outcomes. In the two asymmetrical distributions, the small contribution of the long tail pulls the average a bit toward the tail and away from the most likely value at the peak of the distribution. In the top figure that represents the far future, it is more likely that less effort is needed—an optimistic outlook on effort.

As the future becomes more near term, the outlook actually becomes more pessimistic because information becomes available, although just enough to cause concern instead of enough to understand the needs. There is some fear of the unknown. Gradually, information is developed in the

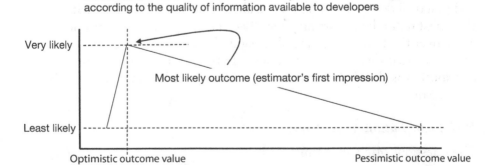

Figure 6.3 Developer's distribution

near present. Usually, about as much is known about the things that could go well as is known about the things that could go wrong. The distribution becomes more symmetric.

Planning Schedule Losses

Have you ever stopped to marvel at how the last minute or two of a basketball game can take 10 minutes to play? How efficient is that? Even measuring over the longer term, the whole game can easily take three times the amount of time shown on the play clock—20 minutes of playing time often consumes one hour of wall-clock time. The fact is: the strategy and mechanics of the game dictate a certain *loss* against the wall clock.

Projects experience this loss as well. The project play clock will seem slower than the wall clock. For instance, people get sick, take personal time, take vacation to refresh and recharge, and need refreshment time during the workday. Over the long run, it is reasonable to assume a 15 percent labor loss in the labor plan. On an eight- or nine-person agile team, the impact of that 15 percent loss is equal to the impact of operating one-person-down almost at all times.

Summary of Planning Drivers

Table 6.2 puts all the ideas together.

Module 1—Discussion for Critical Thinking

Do you find anything inconsistent about this idea: planning takes on more importance the farther up the hierarchy the planning is done, such that at the agile project level and iteration, plans are all but informal—whereas, about the same project at the enterprise level, plans are structured and somewhat inelastic?

Module 2: Scheduling

Not only must we schedule what we know needs to be done, but predictability requires we provide relief for the unknown

Module 2—Objectives

- Discuss and explain what is meant by the rhythm of the schedule
- Discuss and explain timelines in the context of enterprise agile

Table 6.2 Summary of planning ideas

Planning feature	Commentary
The principle of subsidiary function	• A central and higher-level organization has a responsibility to not intrude on its subordinate where that subordinate unit is competent and capable • By extension, plans must not direct and specify the actions of subordinate units • High-level units have a right to expect responsible planning by subordinates • Subordinates must act responsibly to plan and estimate their activities to a sufficiency of detail that intrusion by superior units is not required, except for verification and validation
The cone of uncertainty	• A good plan respects the concept that uncertainty is greatest when the least effort has been accomplished in the project • A good estimating practice is to adopt standard estimating ranges at different points of maturity in the project • Transparency—increasing certainty—is not automatic; specific plans must be put in place to drive out the unknowns
Planning throughput	• Throughput is governed by the complexity of the user story backlog and the team velocity • Throughput is the product finished and ready for production produced by a team in the duration of one iteration • Throughput accounting evaluates the value-add of the team's effort
Risk distribution	• No estimate should be provided as a single-point estimate unless it is the expected value of a distribution of possible outcomes • Every estimate should be presented as having a range for which there is a confidence that the true value will be distributed within the range
Planning for "losses"	• A 15% labor loss over the long term is a conservative planning parameter • On an 8-person team, a 15% loss is like one full-time equivalent labor loss

Rhythm of the Schedule

One objective of agile methods is to vigorously defend the schedule's rhythm to prevent the last-minute press, but also to maintain a near constant pace that can be sustained almost indefinitely.

What do we mean by rhythm? Rhythm is the periodic and repetitive nature of the schedule, almost a melody in the sense of the cycle of release planning, iterations, and releases. Though not the same pace at each task in the cycle, nonetheless each task in the cycle has its own pace.

Sustainable Rhythm

One of the helpful consequences of Agile Principle 8—*maintaining a constant pace nearly indefinitely*—is that there is a certain rhythm to the work pace of the project. Elsewhere, the rhythm of red-green-refactor is explained. And to be sure, if the rhythm is off a few beats, it will be easily felt by hurry-up-and-wait, unscheduled downtime, and other nonrhythmic responses. Constraints imposed by stakeholders and outside authorities may upset the rhythm. Maintaining the rhythm by managing constraints is project management's task.

Drum-buffer-rope

Agile plans take a page from the Theory of Constraints, and the concept of the drum-buffer-rope made popular by the research of Eliyahu M. Goldratt.[11] To maintain rhythm, Goldratt posits the drum as the source of the beat. In the agile project, the agile plan-do-check-act (Ag-PDCA) cycle is the drum. The buffer is just that—a time buffer to absorb unforeseen events so that the beat—the Ag-PDCA cycle—can be maintained. Workflow is the rope that ties it all together. Workflow authorizes cycles to begin and end and authorizes releases to production.

Velocity and Iterations

At each task in the cycle, by experience and similar circumstances, we should be able to predict velocity—the rate of throughput—perhaps the most useful planning parameter for agile projects. But if circumstances at each iteration, or each integration task at release time, cause the team to run fast and slow, energetic and then exhausted, the velocity figure will be meaningless for planning.

And, as we note elsewhere in this book, predictable velocity is a component of a successful Kanban, and velocity figures strongly into the use of the burndown chart and other work-tracking systems. Consequently, the establishment and maintenance of a project environment that allows for predictable velocity, is an important project management task for the agile project manager.

Reflection

Check-act means to measure results, and compare results to intentions and expectations, report findings, and then assess how the iteration could have been done better. Evaluate what should be retained as good practice and what should be improved for the next iteration. Check-act enables emergent processes and practices because the team is influenced and changed by experience and feedback.

Agile principle 12	*At regular intervals, the team reflects on how to become more effective, then tunes and adjusts its behavior accordingly.*

The *check* portion provides an opportunity for customer evaluations to be analyzed. With the product evolution expected in agile methods, *check* provides a fuzzy front-end opportunity for the next iteration's requirements planning. There is an opportunity to restack requirements and add, change, or delete existing requirements. Reflection on the quality of the iteration experience is a lessons-learned opportunity.

Ask why five times:[12] "Why did X happen? *It is because of Z.* Why did Z happen?" And so on. From the five answers, fashion a team response to improve the next iteration outcome.

Time-Box Timelines and Calendars

As a matter of terminology, we distinguish between a timeline and a schedule. A timeline is measured in units of time but has no reference to a calendar. When a timeline is affixed to a calendar, it becomes a schedule.

Time boxes are planned to synchronize not only with business milestones but also with the activities of other teams working similar time-boxed iterations. High-level network schedules tie together the major dependencies between teams. Within the team, the team leadership assigns schedule-constrained work to team members. Trend lines and work-remaining calculations forecast progress over the course of the iteration.

	Scheduling with time boxes
A project management tip	• The most important point to grasp is that schedules are constructed from a number of fixed-duration cycles, somewhat like building a train from many same-length freight cars. • Each cycle contains the same number of calendar days, has nearly constant throughput, and all are networked in finish-to-start in precedence. • Scope is constantly adjusted, making scheduling adjustments possible to fit the time-boxed cycles precisely. • The total duration of the schedule is capped by the time required to execute the requirements deck or by the funding available to sustain the teams that are working.

One way to display the agile schedule concept is with a grid as shown in Figure 6.4. The gridlines align with development and planning wave cycles. Some number of cycles produces a release either on a business-plan milestone or on a milestone planned by the work stream. Each grid space is buffered to absorb small variations in performance; the final release milestone is likewise buffered to better ensure on-time delivery. If there are dependencies between one or more teams, those dependencies are felt at the grid boundaries.

Milestones from the Business Plan

The business plan is the top-level milestone plan. Schedules are nested in the same hierarchy as plans, as given in Table 6.1. So, the place to begin is

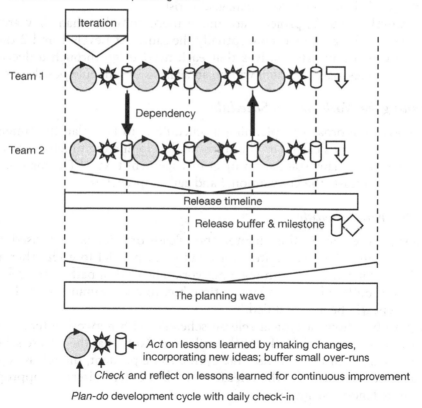

Figure 6.4 Agile schedule grid

with the business case, Level 0, 1, or 2. Milestones are given top-down to the project. In each case, Level 0, 1, or 2, the project accepts and respects business drivers that determine when capabilities are needed. An agile business case does not intrude on the prerogatives of the project manager and the team leads to set tactical schedules, so the schedule detail in the business case is not more than business milestones.

Some milestones may have calendar-specific event dates that carry a very definite value; other milestones are simply made relative to project kickoff. They are scheduled after receipt of order.

At Level 0 there are few milestones, perhaps no more than one or two, and likely these will be established and validated as part of the business-case governance process. Governance is collaborative by design and intent, so there will be an opportunity for the project team and the product owner or business representative to discuss, negotiate, and agree to the business milestones. Such socialization of the schedule is integral to reducing the gap on the project balance sheet to a manageable risk.

At Levels 1 and 2, projects are much more complex than they are at Level 0, but the process is conceptually the same. At Levels 1 and 2 there may be competitive alternatives that each need to go through a decision analysis process, part of which will be an analysis of schedule possibilities.

Planning the Work-stream Schedule

The classical approach to planning a schedule is to first plan the timeline and then put it to a calendar. The steps for developing the timeline are well documented in many standard project management texts.[13] The material in Table 6.3 contrasts the conventional and agile approaches.

The Network Schedule

As discussed earlier in this chapter, the release timeline is comprised of a number of iterations; some iterations will be in parallel to each other and will join results, thereby forming a network. The critical path in the release network is buffered with an empty time box to add assurance that the release event will be as scheduled.[14]

Figure 6.5 shows a typical release schedule with network interconnections and a critical-path buffer at the milestone. Note that the release schedule is a number of *plan-do-check-act* cycles. To be prudent, the release cycle has at least one buffer for the release event, but other buffers are appropriate where tandem strings join.

Table 6.3 Work-stream planning

Conventional planning step	Agile planning step
Develop the work plan to a work-package level of a few weeks' work	Decompose the business-case product vision into major capabilities for each planning wave and release according to customer priority and benefit plan
Sequence the work breakdown structure (WBS) deliverables—do the foundation before the walls, etc. Caution: Keep it simple!	• The primary sequencing comes from priorities set by the customer/user during planning for waves and then releases within waves • Architecture and technical feasibility determine sequencing that is fundamental, such as foundations and walls
Determine the dependencies among the WBS deliverables, and modify the sequencing if necessary	Dependencies may happen at a high level between teams and are adjusted after every release
• If developing an effort-driven schedule, estimate the effort for each task and normalize to the number of individuals according to an effort/day metric. • If developing a duration-driven schedule, estimate the affordable duration, and then compute the effort required to affect the duration	• A fixed effort is assigned to each team. • The number of teams is derived from throughput demands to meet business milestones
Apply durations to the ordered-sequenced list to make a timeline, using dummy tasks for buffers	• Schedules are built-up from time-boxed iterations • Each iteration is characterized by units of throughput—product that can go to production • The schedule is derived from the summation of the iteration durations needed to produce all the product • Detailed planning is apportioned among planning horizons
Apply the calendar to the timeline, blacking out non-work days	The calendar is driven in part by the business plan, in part by the derived durations, and in part by the rolling wave planning process

Module 2—Discussion for Critical Thinking

It's one thing to establish a rhythm when the project is small and self-contained to a nearly green-field environment, but how would you keep a rhythm in a larger-scale project set in the context of an enterprise with many functional and technical interfaces to the project?

A network of teams handles the scope of multiple iterations that feed into one release

Team 1 is the critical path; teams 2 and 3 are buffered to the critical path

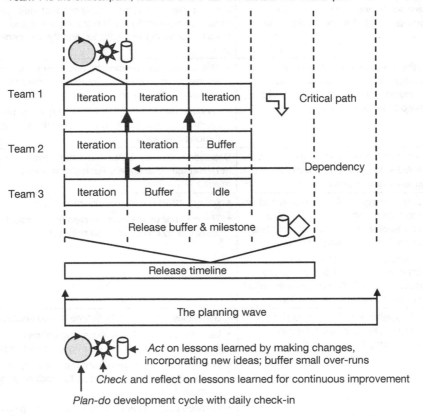

Figure 6.5   Release network grid

Module 3: Other Plans in the Enterprise Agile Project

Projects of any reasonable scale in an enterprise context will have many plans

Module 3—Objectives

- Familiarize the reader with other plans that could impact the agile project

Planning for Architecture and Nonfunctional Deliverables

Architecture is present in every project, whether formally acknowledged or not. A good practice is to make the architecture visible and effective for guiding the product development. Consideration of architecture will certainly appear as part of the governance process for the business case. At Level 0, many projects will conform to an existing architecture. At Levels 1 and 2 (especially at Level 2) consideration of new architecture may be very prominent.

Architecture is best developed by a team effort. The architect, if there is an individual in the project operating model with that portfolio, as well as other subject-matter experts, mentors and coaches the teams. Agile Principle 11 is noteworthy:

Agile Principle 11	The best architectures, requirements, and designs emerge from self-organizing teams.

In this book, we take exception to Principle 11 as it is written. In the business case or project charter, a strategic architecture is provided. It is intended to be stationary. It is typically not an emergent product of development teams.

We take Principle 11 as applying to a lower-level constituent of the top-level architecture that supports the strategic intent of the project. That said, as previously discussed, *Iteration-0* is the time to put in place system components that have no direct customer value.

Nonfunctional requirements should not delay the development iterations needlessly, especially for nonfunctional needs that might be sequenced later in the project lifecycle. Nonfunctional deliverables often accompany the functional products delivered to the customer and often they are a prerequisite to the development of the functional product.

The nonfunctionality deliverables are often on the horizontal axis of the Kano chart as discussed in Chapter 5. Nonfunctional needs include all manner of infrastructure to include computers, networks, storage, security protocols, manufacturing setups, tools and jigs or templates, scorecards and dashboards, and many others.

Planning for Uncertainty

Agile methods are themselves a risk response to the uncertainty and general unpredictability of software requirements, since there are few physical boundaries to contain imagination. And so the general context of agile projects is uncertainty and thus, risk to project objectives.

We make a distinction between risk and uncertainty this way:

- Risk is an event, condition, or set of circumstances having both a range of impacts that could affect project objectives and a range of probabilities. About each of these we may have some insight, even if imperfect. For instance, to have a probability, a risk must have some history to establish the statistics of probability. If there really is no history, thus no insight into probability, we would move such a risk to *uncertainty*.

- Uncertainty is all the rest for which we have little or no insight, or perhaps no knowledge at all—the infamous *unknown unknowns*—but yet, from experience we know there are going to be unpredictable events or conditions that could be troublesome.

Balance Sheet for Uncertainty

Consider again the project balance sheet introduced in Chapter 2. The business plan is represented on the left side. The plan not only provides the goal and the product vision, but specifies the investment and lays down milestones for beneficial outcomes. In effect, the business side of the project balance sheet is about targets and goals—targets for cost, schedule, scope, and benefits.

Even for relatively simple Level 0 plans, it is very likely that the business planners are indifferent—perhaps even unwitting—about how practical and achievable their plan is. At least initially that is why the project balance sheet inevitably shows a gap between the business objectives and the project's capacity and capability to meet those objectives. The business may constrain too many variables fixing milestones, scope, and budget. If one variable is most important, then other variables must forcibly adapt. If one of the other variables is not within the control and discretion of the business, then those that the business can control must forcibly adapt.

As an example: industry tradeshows are milestone inflexible—their dates cannot be moved, but the scope for presentations at the tradeshow can be adjusted. And another example: consider a project to submit a competitive proposal that includes a product demonstration—the proposal cannot be late, but some product demonstration details can be deferred until negotiations take place. And a final example: remember the millennium—the year 2000 could not be moved to accommodate a late project, but some program modifications could wait one or two quarters past January 1 before a date issue became problematic.

It is necessary for the project to respond to the business plan; first with estimates and then with its own plan that operates with those estimates. A project without a plan leaves the project vulnerable to impracticalities that may be embedded in the business plan. Following the wisdom of Fred

Brooks, *hunches are not a plan and are no defense if events do not unfold favorably.*[4]

A project management tip	Planning is more important than the plan
	• The best use of the plan is to establish the correct starting direction and provide a framework to guide the teams to the next horizon. • With the first unforeseen difficulty, some aspect of the plan will have to change. That is the time that the planning experience will pay dividends—when alternatives are required.

Shift Right

There is a chance that joining paths will cause the schedule to slip to the right. This *chance* is the risk of simultaneity; it is calculated as the product of the probabilities of all the joining paths, given that they should finish all at the same time. If, for example, all paths should finish together with probability very high, say 95 out of 100 opportunities, and then the probability of making the milestone with three joining paths is equal to their product: $0.95 \times 0.95 \times 0.95$, or 0.86—which is a shade less than 7 chances in 8.

To raise the milestone probability to 95 out of 100, the schedule must move to the right by adding a buffer before the shifted milestone. The size of the buffer should be large enough to catch the most likely overrun.

The shift-right phenomenon is also known as *merge bias*. The name connotes the fact that there is a bias toward the schedule shifting when paths join. The problem arises if one or more joining paths are tardy. In that event, the schedule will slip to the right awaiting the tardy iteration to finish. Now of course, with rigid time boxes bounding each team's work, a tardy iteration should not happen.

A project management tip	Shift right phenomenon
	• Whenever two or more strings join at a completion milestone, or join as the predecessor iterations of a successor iteration, there is a chance for the timeline to shift to the right. • Because one or more joining paths may join late, the effect is to shift the joining point to the right.

By design and by doctrine, all time-boxed iterations finish as prescribed on the timeline. However, mindful of von Moltke's observation that no plan survives contact with reality, a prudent practice is to provide a small buffer on the off-chance that an iteration goes a bit long. In the extreme case of some calamity where it appears a team is not converging to a finish, the project manager is expected to step in and stop work.[15]

	Getting *done* at milestones
A project management tip	• In general, regardless of where placed, buffers protect the integrity of the milestone schedule. • Of course, many Level 0 projects will be a much-simplified network of perhaps only one tandem string of iterations or sprints. • All projects, regardless of level, should buffer the release event.

Take note that the release event is not a point in time but rather an iteration in itself, wherein a number of go-live production tasks are executed. Depending on accepted conventions and the nature of the product base—whether internal or external—and the support structure for the product, the go-live iteration could be quite varied. Go-live could be anywhere from a simple script that loads and links files to a quite complex iteration requiring dedicated, careful planning with the business, infrastructure managers, and application developers. To be lean and efficient, develop a go-live template that is repetitively used from one release to the next.

How long should an iteration be? There is no fixed prescription, but each methodology has its own recommendation. A principle of agile projects is that releases should be frequent. Take note of Principle 3:

Agile Principle 3	Deliver working software frequently, from a couple of weeks to a couple of months, with a preference to the shorter timescale.

Putting aside any truly Covey-like Category I *most important-most urgent* imperatives that would drive the schedule—or for that matter any immovable milestones—Schawber, for one, recommends fixing a Scrum sprint to 30 consecutive days on the calendar, or 30 days on the wall clock.[16] Refer back to Table 1.5 for recommendations from all the methodologies.

Voice of the Business in Plans

Agile methodologists respect the fact that the business speaks for both itself and the customer through the business plan. The business is the recognized authority on the project's value proposition, and from that authority come the top-level milestones that frame all other plans. The teams can challenge these milestones, but the teams cannot unilaterally set them aside.

Agile plans accept conventions, standards, and practices that collectively are the organizational culture. The business may require conformance to outside regulation and adherence to certain models of behavior. Team behavior may have to conform to various maturity models. These and others will influence and color project planning.

Module 3—Discussion for Critical Thinking

Though the Agile Manifesto values doing things over planning things, the fact remains that the enterprise is driven by various plans, some of which were discussed in Module 1 and some in this module. Do you see any inconsistency with being an advocate for agile, even though a fair amount of planning may come your way?

Summary and Takeaway Points

The theme we developed in this chapter is that *adapting plans and estimates to changing customer needs, and maximizing value and at an affordable cost are the planning imperatives for agile projects*.

From Module 1, we see that there are actually all manner of plans that apply to agile methods. The myth that there is no planning in agile projects is just that—a myth. And, for the hybrid project, work-stream plans are synchronized for the important project and business milestones.

Of course, these plans are not isolated from the myriad of planning drivers that are part of any practical project. In Module 1, we see risk as a driver, along with other factors, to include the efficiency of working at the lowest possible level, in accord with the principle of subsidiarity.

In Module 2, scheduling, we examine the so-called *rhythm of the schedule* that contributes to success in sustaining a work pace that does not burn out the team, certainly one of the Agile Principles. Other scheduling contributors are, of course, the time box, the velocity of the team work, and the impact that reflection and lessons learned imparts to the schedule.

Ultimately, of course, the team must commit to a calendar, especially if working in hybrid, where synchronized milestones are a critical part of project schedule success.

In Module 3, we learn that agile projects are not immune to other planning needs, to include architecture for the entire project, the nonfunctionals that customer/users may not even know about, as well as representing the voice of the business in the project plans.

Chapter Endnotes

1. Paraphrased from Malotaux's, *Timeline, Getting and Keeping Control over Your Project*, a whitepaper that was originally prepared for the Annual Pacific Northwest Software Conference, Portland, OR, 2008.

2. Anderson, *Agile Management for Software Engineering*, 9-10.

3. The Gantt chart is a bar chart with individual bars representing activities. The length of the bar is the scheduled duration for that activity. The overall timeline of the project can be computed by summing the non-overlapping bar segments. Dependencies between bars are not usually shown. The chart is named after its inventor Henry Gantt, mechanical engineer and industrialist, who introduced the chart in the 1910s. Gantt was a college roommate and professional associate of F. W. Taylor, the father of Taylorism, who is discussed in other chapters.

4. Velocity is an XP term and a measure of rate of throughput that is applied generally to all agile methods: objects actually put into production.

5. A time box is a prescribed length of time for a set of multifunctional activities. Scope is modified to fit the time box, not the other way a round. The daily stand-up meeting is done with a time box. Each development iteration and planning wave is time-boxed.

6. The chargeback rate is the rate per unit of time that the individual is charged to the paying organization. The rate may be the base salary or the salary lifted by a factor for benefits, or it could be a rate that includes a lift for both benefits and overhead. In some organizations, and particularly if contracted, the chargeback rate may be a standard cost. A standard cost is a fixed rate by labor or job category regardless of the person's paid-out compensation. In some cases, the standard cost is greater than the actual compensation, and in other times, it is not.

7. Boehm, *Software Engineering Economics*, 311, presents Figure 21-1, which illustrates estimation accuracy versus project phase. The figure is cone-shaped, but Boehm does not use that wording in his text. The estimation accuracy by phase diagram is reproduced as Figure 1-2 in Boehm et al, *Software Cost Estimation with* COCOMO II, 10.

8. McConnell, *Software Estimation: Demystifying the Black Art*, 35-40.

9. Anderson, *Agile Management for Software Engineering*, Chapter 2.

10. Readers can prove this phenomenon for themselves by histogramming various phenomena in the project. There will tend to be a clustering around a central value.

11. Goldratt and Fox, *The Race*, 179; Goldratt and Cox, *The Goal: A Process of Ongoing Improvement*.

12. "5-Whys," developed by Sakichi Toyoda of Toyota Motor Corporation.

13. Project Management Institute, *Project Management Body of Knowledge (PMBOK® Guide—Fifth Edition)*, Chapter 6.

14. Recall that the critical path is the longest connected path through the network. See Goodpasture, *Quantitative Methods in Project Management*, 187-192.

15. Schwaber, *Agile Project Management with SCRUM*, 136. According to Schwaber's Sprint Rules, Scrum masters stop work when the sprint appears to be no longer viable. A subsequent planning meeting is called to evaluate next steps.

16. Ibid, 8.

7

Estimating Cost and Schedule

There are no facts about the future, only estimates.[1]

> *It is very difficult to make a vigorous, plausible, job-risking defense of an estimate that is derived by no quantitative method, supported by little data, and certified chiefly by the hunches of the managers.*
>
> Dr. Fred P. Brooks, Jr.[2]

Module 1: The Nature of Estimates
Making a judgment about the future, even with uncertainty

Module 1—Objectives
- Discuss and explain the unique aspects of agile estimates
- Discuss and explain how complexity finds its way into agile estimates
- Discuss and explain why good enough is good enough

Introduction to Estimates
So, what's an estimate? We have the dictionary version easy enough, as given via google.com:

Estimate: *An approximate calculation or judgment of the value, number, quantity, or extent of something.*

There's a lot we can work with there:

- Only approximations are needed about the future, so we can apply the Agile Principle of *just enough* precision and accuracy to serve our purposes.

- Estimates can be a calculation or a judgment, so that works for agile as well. Some sponsors like the numbers, but other rely more on subjective factors.
- They can be applied to about anything. Again, from an unrestricted backlog perspective, that's good for agile as well.

Here's one more:

- They must include and be consistent with facts from the past. Certainly this is the point of Dr. Brooks' admonishment in the opening quote.

Estimates speak to future events which can *only* be described probabilistically. Some managers may think they can stake the future by estimating that the cost or schedule will hit a single planned point value, but estimating point solutions is usually a fool's errand. More realistically, the estimating objective should be to estimate the limits of a range that should encompass the outcome—and for that range, provide a confidence estimate of whether the true outcome will fall within the range.

Here's an example: *The team is confident that in 8 trials out of 10, the backlog will be burned down completely within a range of six to eight weeks.*

What happens in the other two trials? We're given no information. We can only take from the estimate that in 2 trials out of 10, either the project will take longer than eight weeks; or the project could be shorter than six weeks. In all cases, however, the standard is that the backlog is *burned down completely*.

	Estimates are not facts
A project management tip	Invariably, the most vexing thing about estimates is their propensity to be mistaken for facts, or worse—a commitment!

Agile Estimates

Next to requirements, estimates are probably the most influential factor on the predictability of the project outcomes. Agile projects are managed for throughput and outcomes, not for activity, and not so much for input, either (that is, cost, schedule, scope). As discussed in Chapter 4, the dominant management focus is on delivering a working product.

	Agile estimates
A project management tip	The first principle of estimating for agile projects is to estimate for outcomes, not activity.

Activity and Throughput

Estimating outcomes will bring to the surface the ageless tension between good-faith effort and completion. Good-faith effort is a commitment to work diligently and thoughtfully—in effect, engage in activity. Completion, on the other hand, is a commitment to produce a measurable and valuable outcome—in a word, throughput:

- Every project includes some activity that is a good-faith effort, in effect a level-of-effort
- The point to grasp is that activity is only a means and not the end
- Because the *end* is the only thing valued by customers, agile estimating shifts focus to the end items that are useful and wanted

Traditional activity-oriented Gantt charts and activity networks give way to scheduling throughput-oriented iterations and releases. Instead of being activity-centric, the end game is to achieve throughput as effectively as possible.

As previously established, throughput and backlog complexity are the two parameters that govern team production. If it is hard or even impossible to imagine all the requirements, it is equally hard to imagine the efforts needed to implement the requirements. These issues are summarized in two words: complexity and uncertainty.

	Complexity and uncertainty
A project management tip	• Complexity is quality described by how many ways units can interact, a measure of how many unique states a system can be in, and how many responses one stimulus causes. • Complexity is what transforms a cost-to-benefit opportunity into a cost-to-consequences threat. • Uncertainty is what is unknowable until just-in-time. • Uncertainty is risk without knowledge of an unfavorable event or neutralizing mitigation.

Understanding Complexity

To get a handle on complexity requires some understanding of its properties. Complexity has no better than an imprecise definition. Indeed, there are dozens of definitions. However, to simplify matters we say that it is the known, knowable, and possibly unknowable interactions of a large number of system elements.

Complexity can also mean redundancy; more than one system element is capable of handling a function. However, it may not be known or knowable which element acts at what time and under which conditions. It can also mean unnecessary design and functionality asked for but not actually used. Complexity is not the absence of simplicity.

A project management tip	Complex and simple
	The simplest system that is minimally satisfactory may be complex, but the corollary is true: simplicity is the absence of unnecessary complexity.

Complexity puts systems on the edge of chaos, meaning that a relatively minor stimulus could create unwieldy and unpredictable outcomes. Complex systems have high entropy, meaning that complex systems can acquire or be in many states—some more stable than others—and not all known to developers and testers. Complexity is influenced by the N^2 effect (discussed in Chapter 11 and the glossary), whereby the number of interactions between elements increases nearly as the square of the number of elements. Even a small N, say 20, means almost 400 ways for an interaction to occur, and each of these has conditions, triggers, and subsequent effects.

The systems we are concerned about have many elements, in fact very many elements, more than any one person can keep in mind. Extended to their interdependencies, the numbers can be overwhelming. As discussed in Chapter 4, complexity influences testing, quality assurance, and post-product support.

A project management tip	Organized complexity
	• Warren Weaver describes systems of interrelated elements as having organized complexity.[3]
	• Organized complexity means that over time, certain interactions will dominate; their properties can be observed, tested, and measured.
	• Other interactions, although possible, happen so infrequently that they are operationally inconsequential.

Complexity complicates estimating:

- Key estimating parameters, like velocity, are subject to uncertainty arising from unforeseen interactions among the solution elements.

- Interactions with legacy systems bring many more elements into play, driving the N^2 effects higher, and making testing much more complicated.
- Simple automated unit tests are less revealing; integration with the installed base, always more complicated than unit testing, becomes an ever-larger factor in throughput.
- Allowing for the unforeseeable requires discounting throughput, much like discounting future benefits for unforeseeable circumstances.

In the agile domain, complexity is an economic issue and a throughput issue. The more complex the backlog, the more time is needed for a given throughput to burn off the backlog. Time, in turn, affects the present value of benefits and the operating expenses of the project. Tradeoffs between good, better, and best will be required.

Estimates Become Commitments—a Problem for Managers

Every project sponsor asks for estimates—estimates of required funds resources, estimates of major milestones, and estimates to support other scorecard key performance indicators.

The latter is where the problem comes in; care must be taken. Every project manager knows that estimates do not stay estimates very long. Even if the sponsor has used the word estimate, more often they are thinking, do not exceed, or tell me what it's going to cost and when I am going to get it. And the farther up the chain the estimate is forwarded, the more it loses caveats.

Unfortunately, all too frequently estimates become commitments almost as soon as they are uttered. Knowing this, prudence demands some adjustment for risk to set a proper confidence interval. In the agile context, several techniques are available:

- Only provide *range of possibilities* estimates; avoid single-point commitments
- Buffer every release with a *no content* time box to guard the outcome milestone
- Schedule less than 80% of the throughput benchmark in order to leave *white space* to absorb unforeseen outcomes
- Estimate tasks based on consensus of independent estimators, thereby to reduce bias
- Factor in prior experience to adjust benchmarks to the current situation

A project management tip	Confidence interval
	• A confidence interval expresses the probability that an estimate will fall within the limits of a range, called the confidence interval. • Usually, there is a confidence expressed about how likely an estimate will exceed the interval's maximum value, and another confidence expression about how likely an estimate will be less than the interval's minimum value. An example is shown in the Appendix to this chapter.

Following Agile Principles, the best way to convey understanding and resolve differences is face-to-face with the business. Even so, there will likely be a residual gap between the project plan and the business plan. When the residual gap is close enough, the project manager moves on, accepting some risk. What risk? The risk is that by adapting to opportunity, iteration by iteration, the means will be found to achieve business objectives and satisfy the customer. Close enough is often as much accuracy as a project needs; close enough is agile.

Estimates Fall within a Range

All estimates regardless of methodology are, by definition, probabilistic—meaning that an actual outcome is not known with certainty, but is likely contained within a range of values. As an example, a developer might estimate that an object requires 100 hours + 20 − 10 hours, meaning that the developer has high confidence that the range from 90 to 120 hours covers the actual effort.

One way to take all possibilities into consideration is to average all the possibilities, but a simple arithmetic average assumes all values in the range are equally likely, even though they are usually not. A better estimate is obtained when the information about probabilities within the range is taken into account. So rather than simply adding all the values and dividing by the number of possibilities, do this:

- Take the number of possibilities as a pool of points
- Weight each value, using points, to your judgment about its overall weight or contribution in the sum (the total of weights should add to the pool total)
- Multiply each range value by the points assigned and sum the value-points products
- Then, as before, divide the sum total by the number of points

The result is a risk-weighted average called the expected value. The expected value is that one number that best represents the whole range of possibilities from 90 to 120 hours.

An example of this approach is in the Appendix to this chapter.

Good Enough

All of this suggests that precision and accuracy in estimates need only be *good enough*—in other words, good enough to serve the project purpose of allocating enough resources but not too many, and certainly not too few.

There is no objective definition of *good enough*. For agile purposes, *good enough* means having only enough estimate precision and accuracy such that a reasonable understanding of the range is reached. There is no point in putting effort into estimating a 98 percent—or even greater—certainty about a number that is very likely to change. The nature of agile projects is to be flexible and adaptable about requirements, thereby requiring adaptable and flexible estimates.

	Estimates are valuable even if imprecise and inaccurate
A project management tip	• Money is not to be spent and effort is not be exerted without a close eye on the value returned. • In all respects, the project objective and purpose is to make things better for all its beneficiaries. • Even though the estimates are, by design, not too precise, they nevertheless serve a valuable purpose to frame value.

Module 1—Discussion for Critical Thinking

If you've experienced the business holding you firmly to estimates, rather than understanding that there is a degree of uncertainty around any estimate, do you think the agile practice of estimating to a granularity of an iteration or release would help mitigate misunderstandings?

Module 2: Drivers on Cost and Schedule

Backlog complexity, productivity, and scale of teams

Module 2—Objectives

- Examine the factors that drive cost and schedule resource consumption in agile methods

Backlog and Productivity

The backlog, the productivity of teams, and the number of teams working largely drive cost and schedule. Here are the most important points:

- Team productivity is only stable for a planning wave; thereafter, circumstances may change.
- Estimates are deferred until *just-in-time* based on a detailed examination of the backlog.
- Estimates are then extended to subsequent iterations in the wave, understanding that the check-act portion of the iteration cycle will affect requirements backlog and require refinements of the estimates.

The highest uncertainty is the number of actionable requirements, stories, and use cases and their complexity. The project backlog is the beginning point, but teams expect the backlog to be changed during the course of the project.

A project management tip	Forecasting change
	There is usually no reliable forecast for the degree of expected change.

On the other hand, there are some constituents of productivity that go into an estimate that are relatively stable:

- Time boxes are fixed and deterministic.
- Kanban work in progress (WIP) is controllable.
- All teams expect low turnover and are populated within a small range of 7 to 12 members.
- Each team has a throughput capacity—velocity—that is estimated or known by benchmarking within a reasonably small range.
- Confidence in the expected value of velocity is high.

So the estimated schedule, and to a large extent the estimated cost, is driven either by the number of iterations required to liquidate the backlog, by the number of iterations the sponsor chooses to afford, or by the productivity of the team during an iteration. The material in Table 7.1 summarizes these ideas.

Environmental factors that influence productivity estimates are summarized in Table 7.2.

Table 7.1   Summary of complexity drivers on cost and schedule

Parameter	Strength of influence	Cost and schedule effects
Estimated number of requirements at the user-story level	• High on cost • Moderate on timeline	• Directly drives the total number of units of throughput needed to liquidate the backlog • Each unit has a cost • Each unit is developed within an iteration
Estimated complexity of individual requirements	• High on cost • Moderate on timeline	• Directly drives the total number of throughput units needed to liquidate the backlog • Each unit has a cost • Each unit is developed within an iteration
Estimated velocity—units of throughput per unit of time	High on cost and schedule	• Directly drives the timeline and overall cost • The range of the velocity estimate affects the predictability of the iteration success

Table 7.2   Summary of environmental drivers on cost and schedule

Parameter	Strength of influence	Cost and schedule effects
Number of members in the team and the mix of skills, experience, and cohesiveness	High influence on velocity	• Performance above or below expectation affects velocity • Labor loss of 15 percent is a good practice metric for projects lasting seven months or longer
Availability of favorable environmental factors such as colocation, tools, coaching, and infrastructure support	Moderate influence on velocity	Environment affects team performance
Dependencies with other teams and work streams	• Low if properly sequenced and buffered • Not included in the velocity estimates	• Dependencies affect the ability of an iteration to begin as planned • Inter-team dependences may affect the order of delivered functionality without affecting overall cost and schedule
Critical path or noncritical path	Not every iteration is on the critical path	Resource scarcity of subject matter experts affects delivered scope Opportunity may arise to make up the shortfall in scope without affecting the schedule, but at a cost If the iteration is not part of the critical path, it may be starved of a required resource and might miss the scope objective

Scope, Complexity, and Velocity

Estimating in the agile space focuses on three parameters:

1. *Scope*: Number of requirements, stories, or use cases—to include technical and functional debt—in the project backlog at the outset of the project, plus the other ancillary iterations for planning and engineering, and release to integration and production
2. *Complexity*: The interrelationships of backlog constituents, and the interrelationships with the installed base with which integration must occur
3. *Team velocity*: The pace at which throughput can be delivered; the pace at which the WIP can move through the Kanban steps

From these three, the beginning project timeline and cost can be estimated. But, as the point was made earlier, change to the project backlog is simply not forecastable. As each planning wave matures, the estimating begins again for the next wave that rolls in.

Of course, this returns us to the discussion in Chapter 4 about when the project is *done*. Certainly one estimate of schedule is the number of iterations of duration T that can be fit within the budget. And, the number of iterations must include all of the planning, architecting and engineering, buffers, and release iterations—in other words, the complete package of scope. Table 7.3 lists estimating practices that are mainstream in the industry.

Cost and Schedule Derivations

Every project manager has experience managing both cost and schedule—and all know that one affects the other. We all know that cost and schedule are interdependent, so their plans and estimates are intertwined. For reasons to be discussed and as would be expected, labor cost tracks effort very closely. As effort increases, so does its cost in about the same way—double the effort, double its cost, at least to a first approximation. But effort does not have that same effect on the schedule. To be sure, the schedule often extends when effort goes above plan. What project manager has not heard of Brooks' Law?[4]

Brooks' Law
Adding manpower to a late software project makes it later.

Table 7.3 Mainstream estimating practices

Practice	Commentary
Top-down allocation	Not so much an estimate as a value judgment, a budget of time, dollars, or both is spread proportionally among features and functions according to the customer's attitude about importance and urgency.
Similar-to or analogous	• The estimate is taken from the cost history of a similar system, product, or task. • The estimate is adjusted for drivers that may have changed such as inflation, environment, and specific requirements that are no longer relevant. New requirements are estimated proportionally to their nearest analog.
Parameter or model driven	• The estimate is taken based on multiplying units by a parameter, like dollars per page by the number of pages. • The parameters come from historical benchmarks. Models such as COCOMO II are populated with parametric data, various multipliers are applied, and the results of many parametric factors are summed into a final result.[1]
Stick-built bottoms-up	• Each element is individually evaluated for the likely cost. • Similar-to estimates, parameter estimates, models, and simulations may be combined with detailed evaluations, analysis, and prototyping to build up an estimate from the lowest non-divisible element.

Since Brooks proclaimed his law in 1975, many analysts have examined the behavior of schedules as more individuals are added into the project mix. From their work, much empirical evidence is now available to support forecasting. Some of that information will be used in the material that follows.

Chapter 6 discussed the planning process for agile projects beginning with the business plan. The top-level business milestones and affordability targets originate in the business plan. However, that is the business side of the project balance sheet. The corresponding cost and schedule estimates made by the project fill out the other side, according to these two important points:

1. Schedule duration is derived by applying available throughput to the business case scope, and continues to be derived after every iteration!

2. Cost is derived from the effort to meet requirements, as in all methodologies, but the agile twist is that requirements are never frozen; the requirements deck remains open for nearly the whole duration of the project.

In the big picture, requirements are changeable as the product master seeks a best-value solution. Obviously, an open requirements deck means that cost and duration are always in play, ultimately limited by the cap on affordability established in the business plan. Duration is not estimated in the manner that is customary in plan-driven project development lifecycle methodologies because requirements are only incrementally stabilized for each iteration.

	Cost and duration
A project management tip	• Plans change with each iteration. • Cost and schedule duration are derived from the total throughput required to work down all the requirements. • Requirements, however, are not fixed; in the agile methodologies, the customer, whether internal or external, is encouraged to constantly interpret what is needed. • The cost and duration are not fixed, but the stakeholders get to vote after every release whether to continue.

Module 2—Discussion for Critical Thinking

We say in this module that estimates are deferred until just in time, so that the estimate applies to the backlog in its most stable makeup. Some might say that such just-in-time practices are tantamount to no estimate at all, arguing that if you have not made an estimate when the work is uncertain, what's the point of making an estimate just before work begins when the work is known? What would you say to the critics of making estimates?

Module 3: Building Estimates

No estimate survives contact with reality

Module 3—Objectives

- Discuss and explain several estimating practices common in agile projects
- Discuss and explain staffing effects on estimates

Building an Estimate: Metric and Scale

To build an estimate, focus first on the elements from Table 7.1, which require estimating or benchmarking—requirements complexity and velocity. The fundamental approach to estimating is built on two principles:

1. Diversification reduces risk
2. Benchmarks provide a safe port in a storm

To diversify the risk that an estimator may be wrong, engage many independent estimators. Direct each expert to look at the same problem at the same time and provide an estimate. Then combine all the independent estimates in some agreed upon way to arrive at a consensus.

To incorporate benchmarks, compare your effort with an understood standard, making adjustments for unique circumstances. Four elements are needed to diversify and benchmark:

- A process for independent evaluation by more than one estimator
- A process and a means to combine estimator results to get a consensus estimate
- A process to compare and make adjustments to a benchmark
- A relative-weight scoring system for complexity

These elements are further expanded:

- Process for evaluation and consensus: A recommended process for independent evaluation with combined results is called wideband Delphi. Wideband Delphi will be described in subsequent sections.
- Compare and make adjustments: A good benchmark will be a unit of scope already completed and in production about which the team has a good understanding. Make proportional adjustments for functional and feature complexity, the state of requirements as they were going-in, the environment that prevailed, the experience and cohesion of the team at that time, and the customer involvement.
- Scoring system: A scoring system will have two elements:
   1. An unambiguous definition of what to score
   2. The scale and metric for the score

There are many ideas about what to score—business stories, scenarios and themes, use cases and user stories—all of these and any of these are candidates.

A project management tip	Consistency over metric
	The important point is not which metric to pick, but to pick one and thereafter be consistent and repeatable!

The metric, or unit of measure, can be any of many possibilities. The common list is function points, feature points, story points, or standard or ideal days. These are not measures of activity; they are measures of product produced.

A project management tip	Activity versus product
	• Do not fall into the trap of focusing estimates on activity. • What is needed for a unit estimate is the effort to be expended within a prescribed time box to produce one unit of product at an estimated level of complexity.

Story Point Estimating

For purposes of discussion and illustration, we will focus on the story point. Story points are not particularly better than the others, but in the spirit of *pick one!*, story point is our choice. There is no dimension assigned to a story point—the metric is a dimensionless number. There is no exact definition of a story point, but we define a story point this way:

Story Point
A story point is a quantity of effort to develop one unit of product with minimum relative complexity; in effect, a story point results in a unit of outcome.

In this sense, we think of an iteration delivering so many story points of outcome. The more a requirement is valued in story points, the more scope and complexity is represented. Effort tracks points with a 1-to-1 ratio—double the points, double the effort.

Calibration Required

To calibrate the effort of one story point, the team does these things:

- First, agree on granularity—the grain of the requirements decomposition. Too fine a grain loses cohesion; too large a grain obscures detail. Deciding the grain is a judgment to be considered, debated, and agreed to by the team.
- Once the requirements have been decomposed, the team selects an example of the simplest requirement and also one that seems about midpoint in complexity.
- Then, the simplest requirement is assigned the lowest value of points on the scale and becomes a benchmark for lowest complexity.

- Similarly, the mid-complexity requirement is given a midscale value. The actual numerical values are completely dependent on the scale chosen.

The scale is the number of points assignable. Scale is simply a means to establish the relative difference between units. The scale could be the numbers from 1 to 20, or from 10 to 200; the actual scale is irrelevant to the results.

	Coping with magnitude
A project management tip	It is generally accepted that people effectively can cope with an order of magnitude—1 to 10. Beyond that range, people find it very hard to meaningfully assign different values.[5]

An important idea to keep in mind is that, if an object being estimated does not seem to fit within the range, then the object is judged *very complex* and thereby out of range. In this case, a best practice is to decompose the very complex object into less complex components and estimate them as a collection.

Recall from Chapter 4 that decomposition is a form of diversity. Diversifying a complex object by decomposition will reduce the overall uncertainty surrounding the object. However, the performance of the decomposed objects may be misleading with regard to how the complex object will behave when all the parts are present and interworking.

Estimating Velocity

In the foregoing example, it was assumed that the team had benchmarked itself to a throughput of 20 story points per iteration, ±2 points. There are a few ways to establish this benchmark:

- If the team has been together for a while, then past performance on other iterations is the best indicator
- If the team has not been together or if the environment has been frequently changed, then the team could execute a practice development or run a simulation on a couple of stories to benchmark their performance
- The team lead and the project manager might agree that the team is similar to other teams for which there is a good benchmark. After the first couple of iterations, the team will find its own mark.

Estimating Complexity

When making estimates, consistency is valued more than accuracy for the first couple of iterations, because with a consistent approach, continuous improvement is possible. Consider these two points:

1. The same people should do the estimating each time. The experiences and biases of the estimators will have a large influence on the outcomes. Agile methods count on adaptive correction to smooth things out—but such adaptation requires the team to stay together and to be consistently involved in all estimating.

2. The same estimating tools or practice should be used, because again, there are biases in any practice that can only be neutralized over time and with experience.

There are several alternatives for scale. The more popular alternatives are given in Table 7.4. Two of the three scales shown are nonlinear. The purpose of the nonlinearity is to force some separation between complexity estimates. In other words, it is more meaningful to say something is two or three times as complex, than it is to say something is 1.25 times as complex. Accuracy need only be good enough for the team to do its work; too much precision is unwarranted. For these reasons, either the binary or Fibonacci scales are used most often.

Table 7.4　Popular estimating scales

Scale	Commentary
Linear	• A linear scale from about 1-10, all the integers available as a possible complexity score • Does not directly "help" separate course grades of complexity between low, medium, and high. • However, grouping as shown is an effective way to use the linear scale: 　Low 1, 2, 3 ... Medium 4, 5, 7 ... High 7, 8, 9 ...Very High 10
Binary	• A binary scale from about 1-32, the sequence being 1, 2, 4, 8, 16, 32 as the only possible complexity scores • Helps separate course grades of complexity by only allowing the specific values in the scale
Fibonacci	• A Fibonacci scale from about 1-21, the sequence being 1, 2, 3, 5, 8, 13, 21. In this scale, each number is the sum of the preceding two numbers • Some like this scale better than the binary for separating complexity values, but it's a judgment call • The Fibonacci sequence is used in many types of analysis, but in the context of requirements complexity, its properties are not materially superior to the binary scale

An Estimating Process: Delphi and Poker

Estimating practices—like the Delphi method and planning poker—provide assistance to the estimating process. To see how they are used, we will apply them to the *estimate complexity step* in the scenario given in the Appendix, Table A7.1.

Delphi Method

The Delphi method is a tried-and-true approach developed in 1948 by the Rand Corporation to address uncertainties surrounding emerging defense technologies. In a more up-to-date variant, Barry Boehm and John Farquhar expanded and made popular study work that was done in 1970 by Farquhar.

Farquhar's study compared the accuracy of the Delphi estimates with estimates of the same problem from simple group collaboration. Boehm and Farquhar arrived at a process they called *wideband Delphi*, which itself has been more recently adapted and updated by other practitioners.[6]

	The Delphi method
A project management tip	• In any variant of the Delphi method, the gist of the matter is that each team member estimates independently. • A process of consensus building provides a means to arrive at a team estimate from all the independent estimates.

In a conventional Delphi approach, the process works like this:

- A facilitator gives each estimator information about the estimation task; there may be preliminary discussion with the facilitator to understand the issues.
- Estimators work independently and privately to arrive at an estimate. Privacy ensures that the estimator is not influenced by the reputation and biases of the other estimators, or off-put by any personal loyalties and organizational politics.
- A facilitator works privately with each estimator to understand their point of view; the facilitator provides each with the benefit of the other estimates, albeit anonymously.
- Estimators are allowed to reconsider and change their estimate based on the new information. The process continues until the facilitator has enough information to recommend an estimate.

There is no requirement stating that all estimators agree with the estimate taken away by the project manager.

Delphi in Systems Design

In high-reliability systems, independently developed redundant software pro-grams can be employed to vote on a proper system response to a stimulus. This is a form of a Delphi methodology applied to system design.

The theory is that if one version of a program executes and returns a wrong answer, other redundant but independent program versions will not have the error and will collectively out vote the one incorrect representation.

Delphi and Agile

In its original form, Delphi is inconsistent with Agile Principles. Agile Prin-ciples require public collaboration between team members. On the other hand, simply averaging the answers of a simple collaboration has some struc-tural problems. For instance, in a simple average, one outlier can skew the average. And there are the intangibles to consider. By force of personality, one aggressive estimator can bias the whole team to a single point of view.

Wideband Delphi is the middle ground between Delphi and simple col-laboration. It is slightly different from its parent; the wideband label comes from increased communications and collaboration added to the more pri-vate Delphi method.

Here is how wideband Delphi works:

- The project manager calls the estimating team together for an initial collaboration and group discussion.
- Information from the backlog, narrative, and other sources is provided.
- Each estimator then works privately and independently on the first estimate.
- Subsequent rounds of re-estimation are collaborative, with each esti-mator given an opportunity to explain their estimate.
- The process ends when the group develops a satisfactory consensus.

Planning Poker

In a popular implementation of wideband Delphi for agile projects, a game called agile planning poker is played.[7] Each player holds a hand of cards with all the numbers from the scale. Typically, either the binary or Fibonacci scale is used but, as we know, the scale is largely immaterial if applied con-sistently from one team to the next.

Here are the steps:

1. In the first step of the game, after an initial discussion with the fa-cilitator and after being dealt a hand, each player makes their first

estimate by turning over his or her card choice. To make it closer to the way real poker is played, everyone shows his or her card at the same time. In part, the simultaneous turnover of cards is to avoid estimators changing their estimate after viewing the other cards.

2. In the second step of the game, just like in any variant of wideband Delphi, the team discusses the estimates. Usually, only the extreme estimates are discussed to save time.

3. Following the first play and the group discussion, a second hand can be played—or the team might have enough information to arrive at a consensus without playing a second hand.

In a study of planning poker versus just a simple average of the estimates, researchers found that poker estimates, after completing the game, were less optimistic and generally more accurate than a simple arithmetic combination of independent estimates.

Staffing Effects on Estimates

A useful rule that has emerged from those who have studied Brooks' Law in real situations is that, although the schedule does extend when effort is added, the sensitivity is much less than a 1-to-1 ratio. Empirical results show that the schedule extends approximately by the cube root of the effort increase.

A project management tip	Effort effect on schedule duration
	Doubling the effort likely increases the scheduling duration only by a factor of 1.27.[8]

Team Effects Versus Headcount

Brooks envisioned adding effort in a way that would increase team size (headcount on each team), thereby threatening team cohesion and impacting communications because of the N^2 communication problem discussed in prior chapters. In agile methods, team sizes are fixed, except for the occasional addition of a subject matter expert on a temporary basis. Therefore, the way to add effort is to add whole teams. Certainly, another team will complicate communication and collaboration with all other teams, but the impact will not be as interpersonal as making existing teams larger.

In traditional project management with activity-driven network schedules, leveling the workload of individuals is always a difficult task. In agile methods, this problem all but goes away since the basic building block is a team and not an individual. Team workload is designed to be nearly constant so that pace and productivity are maintainable over a long period. There will be exceptions for special talents in short supply that must be shared across teams, but the problem of resource leveling is greatly diminished.

Resource Deployment

Even without increasing effort, schedule can be impacted by the way re-sources are deployed—that is, the way teams are applied to requirements. The fact is that just as Brooks debunked the man-month by showing that ef-fort and calendar are not interchangeable because of sequencing constraints and indivisible tasks, the same is true when scaled up to the team and iter-ation.[9]

Everything else being equal, the schedule always extends when otherwise independently acting resources become correlated by dependencies. This we know intuitively and by observation, but there is also a mathematical basis for the phenomenon which is beyond the scope of this section.

The mitigation choices are:

- Planned-in time buffers for each team to finish their work and thereby not delay the start of the next development cycle
- Planned-in complexity to allow for logical sequencing required by ar-chitecture, functional dependencies, and technical feasibility

Module 3—Discussion for Critical Thinking

Over the past few years, leading up to this second edition of this book, some of the abstract methods of estimating (such as story points) have fallen out of favor, thereby ushering in a return to the concrete estimates of hours and/ or funding. From your experience, could you work easily in the abstract with story points or would you be so uncomfortable that only a concrete estimate with hours will do?

Summary and Takeaway Points

There are no facts about the future, only estimates. A good agile estimate accounts for the complexity of intangibles and the uncertainty of require-ments. A good estimate melds the facts from history with a judgment about likely future outcomes.

From Module 1, we examine many factors—like complexity, through-put, and commitment—as they affect estimates. We develop the idea that every good estimate is really a range of possibilities—some very likely and others not so likely. Range is made more meaningful with an estimate of confidence.

From Module 2, it is evident that there are a number of drivers that affect estimates, but there is no magic bullet or algorithm that substitutes for judgment and consideration when facing the complexity of intangible requirements. Experience shows that a myriad of interactions hide many effects, until the product is tested, sometimes until it is first used. This is where the power of incremental development and delivery comes to bear. Complexity is best addressed in digestible chunks that are amenable to planning in waves and estimating in segments that can be stabilized for development.

From Module 3, we learn that there are multiple practices for estimating in agile methods, several of which apply abstract estimators, like story points. But of course, abstract methods don't have to be used; traditional estimating methods are applicable as well.

Appendix to Chapter 7

Appendix Example 1: Estimating with Story Points

Here is a quick example of how estimating with story points works. Process steps and data are shown in Table A7.1, and continue in Table A7.2.

Once estimates are made, it may be required to reprioritize and resequence stories to optimize a benefit stream or fit effort within the limits of an iteration. A summary of steps is given in Table A7.2.

Estimating in this manner is more of an art than a science. The first one or two iterations may be off a bit if there is not a good benchmark for a reference model. But accuracy will correct itself after the first couple of iterations as the teams go through self-inspection, reflection, and adaptation to measured results, updating the reference model with each iteration.[10]

Table A7.1 Estimation example

Example step	Commentary
Benchmark team throughput	Assume there is one team working, and that the team has benchmarked its velocity-team throughput
	Benchmark: 20 story points per iteration, ±2 points, for a range of 18 to 22
	(Note: without an objective reference model in the form of a benchmark, estimating with story points is just guessing)
Set a throughput goal for the iteration	Goal: The team elects to take on 17 points of the highest-priority work, leaving the remaining capacity relative to benchmark as whitespace for unforeseen problem resolution
	By selecting only 17 points rather than 18 to 22, the team takes into account that a buffer is needed to guarantee success
	A buffer provides an allowance for the user to have some flexibility to interpret requirements during the iteration
Count requirements in backlog for the first iteration	A candidate set of requirements for the iteration backlog has been assembled according to priority
	Count: the selection is about 20 percent of the total backlog, thus the total backlog is about 5 times larger than the selection
Estimate complexity	The estimated complexity of the selection is 25 story points, ±3 points; too much for this team for a single iteration
	Also: the total backlog is about 5 times larger, or 125, ±15
	The iteration backlog will have to be reprioritized to only 17 story points

Table A7.2 Managing estimates

Example step	Commentary
Estimate project duration	The project manager makes estimates of the project backlog: 125 points, ± 15 points
	Using the benchmark in Table A7.1, to burn down 125 points, ± 15 points, it could take as many as 9 iterations, calculated as (125 + 15) / 17 iterations, and rounding up to the next whole number
Select iteration backlog and set priorities	The product master selects an iteration backlog that fits the throughput benchmark of the team (See Table A7.1 regarding benchmark)
	The product master sets a priority for the requirements in the iteration backlog capacity of the team

Appendix Example 2: Risk-weighted Average (Expected Value)

Set-up (everything is assumed for this example):

- Range values (six in total), in order: 90, 95, 100, 105, 110, 120
- Pool weights for each range value (as a proportion of a pool of 6 points) in order: 0.25, 0.75, 2.0, 1.75, 1.0, 0.25

Calculations:

- <u>Average</u> of range values: $(1/6) \times (90 + 95 + 100 + 105 + 110 + 120) = \mathbf{103.3}$
- <u>Risk-weighted average (expected value)</u> calculation, taking into account weighted values
  - ◆ Summation of range values multiplied by pool weights: $(90 \times 0.25) + (95 \times 0.75) + (100 \times 2.0) + (105 \times 1.75) + (110 \times 1.0) + (120 \times 0.25) = 617.5$
  - ◆ Risk-weighted average: $617/6 = \mathbf{102.9}$

Appendix Example 3: Confidence Estimate

The estimating range is not absolutely bounded—that is, the possibility exists for the real outcome to fall outside the range. The word to describe how well the range is where we will find the real outcome is confidence.

Confidence is the likelihood that the real value will actually be within the estimate range.

- Confidence estimates always have an upper range boundary and a lower range boundary
- Confidence estimates have probabilities about each boundary

For example, one might estimate that the outcome will be less than 120 hours but greater than 90 hours with a confidence of 90 and 80 percent, respectively. This means that:

- Out of 100 available similar project development opportunities, 90 instances should take less than 120 hours; in 10 instances, the effort might be more than 120 hours
- In 80 instances the effort will be more than 90 hours; in 20 instances, the effort might take less than 90 hours

Figure A7.1 illustrates this confidence estimate discussion. The figure shows many measurements or estimates that cluster about a center value. The

Confidence is an estimate of a value being within a range

Value probabilities, %

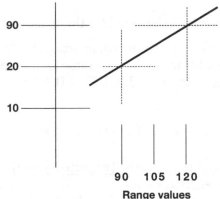

- 90% confidence the outcome will be less than 120;
  10% confidence the outcome will be greater than 120
- 20% confidence the outcome will be less than 90;
  80% chance it will be greater than 90

Figure A7.1   Confidence estimate

estimates near the center value are more probable than are the estimates farther out and near the tails.

The bell curve is a depiction of probability versus the range value. The other curve is the S curve, which is a depiction of accumulating probability from 0 to 1. Confidence is expressed by the probability accumulation from one range point to another.

Chapter Endnotes

1. The quotation is a favorite saying of Dr. David Hulett, given to the author in 1997 during an engagement assessing the risk of a millennium project.
2. Brooks, *The Mythical Man-month*, 21.
3. Weaver, *Science and Complexity*.
4. Ibid,25.
5. Cohn, *Agile Estimating and Planning*, 52. For authority, Cohn references the 1997 work of Thomas Saaty, a renowned researcher in the field of decision-making and analysis. Saaty calls his body of work the Analytical Hierarchy Process (AHP); See Saaty, *The Analytic Hierarchy Process*. Saaty has documented his work in many papers. For example, see Saaty. *Decision Making with the An-*

alytic Hierarchy Process, 83-98, in which Saaty uses the linear scale of 1 to 9 to demonstrate the assignment of values to decision elements.

6. Boehm, *Software Engineering Economics*, Chapter 22. The method is summarized on pg 335. Farquhar, *A Preliminary Inquiry into the Software Estimation Process*. See also a good explanation for practitioners. Stellman and Greene, *Applied Software Project Management*, Chapter 3.

7. Planning poker was first written about in a short paper by James Grenning. It was then made more popular by authorities such as Mike Cohn. See Cohn, *Agile Estimating and Planning*, Chapter 6; Grenning, *Planning Poker, or How to Avoid Analysis Paralysis while Release Planning*. Now, commercial and online versions of the game are available.

8. McConnell, *Software Estimating: Demystifying the Black Art*, 223. The cube root of 2 is approximately 1.27, meaning $2 = 1.27 \times 1.27 \times 1.27$ to a pretty close approximation. The equation for schedule duration increase is: new duration = old duration × (new effort/old effort), 173.

9. Brooks, *The Mythical Man-month*, 17-19.

10. For a more comprehensive discussion of story points and velocity, see Cohn, *Agile Estimating and Planning*, 35-40.

8

Teams Are Everything

Small teams that are faithful to frequent, incremental releases, and capable of self-organization, are the performance-unit building blocks of agile methods.

> *Problem 1: The people on the projects were not interested in learning our system.*
>
> *Problem 2: They were successfully able to ignore us, and were still delivering software, anyway.*
>
> *Alistair Cockburn*

There has always been a place for lone eccentrics: brilliant, unpredictable, innovative, and occasionally delightful in their genius. But the essence of agile methods is teamwork. And why not? Patrick Lencioni writes, "… teamwork is the ultimate competitive advantage…."[1] And, not only teams, but teams of professionals, with multiple skills and who can act redundantly and work collectively.

And more good news—agile teams will not be working alone. Teams in enterprise projects will be surrounded by other work streams, a project office, a generous number of stakeholders, and people positioned up and down the supply chain. There will be members of the marketing and sales teams, executives, post-production support, and others who have both an interest and a stake in the outcome. All will offer help and support, a few will be deeply committed, some will set constraints, and others will cause delays (perhaps unwittingly), but all around there will be help.

However, there are reasons to pause. It is hard work to develop the kind of teams that work well in agile methods:

- Teams that are self-leading and self-organizing
- Teams that march productively to their own drum
- And teams that can handle unique circumstances (the customer is embedded with the developers)

The impact of having the product master embedded in the midst of team operations can be profound—instant interpretation, timely feedback, and a single voice. But, sometimes close is too close!

- The line between technical and functional requirements becomes blurred
- The stability required to meet tight iteration time boxes is disturbed
- A compelling personality might unduly bias decisions

Module 1: The Social Unit

People are naturally sociable. People draw comfort, security, strength, and reinforcement, both from others around them and from networks they join. In businesses and organizations of all types, the sociability of people enables successful teamwork.

Module 1—Objectives

- Discuss and show the differences between a team and other social structures
- Discuss and explain means to transition from a group to a team

Groups as the Genesis of Teams

In a manner of speaking, family is the first group we join. Family members learn about networking and learn to interact. They learn behaviors that enable group participation. As a group, family members communicate, exchange information, support group activities, and bestow rewards.

Group Formation

For a group to form there must be opportunity and motivation for interaction among the participants, but a crowd is not a group, nor is a cocktail party. To have a group, there must be:

- A common purpose that attracts members to join and stay
- Some division of responsibility and some distinguished roles—such as leader and functional contributor

- Accepted norms for behavior and participation
- Defined operating processes
- A set of protocols for reward, discipline, or sanction; these protocols provide a means for attaching incentives to group membership and for dismissing undesirables[2]

Attitudes about territory, space, and identity shaped by culture and experience affect behavior within groups. Everyone has his or her own tolerance for closeness and a need for a place to call his or her own—a phenomenon called territory dominance. But there is personality dominance also. Dominance must be settled before a group can act effectively.

Group membership sharpens feelings about self-identity: Who am I and how do I fit in? People immediately sense those who have command presence and who are going to emerge naturally as leaders. When we address virtual teams in this chapter, some of the issues of identity and space will take on new meaning.

Groups are not teams; however, forming a group is often the first step in forming a team. Populations, partnerships, bureaucracies, associations, and committees are not teams. Teams are different from all of these—and some teams are really not teams at all. For example, business executive teams are frequently criticized for behaving more like groups than like teams. The problem with executive teams is dominance. Teamwork is inhibited by unsettled dominance of person and territory—the power and influence that comes from an organizational position is not easily set aside.

Partnerships, Bureaucracies, and Population

- Partnerships are shared-risk and shared-reward relationships; partners operate independently but pool their outcomes for a common reward.
- Bureaucracies are hierarchical command-control structures that organize resources in parent-child relationships. But mutual support up and down the chain is often begrudged and is present only because the command regimen requires it. Nevertheless, bureaucracies are the model of choice when organizing large populations.
- Populations and associations are farther still from the idea of a team. In most cases, they also lack the structures of a group or bureaucracy. People are members of associations by choice, choosing according to a few common attributes, such as a professional affinity.
- Committees can be teams of course, but often a committee is just a small-scale bureaucracy, wherein the members do assigned tasks with only a modest commitment to the larger goal.

Team Defined

So, what is a team? Here is our working definition of a team:

A Team Defined
A team is a social structure wherein all members individually and mutually collaborate toward the achievement of a common goal that is possible only by the committed and collective contribution of all members.

We've got some things to work on within that definition:

- **A social structure:** thus, social norms and values are to be expected
- **Individually and mutually collaborate:** thus, many lines of communication with information transparency to be expected
- **Common goal:** thus individual agendas are subordinated to the common goal
- **Commitment and collective contribution:** thus, a certain work ethic is to be expected

In the agile space, a team is a performance unit. A performance unit, viewed from the outside looking in, is a single entity with operational capability described by a performance specification which we take to be a benchmark. Velocity is the preferred performance metric, defined as the amount of constant quality throughput that is produced over the course of one iteration.[3] From a management perspective, a performance unit is an encapsulated body with a defined throughput; its mission is to transform backlog into valuable product.

In Chapter 7, the entire estimating regime rested on the concept of a team as an integrated performance unit. The capabilities of individuals were secondary because working collaboratively and collectively diversified the variances found in individual performances

Teams from Groups

We've just defined a team as a social structure requiring mutual collaboration for a common goal. But it's just for that reason that teams are not the most natural social formation—many people are uncomfortable with, or skeptical of, teams and working on a team, thereby surrendering personal independence for team interactions. Most of us know from our common experiences that teams do not just happen. Tuckman's forming-storming-norming-performing-adjourning behavior model remains relevant since its introduction in 1965.[4]

Bruce Tuckman's Model[5]

- Forming: The team meets and learns about the challenges and opportunities.
- Storming: Different ideas compete for consideration and adoption.
- Norming: Behaviors are adjusted to make teamwork productive.
- Performing: Collective, collaborative work styles reinforce the work of each member; conflicts are about solutions, not people.
- Adjourning: The task is completed and the team's work is archived; the team members are dismissed to their operational units.

So, how to get from a group to a team?

1. The first step is to form a group. Once a group establishes some basic stability, teaming begins—storming and norming in the Tuckman model. The team inherits properties of the group—properties like common purpose or charter, roles and responsibilities, and rules for personal behavior.
2. The second step is to establish standards for personal achievement, commitment, and accountability. Then the hard work to internalize commitment to the team as first priority begins. This shift in loyalty from oneself to the team is the shift from group to team. Energy is to be directed toward outcomes, and not toward individual competitions.

Thereafter, reaching a state of performing requires extending the group parameters in several important ways:[6]

1. Define a compelling, unambiguously identifiable, and measurable team mission.
2. Set an expectation that the team must succeed for each person to be successful.
3. Require work to be collaborative and collective; most deliverables require the integration and application of multiple skills.
4. Develop leadership from within the team. A strong hierarchical leader is not always necessary to organize and manage the work if teammates can comfortably share leadership responsibilities.
5. Develop methods and processes within the team, but adopt and adapt them from the standards and conventions of the enterprise.

Module 1—Discussion for Critical Thinking

Teams are really special when they work because of the feeling of loyalty to the team above loyalty to oneself. Among the five extensions to the group parameters just discussed, which do you think are most important in achieving the state of team and team work?

Module 2: Principle and Values Guide Teams

Individual loyalties become team loyalty

Module 2—Objectives

- Discuss and explain the values that make teams work
- Discuss and explain the principles for successful teams

Reaching a high performance level requires member-to-member cohesion—a willingness and commitment to stick together and see the job through. Team cohesion, sometimes called unit cohesion, depends on shared values and beliefs and commonly accepted principles for day-to-day guidance. In a truly cohesive team, the individual so believes in the welfare of the team that individual loyalties become team loyalties. Cohesion sustains the will and commitment to the mission and to the organization.[7]

But much is required; people must subordinate their individual competitiveness, must be receptive to critique and help, and must join in with others, surrendering a bit of privacy, self-centering, and positional power and authority. An S1 high-task directive management gives way to leadership by relationship: collaborative, bidirectional listening, facilitating, and supporting.

Situational Leadership
• S1 through S4 are the tags for the four situational leadership styles promoted by Hersey, Johnson, and Blanchard.[8]
• S1 is high-task direction projected onto low-capability followers.
• S2, S3, and S4 are less directive and more delegating, assuming a correspondingly greater competence and motivation of followers.

Perhaps most importantly, the success of self-organizing teams—those that are given license and latitude to satisfy the customer rather than to follow a prescription—depends on internalization of team values and principles.

Values That Make Teams Work

Certain values make teams work because they go to the heart of interpersonal relationships: trust, commitment, accountability, continuity, simplicity, clarity, and certainty.

Trust

Trust is believing that others will act not only in their interests, but also in yours. It requires an exchange of power, and power exchange is only enabled by honesty, openness, and a track record of dependability and accountability. "Trust lies at the heart of a functioning, cohesive team. Without it teamwork is all but impossible," writes Patrick Lencioni. In fact, among the five main reasons for team failure, he lists lack of trust as number one.[9]

In the absence of trust, there can be no team, so bureaucracies are built instead. Bureaucracies are inherently oriented to structure, substituting positional power and prescribed command and control for trusting relationships.

One must be free of fear in order to trust. Freedom from fear implies safety in both personal and professional relationships. Safety makes it possible to be vulnerable and consequently willing to join with others for strength and resolve. In fact, personal safety is one of the seven principles of the Crystal method, and is repeated in the Humanity Principle of XP. As defined by Crystal's Alistair Cockburn, personal safety is a step toward trust; personal safety is freedom from the fear of reprisal. Trust, building on safety, is in part giving power over your person to someone else and being comfortable with the power transfer.[10]

Virtual Trust

Virtual teams have their own special circumstances that impact building trust. In spite of many separations—time, distance, location, and organization—trust is just as important as if members were co-located.[11] Trust requires mutual identity—there can be no trust among strangers. There must be effective communication to assess safety and establish the parameters of the power transfer.

Communication depends first on language and second on culture.

- Language fluency starts with a literal understanding of words and grammar; but language goes a good deal further, to include jargon, the structure of expression, and tone of voice.
- Cultural fluency means understanding the meaning of body language and other nonverbal signals present in the culture, and understanding

the intent of words and deeds—when does no mean no; is a nod an actual agreement, an understanding, or just politeness?

*   Culture affects how we convey purpose and priority—does an e-mail attach the same importance as a phone call, and does a phone call mean there is personal rapport?

Consider the fact that to some people, mistakes are evidence of reaching, striving, and going for the near unattainable; while to others with a different cultural outlook, mistakes are evidence of poor planning and execution. Similarly, for some, only facts are trusted; for others, intuition and vision are more valued.

A project management tip	Track records build trust
	Only time and opportunity to build a track record between the virtual members will resolve mistrust.

Commitment and Accountability

Teams value the sincerity and integrity of the commitment and willingness to be held accountable. Who has not approached a team assignment with skepticism, reluctant to join a personal fate with the fate of the team, or harbored a suspicion that more will be asked than given? A real team is *norming* when members offer and pledge unwavering commitment to the team objective. A real team is *performing* when members are willingly open to the judgment of others, agreeing that success is defined by a joint performance.

Continuity, Simplicity, Clarity, and Certainty

Teams value continuity, simplicity, clarity, and certainty of purpose and method. To have clarity and certainty presumes little or no confusion. Effort, ingenuity, and energy are directed toward intended results and are not dissipated by spinning wheels, changing direction, and adopting the flavor of the day. Simplicity is the absence of unnecessary complexity, yet the simplest solution may still be complex.[12] Continuity means that from one moment to the next, change is under control.

Table 8.1 captures the ideas that have been discussed so far.

Table 8.1   Summary of team values

Value	Commentary
Trust	A willingness to be vulnerable to, and accepting of, the performance and commitment of others as they act in your joint interests
Commitment	A pledge to apply all possible effort, energy, and ingenuity to the successful completion of the goal
Accountability	A willingness to be judged by others and an acceptance of a personal responsibility for the completion of tasks assigned
Continuity	A confidence that things remain the same until they are changed for reasonable and justifiable reasons, subordinating change to the completion of the team goal
Simplicity	The absence of unnecessary complexity
Clarity	The absence of confusion
Certainty	The absence of unmitigated risk

Principles of Successful Teams

Principles are the guidance for daily work. Principles channel energy and activity directionally in accord with values. Taking principles to heart is a prerequisite to affect teaming in an agile self-organization model. Table 8.2 lists the universal principles that every team should adopt.

Module 2—Discussion for Critical Thinking

A lot about what makes a team work well is the environment of simplicity, clarity, and certainty. However, every project has its moments of confusion. What practices would you employ at such moments to keep the team working at good efficiency?

Module 3: Teams Are Building Blocks

Teams consume investment and teamwork drives the schedule

Module 3—Objectives

- Discuss and explain the agile model of teams and agile teamwork
- Discuss and explain the team network as a necessary architecture for project design
- Discuss and explain scaling with teams of teams

The team is the operating unit around which the project plan is built. A team is an active performance unit characterized by its ability to develop

Table 8.2 Principles for successful teams

	Principle or guideline	Commentary
1	Teams are the structure of choice to execute complex interdisciplinary projects	Multifunctional teams accept and embrace complexity, disorder, and uncertainty more effectively than individuals working alone because of the mutual support for problem solving and the opportunity for group creativity
2	No team will be chartered without a compelling purpose and mission to accomplish actual work	A compelling mission is the most effective motivator for cohesion and commitment to results
3	Communication and collaboration will be frequent and without reticence	Teams are only better than groups of individuals when teammates achieve synergy Synergistic results require communication and collaboration on a timely basis while there is still opportunity to incorporate advice
4	Teams will be made small, but encouraged to network for scale	Larger teams require internal structures and authority figures to manage the scale Small teams can have the effect of large teams by networking and committing to joint objectives
5	Team assignments will be made with staff disposed to commitment and accountability	Assignments only made on the basis of position and availability are discouraged Assignments focus on completing the compliment of technical, functional, and decision-making skills Assignments recognize high performance people are not plug-compatible replaceable
6	Time and activities to promote trust will be planned into the project timeline	Strangers do not trust. Virtual teams need more time and specific opportunity to overcome factors unique to the displacement of team members
7	A safe working environment will be provided	Safety is the first step to trust Reprisals for speaking out will not be tolerated A role as nemesis will be accepted
8	Team members will be encouraged to listen actively, give the benefit of the doubt, respond constructively, and acknowledge achievements of others[1]	The "golden rule" of team behavior
9	Team results and measurements will be evaluated for collective achievement.	Individuals are valued for their skill and ingenuity; collective achievement is valued for its best value fit to customer expectation
10	Rewards will be applied to collective performance as a priority over individual recognition	The performance of the team is paramount; it transcends the performance of individuals

11	Self-organized teams will be granted a measure of autonomy to select their leaders and formulate their processes	Self-organized teams can actually work with no leader, a leader selected by the team, or a leader role that is rotated[2]
		Processes should conform to the conventions of the enterprise to ensure that all assertions and claims to certifying bodies are valid
		Cost, schedule, and scope are managed external to the team in agile methods.

[1]Katzenbach, J. and Smith, D. *The Discipline of Teams*, Harvard Business Review, Cambridge, MA, March-April 1993 81(2):111-120.

[2]Dyer, W., et al. *Team Building: Proven Strategies for Improving Team Performance*, Josey Bass, John Wiley & Sons, New York, 2007, p. 22.

new product. Recall that product is the surrogate for whatever it is that the team produces, whether tangible or intangible, whether for internal use or external application.

The team is the performance unit that earns value and adds value to the project backlog, bringing reality to the product vision. The team is the primary operating expense of the project; it consumes most of the available investment. The pace of teamwork is the main schedule driver. Time on the calendar is primarily an accumulation of time boxes.

Operating Model of the Agile Team

Operating Model
In the context of a value system, an operating model is the meld of the people, process, and technology chartered as a team to do work.

The operating model of the agile project team conforms generally to the parameters described in Table 8.3.

Teams depend on the project manager for establishing and maintaining a project environment and for managing the relationship with the stakeholders. The material in Table 8.4 explains the project management role with respect to the team-operating model. Customers and end users assist the team during each sprint or iteration, as explained in Table 8.5.

Table 8.3 Operating model of the agile team

Operating principle	Commentary
Teams are small, typically 6-8, but could be as large as 12	• The project manager facilitates the formation of the team. • Subject matter experts that are only needed part time are identified by the team and recruited by the project manager from the resource pool. • An initial team may send its members to other teams to seed those teams with the knowledge of the product base required to maintain coordination.
Team leadership and management is determined by the team	• Leadership is empowered by the team members themselves. The leaders may be elected and may be rotated from iteration to iteration. • Management planning, coordinating, communicating, and reporting need not be vested in one individual. • Teams are self-organizing. Each team member assumes a part of the management work load. • A team representative is required to participate in team-of-teams network coordination and to be a consistent point of contact for the project manager, product master, and other outsiders in the project environment. • The team-of-teams representative typically has a leadership role and is empowered to make decisions. • The team leader ensures effective processes are adopted, a clear and compelling goal is set, and means of accountability and measurement are in place and functioning.[1]
Team processes, practices, and rules are established by the team	• Each team may operate a bit differently; however, every team must operate consistently in order for the throughput benchmark to be meaningful. • Processes must conform to the normal conventions of the organization in order to not invalidate claims and assertions required for certifications. • Each methodology has its own set of rules and recommended practices. • Adopting the rules and practices, and enforcing discipline is a collective activity, driven by commitment and accountability. • Discipline is inversely related to formal control; the more self-discipline, the less formal control is required. • Processes address technical and managerial practices. The team is accountable for measuring and reporting progress, assessing problems, forecasting risk, and determining mitigation. • Project scorecards and dashboards are respected by the team. • Virtual teams require processes for communication and coordination.

| Teams benchmark for productivity | • The objective of agile teams is to produce work product frequently at high quality.
• A productivity benchmark is necessary to have a predictable throughput.
• Each team is responsible for establishing and maintaining a reliable benchmark. |

[1]In the Scrum method, the team itself is one of the only three roles, along with the product master and the Scrum master; there is no specific endorsement of the team leader role. However, having designated representatives to a Scrum of Scrum session is recognized as a means to scale up to multiple teams. See: Schawber, K., *Agile Project Management with SCRUM*, Microsoft Press, Redmond, WA, 2004 pp. 6, 121.

Table 8.4 Project manager role

Operating principle	Commentary
The project manager coaches the team	• The project manager is not a directing authority over the team in the style of a manager enforcing a plan. • The project manager is the responsible manager to the stakeholders for the business case. • The project manager coaches the team to ensure all mechanics are in place, conflicts are being managed, non-performing members are corrected, and all measurements and performance records are timely and accurate. • Scorecards and dashboards are reviewed for completeness. • If there are only one, or a few teams, the project manager facilitates the daily meetings and other meetings where a facilitator is appropriate.
The project manager supports the team	• The project manager is the project-level risk manager, responsible for keeping the gap closed, or nearly so, on the project balance sheet. • Constraints, roadblocks, and commitments of stakeholders and customers are managed by the project manager. • All resources and environments required by the team are acquired, assembled, and deployed by direction of the project office. • If there are several teams operating in a network, the project manager coordinates network activity. • Cost is typically managed outside the team by the project manager. • Rewards and compensation plans are administered by the project manager.
The project manager manages conflict, performance, and administration	• In the event the team cannot resolve conflict, the project manager steps in. • In the event the team fails to perform, the project manager can stop work, dissolve or reorganize the team, or take other measures as required. • The project manager forecasts performance, reports results, and manages cost, scope, and budget with the sponsor. • The project manager is a participant in the governance council.

Table 8.5   Customer role with the team

Operating principle	Commentary
Product master interprets requirements	• The customer has a responsibility to provide a product expert, one or many depending on scale, to interpret requirements and validate test results • The customer has a right to see and evaluate product development at an early enough stage that correction and adjustments are possible. • In the Scrum methodology, the customer representative is called the product master
The customer establishes the value proposition	• The voice of the customer speaks for the value proposition of the project beginning with the business case • A primary task of the customer is to set priorities among features and functions competing for resources • Urgency and importance are the say of the customer; feasibility, architectural consistency, structural sequencing, and affordability are the say of the technical and management staff
The product master is committed to team success	• The product master is the one customer who is committed and accountable for the user input to the product development • For agile teams to be effective with relatively short iterations, the team has a right to expect that a committed customer or user will be at-the-ready, embedded in the team if possible, but always available on very short notice
The product master speaks for the customer community	• The product master represents the customer community • In large-scale projects, the customer community may be organized into one or more teams by functional needs • The project master assists the project manager in coaching the customer community for a coherent picture of requirements

Teams in Networks

Increasing the number of working teams increases capacity, but teams working within a network enable capacity attended with complexity. There will still be sequencing constraints, as there is no network that can enable nine women to have a baby in one month. But architecture elements can be parsed among teams in a network. Dependencies can be coordinated. The branch structure of networks enables decomposition of backlog and recomposition of product.

Networks in Agile Project Management
• A network is a lattice-like structure with nodes, branches, and components. • The node is the location of a component—team or system. The branch is the relationship or interface between nodes. • Relationships depend on how the architecture and the scope is divided and then allocated to teams. • Relationships form the channels between teams that facilitate cross-team communication, collaboration, and coordination.

The interconnection of branches and notes expresses logic. In the case of a project network, logic expresses relationships among teams designing, developing, and producing project deliverables. No timeline, calendar, or durations are required to construct the network. If actual timing requires lead and lag buffers beyond the buffers in each iteration, then they are added as whole iterations. Figure 8.1 illustrates the discussion.

Mind Shifting to Agile Networks

For agile projects, there is a mind shift about networks; networks are about team-to-team relationships, not about developer task-to-task relationships. Most of the discussion about agile projects has not assumed a network

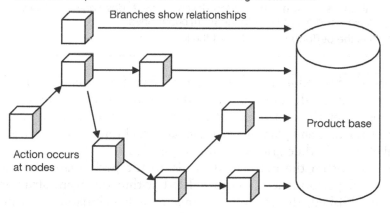

The generic network illustrates the logical relationships between time boxes at nodes, and between time boxes and the product base

Nodes are unique because of the distinct backlog at each node

Branches show relationships

Action occurs at nodes

Product base

Figure 8.1　Generic network

operating model. One team working diligently from one iteration to the next can accomplish much. But sometimes one team cannot get it done in time.

A schedule that is too long might morph calculable risk into incalculable uncertainty. A project stretched too long might endanger the whole benefit stream. A lengthy project is the antithesis of agile: rapid response intended to be faster than the cycle of business and markets.

One remedy is to apply more resources to ramp up development and delivery capacity. But making teams larger is problematic—and making more teams is also problematic. Communications—the lubricant of team productivity—is adversely affected by the addition of more team members. Experienced project managers know that adding more people also adds more person-to-person bidirectional communication links—Karoline needs to talk to Emma, as well as everyone else that is added, and everyone needs to respond to Karoline and Emma, as well as the others.

In fact, the number of links increases by nearly the square of the number of teammates—or the N^2-effect (see chapter endnote 13).[13] Other frictions of coordination and cohesion are likewise amplified. Being mindful of Brooks' Law—adding more people to a late project makes it later—managers hesitate to ramp existing, ongoing teams with additional staff. The operating model with a better chance of success is to add more small teams and network the results.

Agile Network
• The network is about objects, not tasks. The network is a team of teams.
• The usual tasks shown on a plan-driven project development lifecycle activity network are moved inside the team boundaries.
• The team is the performance unit—not the individual.

So, the networked schedule is a connection of team time boxes or units of development, with production objects as the central focus, and a schedule grid. Time boxes or the equivalent of units of development are affixed to the time grid; releases and planning horizons are synchronized with the grid. A pictorial of the schedule grid is given in Figure 8.2.

Performance within the network depends on the performance of each team; individual performance is encapsulated within the team structure. As already established, the team's performance is benchmarked and predictable; the risk to the team of any individual is mitigated by diversifying

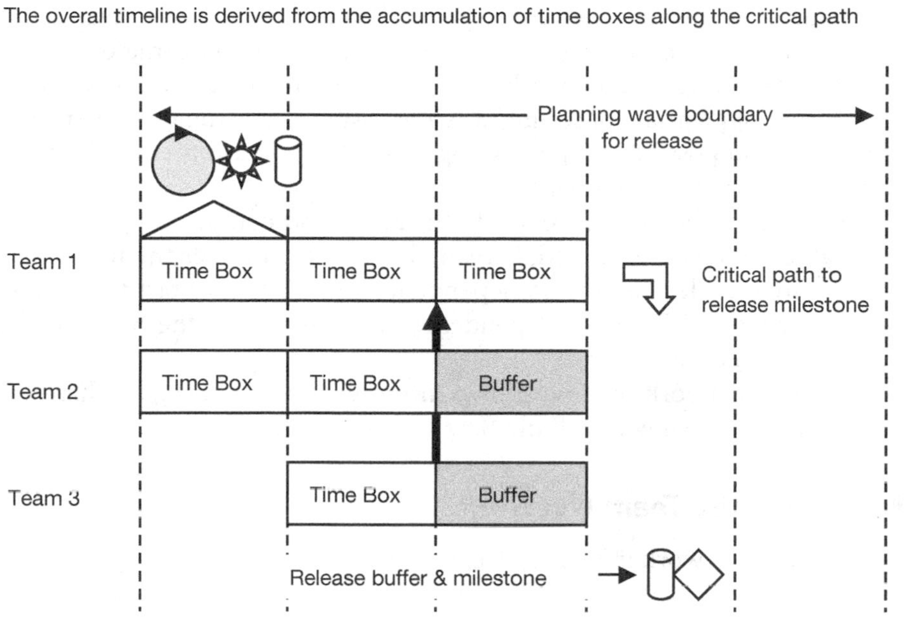
The overall timeline is derived from the accumulation of time boxes along the critical path
Planning wave boundary for release
Team 1
Time Box
Time Box
Time Box
Critical path to release milestone
Team 2
Time Box
Time Box
Buffer
Team 3
Time Box
Buffer
Release buffer & milestone

Figure 8.2 Generic team schedule

among team members. The main tools of diversification are redundancy, multifunctional skills, and collaboration.

Network Logic

Any network is a presentation of logic. Logic captures two ideas:

1. Some deliverables are independent and have no dependency on others. For these, the team's starting point in the network is arbitrary, perhaps only dependent on the importance and urgency expressed by the customer. The logic can be fast-tracked by working independent teams in parallel.[14]
2. Some deliverables have interdependencies. The interdependencies can be complex or simple. By simple, we mean each team develops its own increment to the product base and depends only on other teams to properly integrate their efforts with the product base—the principle of do no harm. In a simple dependency, there is not a functional precedence between teams, but there is a need to be always working with the latest product base so that regression tests validate proper integration.

By complex, we mean there are sequential constraints between teams. Not only does the outcome of one team directly drive the outcome of another with finish-to-start precedence, but also the network logic respects sequencing. With a sequential constraint, it is impossible to rearrange sequence order and it is impossible to speed things up—that is, crash the schedule—by adding more resources earlier.[15]

Look back to Figure 8.2 to see both simple and complex logic concepts illustrated for Teams 1, 2, and 3. Team 3 can start in either the first or second iteration cycle; there is no dependency that fixes the start time. However, Teams 2 and 3 have a dependency with Team 1 at the outset of the third iteration cycle.

Although networks can be shown in more than one form, all share certain attributes, as shown in Table 8.6.

Managing the Team Network

To manage a network in agile space, respect for Principle 2 is required.

Table 8.6   Schedule network attributes for agile methods

Attribute	Commentary
The schedule is a uniform grid	• The grid is based on the duration picked for iteration time boxes • Release dates are synchronized to the grid • Planning horizons are fixed to the grid
Buffers reduce shift-right risk	• Buffers absorb variances in velocity that might force a team to deliver late • Total duration is buffered to absorb additional iterations needed to satisfy customer demands
A critical path is identifiable	• The critical path is the path that determines the last release • All paths in the network may not be connected because of no identifiable dependency
Velocity is not rigidly fixed	• Velocity has some distribution around an expected value • Simple triangular distributions are assumed for individual teams
Total duration of the schedule is derived	• Total duration is derived from schedule logic, overall complexity, and the throughput available to liquidate the complexity
Teams can have simple or complex dependencies on one another	• Simple dependencies means no sequential constraint with another team; complex dependency means there is a sequential constraint with another team

Agile Principle 2
Welcome changing requirements, even late in the development. Agile processes harness change for the customer's competitive advantage.

Begin by constructing the team network diagram for the project logic. Allocate project backlog to each node according to customer priority and sequencing constraints. Then, develop a spreadsheet scorecard to integrate the accomplishments of each team at each node. Figure 8.3 is an example.

As with all scorecards, three elements of information are required:

1. Baseline measure—in Figure 8.3, the baseline is the story point production for each team by iteration
2. Operating plan—that is, the baseline adjusted for up-to-date information
3. Actual accomplishment

Calculations of variances and efficiency to the baseline and operating plan are shown in Figure 8.3 and are given this way:

Variances	Efficiency
Variance = performance − plan	Efficiency = performance / plan

From the network logic, develop a spreadsheet resource plan that can be coordinated with functional managers that provide the team resources.

Team-of-Teams

The team-of-teams is a means to coordinate team activity and product deliverables within a network.

The team-of-teams operates like a management working group. As a working group, it has these attributes:

- An unambiguous charter intended to coordinate product teams within the network.
- A timeline for operations that spans the timeline of all product teams.
- An imperative to meet every day, but to keep deliberations within a prescribed time box.

The team scorecard for STORY POINT production, measured at the end of each iteration, shows early velocity is not up to the planned baseline—there is recovery of the velocity, but not enough to make the planned scope at the first release milestone

	Planning Wave 2										
	Release 1										
	Iteration 1			Iteration 2			Iteration 3			Release 1	Variance to release
	Team 1	Team 2	Team 3	Team 1	Team 2	Team 3	Team 1	Team 2	Team 3		
Baseline	50	55	50	50	55	50	50	55	50	465	
Operating plan	48	50	45	50	53	48	52	55	50	451	14
Actual performance	48	48	45	50	50	48					
Variance to baseline	2	7	5	0	5	2					
Cum variance to baseline	2	9	14	14	19	21					
Efficiency to baseline	96.00%	87.27%	90.00%	100.00%	90.91%	96.00%					
Variance to ops plan	0	2	0	0	3	0					
Cum variance to ops plan	0	2	2	2	5	5					
Efficiency to ops plan	100.00%	96.00%	100.00%	100.00%	94.34%	100.00%					

Figure 8.3   Team scorecard

- A self-organizing and shared leadership.
- A set of self-designed processes for evaluating product team performance in the network.
- A membership from all the product teams and the project management office. With the consent of all members, and being mindful of the daily time box, stakeholders with a particular affinity for the network may be involved. For instance, a key manager responsibility for infrastructure, tool support, or perhaps even vendor management.
- A commitment to open, honest, and safe communications.
- A dashboard for general communication.

The team's administrative assistant publishes a daily agenda. Not only does the administrative assistant manage the agenda, but he or she also updates the dashboard and handles other communications and coordination with the membership.

	Steering the work streams
A project management tip	• On projects with multiple work streams, each work stream will have a network. There will likely be points of coordination required between work streams. • For such coordination, the project manager will have a working group chartered to steer the work stream. • This working group sometimes goes by the name of *steering committee*, after the character of its work. • It meets weekly by common practice. • The work stream team-of-teams is the resource pool for the steering committee. Stakeholders are often invited.

Module 3—Discussion for Critical Thinking

We say that increasing scale by adding teams within a network brings not only capacity but complexity: performance not entirely predictable from the performance of each team alone. Can you imagine what some of the symptoms of complexity might be insofar as they are a consequence of adding teams to add capacity?

Module 4: Some Teams Work; Others Do Not

Among all methodologies, agile is the most heavily dependent on teams

Module 4—Objectives

- Examine the reasons why some teams don't work
- Discuss and explain the issues around virtual teams

Accepted doctrine is that agile teams recruit their members; staff is not arbitrarily assigned by resource managers. And agile teams are coached, not managed. The coach may be a professional agile methodologist specializing in coaching, or the coach could be the project manager.

Agile teams are self-organized and are afforded considerable latitude to get the job done. Teaming sounds great. Why doesn't it work every time?

Why Teams Don't Work

There is a serious body of thought around the idea that teams do not work, do not work well, or do not work in many situations. Many have studied dysfunctional and failed teams and situations where teams cannot seem to succeed. The findings are worth examining for lessons learned.

Teams in Corporate America
In fact, teams as multifunctional performance units have only been around in American corporate life since the late 1960s. In many ways, the team is a reaction to the overwhelming size and impersonal character of the corporate design that evolved from early twentieth-century Taylorism. Taylor's ideas, already addressed in prior chapters, are the seeds that drove bureaucratic design to its pinnacle, featuring multilayered enterprises that treated people as plug-compatible parts. Look only to the popularity of the cartoon strip Dilbert™ to see the evidence. A more extensive read on the history of teams is found in Robbins and Finley's *The New Why Teams Don't Work: What Goes Wrong and How to Make It Right.*[16]

Problems begin with people as individuals. Many people are not naturally predisposed to teamwork, in contrast to individual contributor work. Many who share the deep-seated cultural value that every person is a uniquely talented individual, resist anonymity and subordination. Others who are fiercely and individually competitive find it difficult to accept restraints and constraints, and to put aside their own competitiveness for the greater good.

Teams are about how to organize small numbers of people, and so this is one of the first things that can go wrong. Teams are too large. Anything larger than about a dozen requires overhead structure, management tiers, and bureaucracy to hold the team together in some kind of organizational suspension.

Apart from building the wrong-sized team, there are other management miscues:[17]

- **Boundaries are too often left fuzzy:** Confusion is a productivity killer. Are all members clear on the team's mission, goal, and scope, and what is out?
- **The mission is not made compelling:** People are not naturally attracted to the purpose and goal. Constant encouragement and reinforcement is needed to overcome boredom and disinterest.
- **Team members too often are selected by making the easy choices:** Often members are selected by position and availability. Instead, selection should be by rigorous evaluation that is based on skills and commitment.
- **There is no allowance for a nemesis member to neutralize group think:** Group think is a simple idea—but a grave threat. Commonly held beliefs and biases become enshrined almost as axioms, crowding out alternatives and counterpoints that might be more productive and beneficial.
- **The team membership is allowed to turn over too rapidly:** Rapid turnover ends up diluting cohesion and squandering productivity built on personal relationships.

Researchers Harvey Robbins and Michael Finley have also looked at why teams don't work. They add these reasons, among others:[18]

- There is a bad decision-making process or there are inadequate decision-making skills.
- Even when guided by good decisions, teams habitually execute them poorly.
- The team includes difficult people; talented eccentrics that cannot abide sharing and collective teamwork.
- There is competition among members that often leads to secrecy and compartmentalization—quite opposite to collaboration.
- There are empowerment uncertainties, awkward and untimely decision chains, and confusion about roles, rights, and responsibilities. Empowerment requires great trust and a faith in the decision making and loyalty of the empowered.
- Many personnel issues are left unresolved, not the least of which is compensation and reward. The question, "What do I have to give up?" is not satisfactorily addressed.

With the litany of problems in the lists just given, is it any wonder that some people question if teams can work, if they do work, or if they should even be a part of the operating model?

Why Teams Can Work; Why They Do Work

In the main, teams can work because they are social units compatible with the socializing instincts that all people have to be around like-minded people. And teams draw people in who are attracted to a compelling purpose. But, not too big of a team—no one particularly likes the impersonal nature of *big*. Smaller is more personal and familiar; smaller is closer to the action; smaller is very reinforcing—made so by the opportunity for rapid feedback.

Caution is advised: the values and principles discussed in this chapter need to be genuinely woven into the fabric of the enterprise, not just layered on for the moment. Anything short of honesty will impact trust and threaten safety.

Reengineering for Teams
• Teams are a fortunate consequence of making organizational models flatter—spurred onward by the hugely influential theories of Michael Hammer and James Champy to reengineer the corporation.[19] • One development in business management from the reengineering movement of the early 1990s was acceptance and faith that small multifunctional teams operating as nearly autonomous units can accomplish remarkable things.

Teams do work because small multiskilled performance units are ideal for addressing the unusual complexity and uncertainty that attends even small-scale software systems. Scale may require a team-of-teams, and even work streams each with teams-of-teams. Teamwork fits the proven way to address large problems: to decompose them into the simplest forms for construction and then recompose the product increments to achieve the product vision.

It is perhaps fortunate that the sophistication and capabilities of performance teams have come along at a time of enormously intricate and pervasive systems that envision huge complexity existing in very small and increasingly very mobile platforms.

People Are Not Machines

Perhaps the best point to make is the one made by Crystal's Alistair Cockburn when he declares that people are nonlinear, both in their behavior and in their performance—nonlinear, meaning a little stimulus might produce one result, but a little more might cause either regression or acceleration.[20] It could even be argued that in addition to being nonlinear, people are a bit chaotic—that is, irrational at odd moments, having been set off by some trigger.

How does agile manage staffing?

1. First, get the right people. Approach each person separately to ascertain his or her uniqueness and fit to the team. Specific profiles are not as important as filling out redundancy, ensuring all functional skills are covered, and establishing that candidates are fit for teamwork.

2. Second, be true to Principle 5, trust motivated people to get the job done, and Principle 8, plan for a steady and sustainable pace. A compelling mission and commensurate reward, in the context of a safe and effective environment, will be motivating. But then, do not exploit motivation to the point of staff burnout. Approaching burnout, both nonlinear and chaotic behavior is an ever-present risk. Planning a sustainable pace requires paying attention to labor loss—an amount of time that takes away from the normal working time.

3. Third, diversify the skill base of the team by having more than one person available who is capable of handling a particular task. Cross train among jobs on the team so that more than one person can run a script, examine a database, or fashion a user interface. Switch job responsibilities, such as writer, tester, or verifier, from one iteration to the next. Cross evaluate performance between team members.

	People are not machines
A project management tip	• People are most effective when they are comfortable with the culture. • Culture is the body of values and principles that we believe in and the guidance for the actions we believe is right, honest, fair, and ethical. • Teams have a culture. Forming a team is, in part, recruiting staff with a cultural commonality. • Every team should have a process for evaluating fitness and mitigating the unfit.

Conflict Resolution

Handling conflict effectively goes a long way toward mitigating why teams do not work. The body of knowledge about conflict resolution is deep and wide, covered in many standard texts on project management, and addressed by many who have studied teams.[21]

A few points regarding agile teams:

- **Accepting new members:** Agile teams are expected to stay together throughout the lifecycle of the project; not adjourning and handing over to new teams formed for later planning waves. Over time, turnover is expected, but only modest turnover because of the strength of unit cohesion. With turnover, team productivity will require recalibration; in the short run, productivity may suffer.

  New members require time to form effective relationships with teammates who have bonded through a shared experience. New members will not be plug-in replacements; more likely, their skills will differ from those who have left the team. It is expected that some realignment of roles and responsibilities will follow staff changes. It will take some time for realignments and relationships to fully mature.

- **Trusting new relationships:** Trust must be earned—and earnings take time. A look to Stephen Covey is appropriate: everyone comes into a relationship with a small deposit in their trust account.[22] People naturally assume an optimistic outlook when meeting people they respect. No one will be invited to join a team as a stranger.

  The objective of the new arrival is to build up his or her account balance. Each new team member should be accepted on this basis: he or she can be trusted until proven otherwise. Each new member must appreciate that regaining lost trust is very difficult, and even more time-consuming than was establishing trust in the first place.

- **Competitiveness on the team:** Building complex systems is a competitive business, and the people who do it are competitive. But, intuitively and practically, competition breeds privacy and secrecy. There can be no effective collaboration if things are too compartmentalized. Communications and collaboration are the oil of team processes, and without them, frictions build into conflict and tension. Coach the team to replace secrecy and privacy with collaboration and trust.

- **Not a team player:** Some people cannot abide teamwork and never will. They cannot be won to collective work by trust and safety. They are constantly at odds with team values and principles. Presumably, they would not be knowingly recruited; presumably they would not be assigned to a team by a knowing manager. Nevertheless, teams find themselves with nonplayers, usually because they have an exceptional skill that is in high demand and short supply.

- **Virtual teams:** Virtual teams have their own unique conflicts. Virtual teams are not culturally integrated; members are far apart and they miss the personal gesture. Socialization and bonding with teammates is largely absent; the social component is mostly local.

Conflict arises out of misunderstandings which have their roots in values, language, culture, and purpose. A good practice is for virtual teams to meet face-to-face during the forming stage. If this is impractical, then a limited personal representation is next best—an exchange program. Although teleconferencing and videoconferencing are important technologies, almost nothing replaces personal touch.

Incentives and Compensation

The simple rule is to build rewards, incentives, and compensation around team achievement, not personal achievement. As simple as it is, such a rule goes against the grain of almost all compensation practices in modern enterprises. Human resource departments, procedures, and principles are built around serving the individual, not the team. Almost any team-level compensation and reward is going to be an exception to policy, and therein begins the job of project management. Most projects and teams are rewarded in cash or kind for performance:

- Spot awards for extraordinary performance in unusual or unplanned circumstances
- Performance awards based on successful releases
- Retention rewards for key individuals, conditioned on acceptable performance by the person and his or her team

The more troublesome compensation problems arise for business members who are assigned to the team. Senior business people are usually compensated variably with bonuses, commissions, and incentive packages. How, then, are those persons to be compensated for time away from a variable compensation opportunity? The answer is usually found among these formulations:

- **Commissioned sales staff:** For the dollar component of compensation, pay project compensation based upon the recent track record of commissions smoothed over a reasonable period of time. For the nondollar component, such as credit toward sales trips, the credit can continue to be awarded based on project compensation, or the salesperson can be awarded the trip in the role of sponsor or coordinator based on successful performance on the project.
- **Managers with variable pay or bonus:** If the product master has a bonus that is based on macro parameters, such as enterprise performance, the bonus can continue unchanged. Personal performance bonuses can shift to project performance.

	Compensation and reward
A project management tip	• A fair and transparent compensation plan is unquestionably part of making team members comfortable with moving from a functional environment to a team environment. • Money speaks, and if attached to team performance, it speaks loudly to the value placed on teams by the enterprise. It will partly resolve the oft unspoken question, what am I giving up?

Virtual Team

The virtual team is a special case for agile projects. Virtual teams enable skilled personnel who cannot physically co-locate to work together. In some cases, a virtual team may extend the affordability of the project. In other cases, it may bring technologies within reach that are otherwise unattainable economically. And, the virtual team may be able to bridge disparate boundaries within enterprises and among partners, suppliers, and others in the supply chain.

A number of barriers must be overcome to gain these advantages:

- A common purpose must be compelling to all team members.
- What is inspiring to one, may be ordinary or unappealing to others.
- A means of establishing trust must be found and communications protocol that will facilitate the ever-necessary collaboration is needed.
- A measurement, reward, and celebration system that is culturally compatible at multiple sites is also required.

Cultural influences
At a semiconductor plant in western Europe, team members were overheard exclaiming to their American coaches, "We don't want T-shirts and coffee cups!"

Delegating and trusting leader-follower relationships, encouragement of self-management and self-organization, and peer review accountability are not easy to convey through the virtual network, especially if the virtual team is multicultural. American culture has these characteristics:

- Tolerates challenge to superiors
- Tolerates the anti-group-think nemesis

- Accepts and encourages flat organizations
- Actively discourages discrimination in all forms

But other cultures have other values and respect these matters differently.

So, in spite of ever more effective and efficient electronic networking capabilities to overcome time and distance, the human factor remains paramount. The important parameters on everyone's list are these:[23]

- **Time and distance:** In spite of electronic communications, time and distance produce offsets and discontinuities in creativity, construction, production, and in the flow of thinking. Collectively, these result in an *overall slower velocity and longer schedule*—perhaps one of the most important risks for the project management office that is to be accounted for in planning iterations and releases.
- **Lifestyle, culture, language, and distance:** These all inhibit rapid deposits in Covey's so-called trust account, thus requiring extra time, effort, and opportunity to overcome the barriers and the inertia. Newton's First Law applies: if otherwise undisturbed by an extra and determined effort, things will continue along unchanged and unimproved.[24] Such behaviors are *contra-lean*; they add to the velocity issue discussed previously, and contribute to a larger and more pervasive overhead cost that also must be accounted for in planning.
- **Identity is disturbed:** People have a physical space and a local identity— but then they are expected to have a virtual identity and to be present in a virtual space. In some cases, there could be stresses where two identities must be managed in near real time. Physical space can be made private; virtual space is more open and more vulnerable. These differences may cause tension or a distraction, all contributing to incoherence.
- **When is time-off?** Some virtual teams can take advantage of the world clock and work continuously. But that means problems, issues, and events occur around the clock. Is a 24-hour workday really compatible with Principle 8 to plan for a sustainable pace?

	Virtual teams
A project management tip	• Virtual teams can and do work, but the issues identified in *Why teams do not work* are amplified and more acute. • Plan additional effort to mentor and coach for success. • *Assume that team velocity will be lower and costs will be higher than a similarly staffed co-located team*, until the virtual team gains experience working together.

Module 4—Discussion for Critical Thinking

Given the ubiquitous presence of virtual teams in almost every enterprise-scale project, the slower velocity and extra overhead detract from their advantages. What do you think you could do to recover some of these losses?

Module 5: Matrix Management in the Agile Space

Some say the matrix style and agile are naturally incompatible

Module 5—Objectives

- Examine how the matrix management practice and agile can be compatible

There are several operating models for projects; they can be agile and otherwise. The *PMBOK® Guide* illustrates the most common models in Chapter 2, Project Life Cycles and Organization.[25] The matrix is of interest to project managers with agile teams because it has the potential to impact the concept of a long-life performance unit team.

Matrix Attributes

A management matrix is a two-sided grid with project responsibilities on one side and functional responsibilities on the other. Cross-points represent the intersection of shared responsibilities.

	The matrix introduces conflict
A project management tip	• Matrix management introduces deliberate conflict. • Competition at the cross-point is the source of conflict. • Organizations that are weak in conflict management should avoid the matrix.

The cross-point may also represent the intersection of two bosses for an individual team member. Each boss expects loyalty, commitment, and accountability—a tall order for most. Conflict mitigation requires general managers to decide: Is the project or the functional organization to have primacy? Sometimes it is a pretty tough call; the business of business must go on. In the agile space, there can really be only one practical answer: The performance team must have priority to have a meaningful benchmark for throughput.

By common convention, the project is represented on the top side of the matrix with vertical columns arrayed under the project office. The functional organization is represented on the left side with horizontal rows extending from the functional managers. Figure 8.4 illustrates the discussion.

To develop a matrix when starting a new agile project, make a list of all the management responsibilities for both the project and the organization. Then, allocate the responsibilities to each side of the matrix according to the operating model. The operating model usually takes one of two forms, but the first model is preferred because all the project responsibilities roll up to the project manager.

1. The functional manager is a resource supplier, taking responsibility to provide people to the project.
2. The functional manager becomes a contractor to the project. The functional manager assumes responsibility for team performance; essentially forming performance teams that are contracted units to the project office.

With thoughtful allocation, the same responsibility does not show up on both sides of the matrix. Thus, responsibilities do not overlap, so why should they compete and create conflict? The answer is different missions.

Matrix Managers with Different Missions
The mission of the managers for each side of the matrix is different, and thus, the priority placed on the joint intersection of interests by each side's manager is different.

On the one side, the project mission is to meet an iteration timeline. All hands must be present. On the other side, as an example, the functional mission may be staff development. The functional manager may have a key performance indicator, with compensation attached, to ensure a minimum number of hours of skills training within a budgeted timeframe. A team member, caught in the middle at a cross-point cannot be in two places—the project and the training. A tiebreaker is needed.

The situation just described is made all the worse if each side of the matrix is a different institution. For example, in some contracted situations, a performance team is made up of a mixed staff from both institutions,

Matrix relationships are between the project and the enterprise and its business units

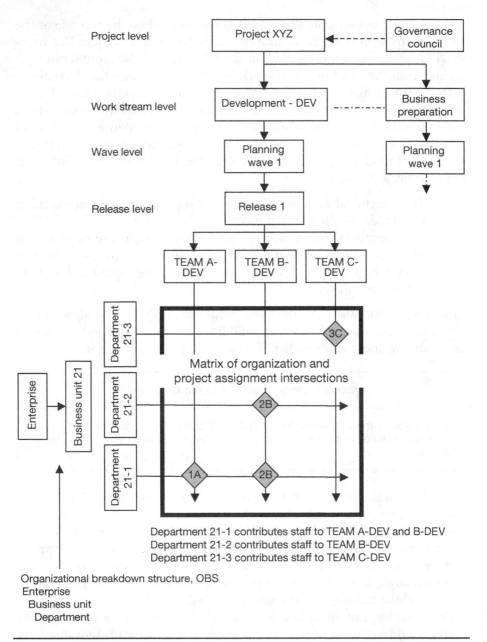

Department 21-1 contributes staff to TEAM A-DEV and B-DEV
Department 21-2 contributes staff to TEAM B-DEV
Department 21-3 contributes staff to TEAM C-DEV

Organizational breakdown structure, OBS
Enterprise
  Business unit
    Department

Figure 8.4   Generic matrix

co-located and otherwise transparently one team. But institutional preroga-tives sometimes intervene and conflicts arise.

Matrix as an Agile Management Tool

Matrix management is a form of risk management.

1. Cost is one risk that is managed. Presumably, team members who are no longer needed by the project are absorbed back into the func-tional side, thereby relieving the project of their cost.
2. Resource supply and demand is the second risk managed. Func-tional managers anticipate demand by looking ahead to the planning horizons. Supply is managed accordingly. In larger organizations, the functional managers recruit for turnover replacement, plan and execute skills training, and locate contract employees who provide on-demand skills.

Functional managers are usually charged with the responsibility to meet and maintain certifications to outside authorities, like the International Organi-zation for Standardization. To do this, functional managers ensure training, indoctrination, and consistency in applied principles and practices.

Agile Teams Recruit Their Members

All agile methodologies work best with highly motivated, well skilled, and experienced team members. All agile methodologies endorse the concept that teams recruit their members, rather than have members assigned to them. Members are recruited for their specific skills and capabilities, and not just because they are available for team assignment.

Any large population is going to have a normal distribution of perform-ers—in other words, a distribution that looks like a bell curve. The center of the bell is the average. Not everyone is a stand-out. Indeed, half of all developers are below average.[26] Not every team can draw from the top per-centiles; there simply will not be enough top performers to go around.

Assignments and recruiting are conformed to the conventions of the enterprise. Nevertheless, even after optimization, teams will be populated with people of varying grades of capability and performance. Fortunately, agile teams are designed to diversify individual performance risks. Common mitigation procedures are given here:

- Cross-train to create redundancies
- Employ pair-programming to reinforce designed-in quality

- Conduct peer reviews to catch problems and inconsistencies early
- Benchmark velocity to get a handle on the actual performance; re-benchmark after experience with the first few iterations
- Buffer the iteration plan for unforeseen variances
- Plan for labor loss

	Not everyone is a superstar
A project management tip	Plan for reality; everyone is not a top performer. A committed effort often overcomes skill shortfalls; See *David and Goliath* and the record of the 1980 U.S. Olympic hockey team.[27]

Module 5—Discussion for Critical Thinking

The matrix idea is certainly a traditional management practice. Some say it has no place in agile methods because it is not "lean"—too much overhead from multiple managers—and because agile teams are recruited for the duration, whereas matrix management envisions opportunistic assignments. What do you say to these critics? Are they right or wrong for the most part?

Summary and Takeaway Points

The theme in this chapter is that small teams, capable of self-organizing, and absolutely committed to frequent and incremental releases, are the performance-unit building blocks of agile methods.

From Module 1, we discussed that a team is a social structure wherein all the members individually and mutually collaborate toward the achievement of a common goal—achievement that is only possible by the committed and collective contribution of every member.

From Module 2, we know that every team has a set of values and principles, but the most important is trust. Without trust that your teammates have not only their own but your interests in mind, there can be no truly collaborative and collective teamwork.

From Module 3, we developed the idea that in the agile space, teams are a building block and a performance unit. The principle performance parameter is velocity, the measure of throughput.

To achieve scale, teams are formed into networks. A team of teams manages the network and ensures coordination and collaboration among teams.

From Module 4, we examined the idea that some teams work and some do not. Apart from trust, the main impediment to successful teams is the lack of a compelling mission and the lack of clear boundaries for action and results. Teams that work do so because there is trust and because their members believe in the mission and are supported by the enterprise.

Incentives and compensation should be at the team level. Team compensation is at odds with most human resource principles that compensate at the individual level.

From Module 5, we discuss the reality that in larger organizations, some form of a matrix is inevitable. The matrix coordinates the project mission with the functional management mission.

In the end, teams work and produce superior results. Agile methods are made possible because of the superior work that is done by teams.

Chapter Endnotes

1. Lencioni, *The Five Dysfunctions of a Team: A Leadership Fable*, vii.
2. Sherif, Muzafer, and Sherif, *An Outline of Social Psychology*, 143-180.
3. A similar concept that a team is better thought of as a unit of performance, although not in terms of velocity and agile methods, is described in Katzenbach and Smith's "The Discipline of Teams," 81(2):111-120, which reports on the run-up studies leading to the publication of their book *The Wisdom of Teams*, 1994.
4. Tuckman, "Developmental Sequences in Small Teams" 384-399. Tuckman subsequently revised the theory adding a fifth stage, *adjourning*, in a 2001 reprint of the 1965 article in *Group Facilitation: A Research and Applications Journal*, Issue #3, Spring 2001.
5. Wikipedia, "Forming-Storming-Norming-Performing."
6. Katzenbach and Smith, *The Discipline of Teams: A Mindbook-Workbook*, 4.
7. Henderson, *Cohesion, the Human Element in Combat*, 4.
8. Hersey, Blanchard, and Johnson, *Management of Organizational Behavior*, 173-174.
9. Lencioni, *The Five Dysfunctions of a Team*, 43, 195.
10. See article "Personal Safety," provided by Alistair Cockburn at http://alistair.cockburn.us/Personal+safety (an excerpt of: Cockburn, *Crystal Clear—A Human-powered Methodology*), 28.
11. Kimble, Li, Barlow, "Effective Virtual Teams through Communities of Practice" Research Paper 2000/9, 5.
12. Beck with Andres, *Extreme Programming Explained*, 18-19.
13. The number of unique communication paths between N individuals is given by the formula $N \times (N - 1)$. When N is large, this formula is effectively N^2. For example, if there are five people on the team, named A, B, C, D, and E,

then there are 20 independent paths that can be used to communicate among the five parties. *A* can talk to *B*, *C*, *D*, and *E*, and *B*, *C*, *D*, or *E* can talk back to *A*, just to identify eight paths. But add three people to the team, and there becomes 56 ways to communicate! A little friction in each communication path will add up quickly and dissipate team productivity.

14. Project Management Institute, *A Guide to the Project Management Body of Knowledge (PMBOK® Guide)*, 155-156.

15. The classic example of a schedule that cannot be crashed is "nine women cannot have a baby in one month." See also The Project Management Institute, *PMBOK® Guide*, 155-156, and Brooks, *The Mythical Man-month*, 16-18.

16. Robbins and Finley, *The New Why Teams Don't Work*, 4-8.

17. Coutu, "Why Teams Don't Work," Interview with Dr. J. Richard Hackman, May 2009.

18. Robbins and Finley, *The New Why Teams Don't Work*, 49, 88, 130, 131, 185, 186, 188.

19. Hammer and Champy, *Reengineering the Corporation: A Manifesto*, 34-52.

20. Cockburn, "Characterizing People as Nonlinear First Order Components," HaT Technical Report presented at the Fourth International Multiconference on Systems, Cybernetics, and Informatics.

21. An excellent treatment for project managers is given in Harold Kerzner's classic textbook *Project Management: A Systems Approach*, Chapter 8. Conflicts in teams from the point of view of general management are well treated in Robbins and Finley, *The New Why Teams Don't Work*, Chapter 11.

22. Covey, *7 Habits of Highly Effective People*, 188-190.

23. For an excellent overview in report form, see Kimble, Li, and Barlow, "Effective Virtual Teams through Communities of Practice," Research Paper 2000/9. In book form, an excellent reference is Haywood, *Managing Virtual Teams: Practical Techniques*, 5-10.

24. Paraphrased from the writings of Sir Isaac Newton who published his laws of classical mechanics in *Philosophic Naturalis Principia Mathematica*.

25. Project Management Institute, *A Guide to the Project Management Body of Knowledge (PMBOK® Guide)*, 28.

26. A *normal curve* is symmetrical about the average. One half of the total population is above average and one half is below.

27. Malcolm Gladwell has a remarkable analysis of effort versus skills in his piece entitled, "Highly Effective Underdogs," 40-49.

9

Governance

Governance brings order and empowers innovation, leveraging the power of the enterprise for project achievement.

> *We always overestimate the change that will occur in the next two years and underestimate the change that will occur in the next ten. Don't let yourself be lulled into inaction.*
>
> *Bill Gates*

Governance and some agile principles in the same paragraph may seem like an oxymoron—but that is not so. A means to govern is essential for orderly project functioning. Without governance, the advantages of adaptive and evolutionary methods could be overwhelmed by functions that are bolted together haphazardly and rendered operationally ineffective, expensive to maintain, and disadvantageous to customers and stakeholders.

Agile practitioners agree that governance is necessary. Indeed, a look through the web yields numerous papers, blogs, and websites that are dedicated to promoting agile governance. Agile methodologists have gone so far as to build in governance practices like retrospective reviews, time boxes, and daily reviews.

A governance program should be purposeful about maximizing the business potential of a project, while at the same time, dedicated to minimizing the risks to business performance. A governance program should enable and promote innovative and imaginative solutions but deter behavior that strays too far from norms. In short, a governance program exists for five reasons that are, in effect, the governance mission statement:

Governance Mission
1. To oversee and approve investment on behalf of business beneficiaries. 2. To codify decision-making rights to enable teams to have autonomy and freedom to maneuver. 3. To enable and promote innovation, evolution, and technical excellence within the framework of architecture and operating norms. 4. To be the ultimate arbiter of risks that affect both business performance and accountability. 5. To provide accountability for compliance to mandatory standards.

Module 1: Governance Is Built on Quality Principles

Governance empowers quality outcomes

Module 1—Objectives

- Examine the elements of governance that empower quality outcomes

Governance Empowers

Empowerment has a foundation in these quality principles:

Quality Principles
1. Governance should be applied proportionately to the amount at stake. 2. Governance should provide clarity for mission and purpose, scope boundaries, decision-making authority, and decision rights. 3. Governance should respect the principle of subsidiary function: governance should not intrude into the management of functions that are best left to functional and project managers. 4. Governance must be lean, timely, and responsive, respecting agile principles to provide enough—but just enough—oversight and control to accomplish the governance mission.

Consider a couple of points:

1. Governance can be the vehicle to moderate supervision and flatten bureaucracy. This is accomplished by conveying rights to teams so they can make their own decisions.

2. Governance can bestow rewards for disciplined behavior. With discipline, trust follows, and trust enables self-determination.

Trust is an absolutely necessary condition for lean governance. Without faith in the actions of others, there is an inclination to add many resources and process steps to check and inspect. The best leaders are trusted by their followers, and the best teams are trusted by their leaders.

Leadership inspires inquisitive minds to question the status quo and to search for a better way; leadership motivates innovation. A trusting organization is a safe organization. A real benefit of trustfulness and discipline is the safety to go about doing really innovative and interesting tasks.[1] In the agile space, safety extends boundaries; wider boundaries often bring new discovery and challenging opportunity within reach, adding to competitive returns.

In its best form, governance empowers action and endows decision-making rights to project management and team leaders.

Leverage Empowers

All governance systems leverage enterprise power on behalf of projects. This is never truer than it is when working with the business case budget. Innovative products and services that feature technical excellence and effective customer service—those in the *ah-hah!* quadrant of the Kano chart—typically return many times their investment. Governance legitimizes activity—that is, spending and resource commitment, research and development, and continuous improvement—in all sectors of the balanced scorecard. Do not lose sight of the fact that funding sources are always in the hands of executives and stakeholders. Executives and stakeholders both sanction and constrain projects; they will loosen their purse strings and provide investment for projects thoughtfully presented, professionally managed, and objectively governed.

Decision Rights Empower

The unambiguous right to make a decision is conveyed by policies. Governance conceives and enforces those policies. As odd as it sounds, governance can actually get the organization out of the way by clearly pushing decision making to the project.

Governance clarifies direction among conflicted constituents. Constituent conflicts and confusion constrain action. All concerned parties have interests they instinctively protect, and they promote only those projects that serve their interest. Governance provides objective arbitration to achieve balance among parties.

Purposeful decisions enable effective project management. Confusion saps power; it is inevitable that there will be choices that are overlapping, contradictory, unaffordable, or inconsistent. But effective governance provides decisions that clarify, instruct, and direct action.

Leadership Empowers

Governance bodies practice situational leadership tailored to the circumstances at hand. Leadership in all forms motivates, inspires, and encourages action. Under the auspices of the governance council, there can be funding and support for research and development, prototyping, experimentation, and modeling. New ideas can be given early exposure and risks can be managed and contained within reasonable limits with methods and practices such as the spiral model described in Chapter 1.

Some Mechanics Are Necessary

Some governance bodies, policies, standards, and certifications are inescapable. Familiar examples: financial governance given by GAAP or the Sarbanes-Oxley standards; and information technology governance rendered by voluntary compliance with CoBIT or ITIL; and quality certifications monitored by the ISO.[2] These agencies and policies are decidedly not Agile.

However, careful application governance for agile projects is at the discretion of the organization; governance can be as little or as great as the risks demand. Governing bodies provide a service to constituent managers. It is really up to those managers to decide how much oversight is enough to protect their interests.

Operating Elements

To make governance work effectively, four operating elements are needed:

1. A policy model for effective dissemination of direction and guidance
2. A management framework for deciding among alternatives and objectively making best-value decisions
3. A protocol for exercising decision rights and situational judgment
4. A mechanism or regimen for accountability that satisfies the oversight responsibilities of business councils and senior managers

Each of these four elements is expanded for discussion in the sections that follow.

Policy Model for Governance

Policy makes effective governing possible. Without a policy regime to provide guidance and boundaries, managers fill the void and make it up along the way. A business may be able to operate in a policy vacuum, but to do so means setting precedents with every major decision. Experience has shown that it is more effective to do these things:

- Establish only those few policies that are necessary to set up behavioral boundaries
- Establish the policies in advance of their need
- Establish polices at a high level
- Allow specific extensions and interpretations to fill in the operating detail

A good policy is brief, unambiguous, operationally relevant, readily available on-demand, and capable of being extended operationally. As given in Table 9.1, effective policies are supported at the highest executive level. A framework holds all the policy instruments. Policies are actively deployed according to a deployment plan; compliance is actively tracked.

As an example of policy, take a look at Table 9.2.

Table 9.1 Policy attributes

Policy feature	Meaning and intent
Charter	Policy, at its highest level, should be chartered and endorsed by the organization's senior executive.
	Policy is incumbent on all by flow-down through the organizational structure.
Framework	A policy library of governing documents should be maintained by each functional unit.
	Dependencies among and across domains should be identified and managed in a policy cross-reference.
Deployment	A communications and deployment plan for governance policies should be developed and implemented among constituents of each functional unit.
	Policies should be easily available to all constituents by organizational network or otherwise.
Compliance	Compliance measurement and accountability should be actively managed.
Operational relevance	Policy must be maintained. As business and the business environment change, so must policy.
	Business units should extend high-level policy to incorporate operating detail.
	In the spirit of continuous improvement, a means to receive feedback and act upon good ideas should be provided. Policy recipients should be encouraged to make policy clear and unambiguous.

Table 9.2 Policy example

Policy component	Meaning and intent
Subject area	Information Technology Assets
Policy statement	Applications, systems, infrastructure, and data are to be shared among business units to maximize their business value.
	• Stand-alone exceptions are allowable with approval
	• Stand-alone renegades are to be actively discouraged
Policy objectives	The policy objectives are to:
	• Improve business operational efficiencies by reducing the cost of business unit interoperability and functional coordination;
	• Mitigate business performance and compliance risks from uncertified systems and data;
	• Provide for disaster recovery, ensure integrity, protect confidentiality of systems and data, and
	• Assure reliability and availability of business systems
Application and dissemination	• Applicable to all business units
	• Disseminate to all managers and team leaders
	• Make available on the company intranet
Compliance	• Mandatory for all systems and data except personal desktop applications not intended for official use
	• Compliance to be certified by managers annually

	Decision policy for the project manager
A project management tip	• The simplest policy for decision making is: always make a best-value decision based on the collective value of the risk-weighted factors.
	• When deciding among alternatives, pick the alternative that informs the business most favorably, even if there is suboptimum results for the project.

A Management Framework

Governance is management executed outside project boundaries that protects objectivity and independence. Objectivity and independence establish fair play and trust in decision making.

Management is provided by a council—a governance council—established and empowered by the organization's executive management. The governance council may also include an independent architecture council who is charged with maintaining coherent architecture for the systems and products being governed, and a business preparation council that represents users, customers, and stakeholders.

The Mission of the Governance Council
• The governance council is the operating executive for the five-point governance mission.   • Day-to-day, the council examines each business case and makes project go/no-go decisions in context with the organization's goals, strategies, and conventions.

To be lean, the governance council may involve only one or two persons for Level 0 business cases. Decision making at Level 0 is amenable to being regulated by electronic workflow; such flow-control systems save time and money and preserve decision-making records. At Level 1 or 2, more elaboration is needed. Recall the principle that governance is applied proportionately to what is at stake: total investment, customer impacts, benefit realization, and business performance.

The staff assigned to the governance council reflects the mission particulars. The number of staff is less important than their skills and authority. Like team members, council members should be recruited for their acumen—their business knowledge, customer familiarity, comfort with technology, and an analytical mindset. The council cannot be tone deaf to politics. Political skills will be necessary to enforce decisions and gain constituent support.

Most governance councils are event-driven, meaning that they act when an event requires attention, rather than meet on a regular schedule. In the spirit of agile methods, governance councils time box their deliberations.

The governance council is responsible for a governance framework. The framework provides the services and functions given in Table 9.3.

A Protocol for Decision Rights

Effective governance embeds its decision-making instructions and limitations in a protocol. Decision-making protocols lay out the rights, responsibilities, and rules for everyone involved in decisions.

Decision rights specify who can be the decision maker, what they can decide, and how much resource they can commit in various circumstances. Here are three examples:

1. *Sponsor rights:* Sponsors approve the business case. Decision rights are conveyed to the project sponsors for each of the three business

Table 9.3   Management and policy framework for governance

Framework component	Commentary
Mechanics and services	• Provides a means to publish, approve, maintain, and access objects, primarily documents. • Provides a document repository. Manages check-in/check-out. • Provides web-based documents, typically policies and decision documents, routed for approval by workflow, and accessible on an internal website after approval. • Makes it easy to access policy and decisions by searching internal web.
Policy support for business case	• Defines and establishes parameters for Level 0, 1, and 2 case. • Enforces business case submittal, approval, and maintenance with workflow. • Defines and establishes the approving authorities and the workflow for approval.
Verification of project compliance	• Enforces trip wire functions that track compliance to policy requirements.[1] • Makes it easy to comply, track, and report compliance by data entry and retrieval by web forms.
Verify other functional compliance, e.g., IT and finance	• Enforces policy compliance according to policy directives. • Utilizes functionality to publish, approve, maintain, and access. • Makes it easy to comply, track, and report compliance by data entry and retrieval by web forms.
Security and integrity of policy library	• Manages access and modifications to content according to security policy and practices. • Enforces authorization, authentication, rights and privileges to create, read, update or modify, and delete documents.

[1]A "trip wire" function is a condition set by the governance council that will cause some governance action to kick-in if the condition becomes true. The trip wire could be set around a financial parameter, a milestone, or some functional need. In some cases a trip wire could be set around a scorecard from the customer.

cases—Levels 0, 1, and 2—according to the investment, impacts, and benefits anticipated at each level.

2. *Project management rights*: Project managers govern performance, accountability, and achievement. Project managers are given rights to affect performance, insist on accountability, and intervene to correct inefficient and ineffective practices.

3. *Team rights*: Teams govern requirements and day-to-day practices. Performance teams are conveyed decision rights for selecting requirements for the backlog, setting priorities, and sequencing features and functions for production. Teams regulate their own practices and decide which are applicable and appropriate to the situation.

Rights come with responsibilities. The decision maker is responsible for:

- Following the decision-making rules of the governance regime
- Making decisions in a timely fashion
- Supporting the team that executes the decision
- Taking responsibility for results

Protocols are rules-based. Rules impose order; rules enable decision making at a distance. Table 9.4 lists some of the more common rules.

Decision makers have been mentioned many times. Table 9.5 addresses the questions of what do they decide and what business case level is affected?

A Mechanism for Accountability

Accountability means taking responsibility for results. Good results require, among other things, compliance with governance direction and guidance. The best evidence of compliance is customer satisfaction with product outcomes.

Table 9.4 Decision-making rules

Rule	Commentary
All decisions respect the value proposition of the project as given in the business case	• It's acknowledged that the voice of the business and the customer is heard in the business case • Funding limits, milestones, and product vision come from the business case • The balanced scorecard is felt through the business case; it represents each sponsor's commitment to the project
Decisions that support outcomes are favored over decisions that support achieving a plan	• Satisfying the customer is a higher priority than meeting the specifics of a plan • The rule assumes there is a non-value gap between the plan and the desired outcome such that the plan is less optimum for the customer
All decisions will be ethical, lawful, and conform to regulatory and policy strictures	• Each decision maker is responsible for the quality of the decisions made • The rule seems objective on its face, but interpretations often complicate matters
All decisions will be evaluated for risk; downside possibilities will be within the decision rights of the decision maker	• Every project decision involves risk; financial risks are customarily evaluated with discounted cash flow methods • The downside of risk—how bad it could be—must not exceed the authority of the decision maker
Decisions among alternatives that are otherwise equal will be decided in favor of best-value for the enterprise	• Best-value always includes a consideration for the customer

Table 9.5   Decision makers

Decision makers	What do they decide?	What business case level is affected?
Executive team	• Highest-level strategy and goals • Capital and expense funding above business case Level 1 • Personnel decisions with strategic impact • Business-to-business relationships that affect high level strategy and goals • Next steps based on strategic benchmarks	• Level 2 always, and • Level 1 when key to executive strategy and goals
Governance council and/or architecture council	• Consistency with legacy business practices, legacy systems, and forward-looking road maps • Strategic technologies, new product direction • Strategic steps based on scorecards and benchmarks • Portfolio sequencing • Priority of limited resources	All levels
Functional managers	• Resource commitments to new activity • Change management to absorb new outcomes • Next steps based on scorecards and benchmarks	All levels
Project managers	• Estimate for new or changed activity • What processes and measures will apply to each team-level activity • Next steps based on scorecards and benchmarks	All levels
Team leaders	• Estimate inputs for new or changed activity • What processes and measures will apply to each activity within the team • Which resources are applied to each team activity	All levels
Subject matter experts	Tactical steps to be taken to solve a specific problem	All levels

However, investment must be recovered and other beneficiaries must be served. Achievement of key performance indicators on the balanced scorecard is the next best evidence of accountability for results.

Outside agencies that convey certification, require proof of compliance. Audits to gather information from scorecards, dashboards, workflow records, and other artifacts provide proof of performance.

In the next section of this chapter, we will address compliance in more detail.

	Accountability to the business case
A project management tip	• Effective accountability metrics always incorporate a results measure. • Avoid measures of input consumption and activity, such as funding and hours; focus governance on outcomes and beneficial results.

Module 1—Discussion for Critical Thinking

Governance in the absence of policy is just making it up as you go along. Governance in the context of policy is empowering. Do you agree with these assertions, and why?

Module 2: Governance Verifies Compliance

Compliance verification: the test of any governance paradigm

Module 2—Objectives

• Discuss and explain scorecards as a tool for governance

Scorecards and Benchmarks for Results

In the agile space, results come periodically and incrementally. During the check-act part of the Agile-plan-do-check-act cycle, there is opportunity to audit compliance to standards, regulations, and conventions, and analyze achievements on scorecards and dashboards.

• **Scorecards are snapshots of achievements:** Scorecard data is temporal, meaning time-sensitive; for governance purposes, data snapshots at milestones usually suffice to show whether governance objectives are being achieved. For example, some scorecard information depicts performance against benchmarks established by the governance council to guide project performance.
• **Dashboards are information portals:** These portals provide not only the temporal scorecard, but also stationary information. Some stationary information, such as when and how standards are deployed, may be useful for certifying compliance.

The architecture council may require technical benchmarking when there are risks identified with technology feasibility, infrastructure performance, or architecture. Technical benchmarks are usually embedded in a process called technical performance measures (TPM). TPM envisions periodic measurements of technical achievement, comparison of achievements to benchmarks, and then actions to mitigate variances.

Team productivity figures, quality measures, and product performance results are typical technical benchmarks. Agile projects lend themselves to benchmarking and TPM because frequent deliveries offer many points of evaluation, provide data to support trend lines and forecasts, and build progressively towards the TPM goal. There is ample time to build a cumulative experience over a range of circumstances that enrich the results.

Lean Scorecard for the Black Box Model

In thinking about the utility of a scorecard for business-case governance, we invoke the black-box model of a project:

- The project is fully encapsulated
- There is no visibility to the internal mechanisms
- Interfaces with defined functionality and technical performance accept resources and triggers, return or deliver processed results, and accept governance controls and environmental support

See Figure 9.1 for the visualization of this concept. At each input and output, there is expected and actual performance. Among these four data elements, variances and efficiencies can be calculated. Recall that a variance is a difference between two data elements; efficiency is a ratio of two data elements.

As a quick example, take a look at the scorecard given in Figure 9.1. The units of measure are arbitrary, but in most cases, they will be dollars on the top half and story points on the bottom half. The calculations in the top half are measuring consumption in the black box. The data in the bottom half of the card shows results. It is instructive in a real project to compare top and bottom half variances and efficiencies to continuously improve forecasting and benchmarks.

When looking at efficiencies, the objective is always for the ratio to be 1.0 or greater, meaning that expectations are met or exceeded. Unfortunately, 100 percent is a tough benchmark to achieve. For any number of reasons, there are often losses that drag the efficiency below 100 percent. After each iteration and release, during check-act reflection, reasons for efficiencies and variances are examined for opportunities for improvement.

To outsiders, the project is a black box, the performance of which is evaluated at its interfaces, input and out.

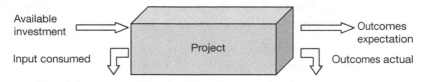

Scorecard		Milestone			
Source	Metric	1	2	3	4
Business	Investment Available	10	15	15	12
Project	Funds [input] Consumed	9	15	16	12
Calculation	Funds variance	1	0	-1	0
	Funds efficiency	111%	100%	94%	100%
Business	Outcomes Expected	5	7	7	6
Project	Actual Outcomes	4	7	8	6
Calculation	Outcomes variance	-1	0	1	0
	Outcomes efficiency	80%	100%	114%	100%

Figure 9.1   Lean scorecard for black box model

Module 2—Discussion for Critical Thinking

Scorecards as governance tools reinforce the agile idea of accountability for outcomes. What scorecards are common in the projects with which you have experience? Have you thought of them as governance tools or simply as a means to communicate progress?

Summary and Takeaway Points

Our theme is: *governance brings order and empowers innovation, leveraging the power of the enterprise for project achievement.*

From Module 1, we find that governance is built on quality principles and empowers quality outcomes. A governance program should be purposeful about maximizing the business potential of a project while, at the same time, dedicated to minimizing the risks to business performance. Governance should encourage innovative and imaginative solutions, but deter behavior that strays too far from the norms of the enterprise. In short, a governance program exists for five reasons:

1. To tie an investment to business value and results
2. To codify decision-making rights
3. To enable and promote innovation, evolution, and technical excellence within the framework of architecture and operating norms
4. To manage risks that affect business performance and accountability
5. To provide accountability for standards compliance

There are four principles that guide an effective governance implementation:

1. Governance is to be applied proportionately to the amount at stake
2. Governance should provide clarity for mission and purpose, scope boundaries, and decision-making authority and rights for approved projects
3. Governance should respect the principle of subsidiary function; governance should not intrude into the management of functions by subsidiary operating units
4. Governance must be lean, timely, and responsive, respecting the Agile Principles to provide enough, but just enough, oversight and control to accomplish the five-point governance mission

To make governance work effectively, four operating elements are needed:

1. Policy model
2. Management framework for deciding among alternatives and objectively making best-value decisions
3. Protocol for exercising decision rights that empowers decision makers to exercise judgment about estimates and to objectively decide among facts
4. Mechanism or regimen for accountability that satisfies the oversight responsibilities of business councils and senior managers

In Module 2, we learn that scorecards and benchmarks provide the data for verification. Every governance system closes the loop on results. After all, obtaining results that benefit the customer and the enterprise is the motivation to regulate performance.

Chapter Endnotes

1. The concept of a safe organization is an important concept in the so-called human-powered methodologies called Crystal methods. See Cockburn, *Crystal Clear—A Human-powered Methodology*, 28.

2. The Generally Accepted Accounting Standards (GAAP) in the United States is administered by the Financial Accounting Standards Board. Sarbanes-Oxley refers to the U.S. law that sets standards for reporting and certifying the accuracy of financial reports. See also COSO, a preferred model for Sarbanes-Oxley compliance; Control Objectives for Information and related Technology (CoBIT) is a set of governance practices for information technology administered by the IT Governance Institute. Information Technology Infrastructure Library (ITIL) refers to the IT practices developed by the U.K. government. The International Standards Organization (ISO) is dedicated to promoting quality under the umbrella of ISO 9000 standard, among others.

Web
Added
Value™

10

Managing Value

Agile projects accumulate value by delivering product incrementally, peri-odically, affordably, and according to the priority of the customer.

> *If the customer is not satisfied, he may not want to pay for our efforts. If the customer is not successful, he may not be able to pay. If he is not more successful than he already was, why should he pay?*
>
> Niels Malotaux

In the agile space, value is always business and customer-centric. Agile doctrine accepts that the business and customer[1] are their own best authority on what is important to them. In the agile space, value accumulates over time—functionalities and features are added to the product base release by release, according to priorities and benefit demands that are reevaluated by the customer iteration by iteration. Value accumulated is value earned. Agile projects add to earnings as the project backlog is burned off.

Value Is Earned

For the project scorecard
  • Each completed backlog entity (story, use case, requirement) is an entity with a value to be earned when *done*
  • Each release package has a value to be earned when the package is integrated with the product base and delivered to the production operation
For the business scorecard
  • Go-live to production earns value for the business scorecard

Module 1: Defining and Accounting for Value

Value: I'll know it when I see it

Module 1—Objectives

- Examine the various definitions and concepts that attend the definition of value

Value Qualities

Agile is all about giving the customer/user license to drive the value proposition. Two qualities we think of as value defining are very much customer oriented and in the eye of the beholder:

1. Esteem value that pleases rather than performs
2. Use value that satisfies because functions work and perform as intended

Getting these two qualities right, and in the right balance, and with the right economics is the value-quality challenge of our time, and is at the center of agile methodologies. In fact, a business model—quite apart from agile as a methodology—has grown up around this challenge; this model goes by the moniker *design thinking*.[2]

And then there is value satisfaction, or the satisfaction that comes with a good value. Generally speaking, value satisfies when quality exceeds price—that is, outcomes meet or exceed expectations and the price seems fair.

Of course value requires a need, and willingness married with capability and capacity on the part of the customer to address that need. Putting all this together leads directly to an ageless definition of value. *It is what the customer is willing to pay for.* The corollary is simply this: if few are willing to pay, then the value is not commanding or compelling.[3]

	Value means
A project management tip	• There is something worth paying for—value anchored to need • Quality in the large sense of fitness and esteem is satisfied • Outcomes meet or exceed the expectations

Objective Measures

Value has objective measures:

- **Investment value—or *cost-of-value*:** the lowest possible cost to produce a satisfactory deliverable.
- **Earned value:** that part of the planned outcome (planned value) that has been completed and delivered, thereby *earned*.
- **Burned value:** that which is *done* is *burned*. Teams burn off the backlog and thereby create value with delivered product. Think of this as agile terminology for the concept of earned value.
- **Benefit value or economic value:** the present value to the business of the benefit stream paid for by the customer, internal or external.
- **Best value:** as given in Chapter 1, *delivering the most scope possible—for the available resources—that most optimizes business effectiveness, importance, and responsiveness to urgency for the customer.*
- **Free-value:** value delivered for essentially a zero price, either because the marginal cost of production is all but zero, as in software; or because the producer makes money, but not directly from the end-customer, as in advertising supported services.[4]

Value Distinctions

Are cost-of-value and best-value distinctions without a difference?

No. The cost-of-value, or investment value, of a simple order-entry function may be very large to develop—and more each year to maintain—but to the customer wanting to buy the system, the simple order-entry function may be a best value at no more than a fraction of the investment value.

- To bring cost-of-value or investment value into alignment with best value requires economy of scale.
- Economy of scale requires larger-scale lean practices not attainable at small scale.
- Production scale recovers the development, production, distribution, and maintenance costs incrementally from many customers.

Accounting for Value

There are three commonly applied practices to account for value:

1. Cost accounting
2. Throughput accounting
3. Earned value accounting

And, there is one that is not: percent complete.

About These Accounting Practices
• It's common practice in all methodologies, whether agile or traditional, to be attentive to cost accounting in one form or another. • Many traditional methodologies apply some form of earned value, as does agile, though an agile team thinks in terms of *burned backlog*. • Throughput accounting is more appropriate to agile than traditional because the focus is strictly on the value added and not the total cost.

In Chapter 4, we discussed *Agile in the Waterfall.* The marriage of methodologies or the coexistence of methodologies in the same project likely brings all of these accounting methods into play in one form or another.

Cost Accounting

Cost accounting is the traditional way to evaluate the cash flow or resource consumption in the project. It is characterized by a budget forecast and an accounting of every expense (or hour) charged to that budget. In agile parlance, cost accounting is input accounting. It keeps a measure on the manner that input budget is consumed.

Because cost accounting is strictly an input measure, there is no customer-oriented value metric per se.

Cost Accounting Focus
The focus is on minimizing the expenses of development and production in order to earn back the investment.

Value in the sense of optimizing input consumption is attained if these three conditions are present:

- Operating expense (in funding or hours) does not exceed the operating budget
- The net present value of monetized project costs and benefit cash flows is positive
- The economic value added of cash commitments is also positive

Throughput Accounting

Throughput accounting focuses on the value added by the team to the baseline value of the pre-project as-is. Throughput, previously defined, is the product produced in one development iteration or one release. In agile projects, the throughput parameter is like that of velocity, measured in story points completed and *done* per iteration.[5] In other words, throughput, and its cousin velocity are rates of production.

The pre-project opportunity and as-is situation usually has some inherent value. For example, there is some value in new ideas conceived but unimplemented, legacy capability existing but unchanged, and bug lists prioritized but unaddressed. The inherent value motivates the business to make some investment to define the opportunity, figure out the benefit possibilities, identify the stakeholder community, and begin to move down the value V shown in Figure 2.2.

Once things get underway and project releases begin, value is earned.

Throughput Value Earnings
In monetary terms, throughput earnings are essentially the present value of the benefit stream associated with the release—net of the initial opportunity value. Thus, the calculation is value-added to the business.

Earnings first recover the initial investment; thereafter, earnings add value in excess of the initial investment.

	Accounting focus
A project management tip	A throughput accountant calculates the value added, and the cost accountant calculates the marginal return on the invested expense. Figure 10.1 depicts the discussion.[6]

From the discussion and Figure 10.1, take note of the different ways that operating expense is handled. In the agile project, the majority of operating expense is the labor cost of the teams; additionally, there are infrastructure expenses, tool licenses, and the like. Once optimized, expenses are nearly a fixed cost to the organization in this sense: when the team finishes one iteration, it goes on to the next; when the project is completed, the project teams go on to the next project.

Throughput accounting focuses on the value add difference between the input opportunity and the output deliverables

The project operating expense is considered a fixed cost

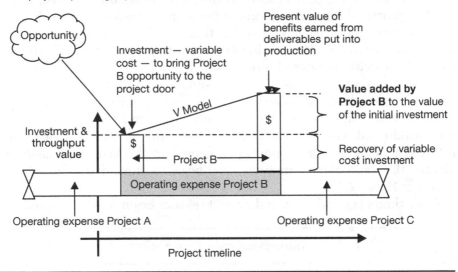

Figure 10.1 The value of throughput

Labor is only marginally variable over the long reach. However, cost accountants usually categorize all project expense as a variable expense. Throughput accountants ignore expense that is fixed in the as-is state; throughput is how much value is added to the as-is.

Percent Complete

Percent complete is not a measure of value; it's really not even a measure of completeness, even if some, but not all, work is completed when the measurement is less than 100%. We say this because, as a ratio, both the denominator and numerator are in play. Thus, *percent complete* suffers from the hazard of a moving baseline—the denominator.

The ratio is dimensionless, whereas value has a dimension. For this reason, value cannot be measured; value requires a metric with dimensions.

In the agile space, percent complete is replaced entirely with *remaining effort*. In other words, the agile management focus is on three questions:

1. How much do I have to do? To wit: how much backlog remains for the iteration, release, or project.
2. How much have I done already—backlog burned and done?

3. How much do I have left to do? Note: how much left includes the work in progress (WIP)?

Since backlog is dynamic—some new things added, some things abandoned, some things left over as debt from prior iterations—you can see that percent complete is meaningless. Measured as a ratio, backlog at any given moment is the denominator (burned, WIP, and not started); the numerator is the backlog burned. Both numerator and denominator change from moment to moment, rendering the ratio useless for management purposes.

Accumulating Value Is Earning Back the Investment

Accumulating value is a straightforward concept that has been around since projects began. In simplest terms, accumulating value is incrementally giving the customer their money's worth:

- In agile projects, customer value accumulates from incremental product releases.
- Traditional projects also accumulate value incrementally, though the traditional project design may deliver the value all at the end if there is not a convenient way to phase deliverables to the customer.
- Hybrid agile-traditional projects rely on synchronized outcomes, as we discussed in Chapter 4, each outcome having some accumulated value.

Business benefits are derived from customer value; although the business accumulates its benefits over time, whereas customers perceive value right away. In other words, there is a timing relationship between an outcome for the customer—here and now—and a benefit for the business to be realized over time. So, at the moment of release, there is:

- A product in production
- A customer who is satisfied, and perhaps value is realized right away because the released entity is usable right away
- A benefit forecast for the business but with unrealized value—value realization takes place over time as mission success is realized or customer/users create business benefits over time

We claim that the business benefit is unrealized at release time—at release time it is a benefit on paper only. Over time, benefit forecasts become benefit realities; benefit accumulation continues until the entire opportunity has been earned.

In project terms, accumulating value and earning value are nearly synonymous:

- Earning or accumulating value mean planning for a beneficial outcome, and then achieving it, whether or not the intended resources are applied and consumed.[7]
- When the project is completed and expectations are met, the entire project scorecard value is earned and accumulated—all requirements are rendered in production and are mapped to benefits.

Agile methods change the bookkeeping a bit, focusing on burning down the backlog as they do, but by Agile Principle 1, delivering value is at the top of the list:

Agile Principle 1
Our highest priority is to satisfy the customer through early and continuous delivery of valuable (product).

Three Components of Earned and Accumulated Value

Conceptually, any earned and accumulated value system has three basic metrics:

1. *The cost-of-value planned or forecast to be earned and delivered*: The cost-of-value (CoV) expresses outcome value in dollar terms and is a surrogate for quality; that is, value at a fair price (or cost).
   a. CoV is synonymous with the budget plan, but not the actual cost (AC).
   b. Traditionally, the CoV is the planned value (PV) or budget.
   c. In conventional traditional terms, the CoV is the PV of outcomes, not a value of requirements per se.
   d. Requirements per se are not valued; outcomes, as a consequence of requirements applied to project processes, are valued.
2. *The value earned, accumulated, or delivered*: The value earned and delivered is synonymous with the value earned.
   a. As explained elsewhere, the value earned may be different from the actual cost.
   b. Agile project teams usually think in terms of what portion of the backlog has been burned down and delivered.
   c. Traditionally, the value earned is the *earned value*.
3. *The actual resources consumed*: An accounting of the actual resources consumed or AC.

a. AC is project operating, development, or construction expense, including any initial opportunity investment that is allocated to the project.

b. Cost accounting is applied to actual resources consumed.

Several other useful metrics are derived from the basic metrics.[8] Table 10.1 gives the important formulas written for both traditional and agile practices. Take note that in Table 10.1:

- Ratios are measures of efficiencies
- Additions and subtractions are measures of variance

Earned and accumulated value mechanics are straightforward and easy to apply. In the appendix to this chapter there is a short example of how these mechanics are applied to an example agile project.

	Earned and accumulated value applied to agile projects
A project management tip	• Earned value (EV) is applied to the team as a performance unit, not to individual tasks • A major difference between EV in a traditional project and an agile project is the difference between valuing the completion of tasks, and valuing completions released to production • Accumulated value can be tracked with burn-down and burn-up charts

Value Accumulation Measurements

In the traditional project plan, there is often serious dispute about the value earned and value added to the accumulation. Disputes arise because:

- Value earned measurements are taken at the end of a reporting period, regardless of whether an outcome is completed
- A judgment, subject to dispute, is made about the partial value earned.

Hybrid Project, Traditional Practices

If the project methodology is hybrid, as described in Chapter 4, the measurements for the work streams applying traditional methodology are relatively simple to take at every milestone:

- **Measure the AC:** The AC comes from the cost accounting applied to the project. Cost accounting is typically parsed by work package, a unit of work roughly equivalent in time and effort to an agile iteration.[9]

Table 10.1   Earned and accumulated value metrics

Formulation	Commentary
Value earned or delivered per unit of cost-of-value (CoV)	• A measure of efficiency. The ratio shows how efficiently the earning plan is being executed. • Traditionally written as EV/PV. • Agile written as Value Earned/Cost-of-value.
Value earned or delivered per unit of actual cost (AC)	• A measure of efficiency. The ratio shows how efficiently a unit of AC creates a unit of value earned. • Traditionally written as EV/AC. • Agile written as Value Earned/Actual Cost.
Value earned or delivered less CoV at a particular point in time	• A variance to a plan to deliver units of value by a certain time. • Traditionally, EV – PV is a measure of being ahead or behind schedule. • Agile written as Value Earned – Cost-of-Value
Value earned or delivered less AC at a particular point in time	• A variance to a plan to deliver units of value at a certain cost. • Traditionally written as EV – AC. • Agile written as Value Earned – Actual Cost

- **Measure the value earned:** Just like in agile, the value earned is that part of the work package task that is finished and deliverable to the successor task or work unit, or another work stream.
- **Calculate variances and efficiencies:** Using the typical EV formulas for cost and schedule variance, and for work and schedule efficiency, calculate all the metrics required for management and reporting.

One version of a value accumulation scorecard applies to the example project given in the appendix. The cost and value earning measurements are scored at each milestone and recorded on the scorecard. From the measured data, the values for calculated metrics are computed using the formulas in Table 10.1. The first example in the appendix illustrates these ideas in a project context. Table 10.2 compares the value measurement practices between traditional and agile methodologies.

Module 1—Discussion for Critical Thinking

Many agile practitioners would say the metrics and measurements for tracking accumulated value in the way we have described—and illustrated in the appendix—is not sufficiently lean for agile methods. Perhaps—but when working as a professional with other people's money, what other, more lean

Table 10.2 Value metrics comparison

Ag-PDLC Practice	PD-PDLC Practice	Commentary
The total monetized value of the opportunity is given in the business plan by the investment commitment and the total affordability cap		The business plan expresses the value proposition of the business, even if all the detailed requirements are not known
Value is planned only over the duration of the current planning wave	Value is planned for the whole project up-front	By Agile Principle 2, requirements are encouraged to change even late in the project
The project baseline is planned in detail only for the current planning wave	The project baseline is planned for the entire project	Agile planners plan for the segment of the timeline where the requirements are stabilized
Requirements are not specifically valued, since requirements change between iterations	Requirements are valued in the sense that the work plan holds all the deliverables traceable to requirements	The embedded product master on each agile team will direct the team only towards valuable, important, and timely requirements
The outcomes are valued	Each deliverable is valued	**Value to the business is not dependent on the project methodology**

metrics would you suggest that will give the sponsor confidence that money and resources are being applied efficiently and effectively?

Module 2: Burn-down Charts and Value Scorecards

It's all about getting a handle on what's left to be done

Module 2—Objectives

- Discuss and explain the burn-down chart as a project management tool
- Discuss and explain the WIP chart, also as a project management tool

The Burn-down Chart

Somewhat different from traditional practices, agile projects usually maintain some version of these two valuation management tools:

1. A *burn-down chart*—sometimes done upside down as a *burn-up chart*—measures backlog completed (a.k.a. burned) and backlog remaining, usually in hours of effort.[10]
2. A *WIP chart* that shows the status of work in process, whether following a Kanban process or not.

Since neither of these charts is intended to directly show the preferred sequence of work within a backlog, usually a planning chart showing sequence of remaining backlog is maintained.

- Such sequence planning may have as inputs, functional or technical constraints—or planning inputs may be a matter of customer priority.
- Since sequence is dynamic, and subject to customer demand as well as other project factors and constraints, a virtual or physical whiteboard is commonly used to keep all the backlog constituents in their proper place in the development or construction queue.

Burn-down Chart Characteristics

The burn-down chart—sometimes implemented as a burn-down table of values rather than a chart of values—has these characteristics and features:

- **Remaining hours:** This is a plot of remaining hours (or effort) versus the project timeline. Usually remaining hours is the vertical scale; the project timeline is the horizontal scale.
- **Velocity:** Unless there is information to the contrary, the slope of the plot is the team's velocity benchmark in units of remaining hours per unit of the project timeline.
- **Discontinuous plot:** As the backlog changes because of new or abandoned items, and the accumulation of technical debt, the plot may have discontinuities as remaining hours step up or down as the backlog steps up or down.
- **Planning plot:** Before work starts, a planning or target plot is made; this plot is of uniform slope and at the team velocity.

Work sequence: There is no work unit sequence shown on the burn-down chart. Sequence is maintained on the WIP board.

Retrospective planning: After the project begins, all estimates and plans about revising the burn-down chart are reviewed during the retrospective review at the end of each iteration or release. Some teams schedule a separate meeting specifically to clean, refurbish, or reorganize the backlog. Like any database, over time it becomes untidy.

Figure 10.2 shows a typical burn-down chart. Perhaps the hardest concept to grasp when looking at Figure 10.2 is that the remaining hours are not what's left in the budget, nor are they some effort derived from percent complete, but rather the remaining hours are the hours of effort required to finish and achieve the status of *done*, as evaluated in the retrospective reviews.

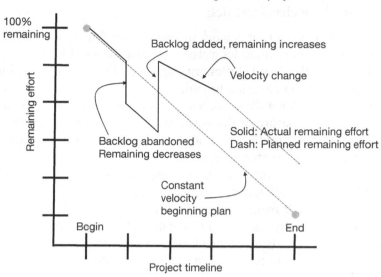

Burn down chart shows remaining effort vs. project timeline

Figure 10.2　Burn-down chart

Burn-down Chart Example

A simple example of a burn-down applied to a project is provided in the Appendix to this chapter. In it, you will see that value accumulates as the backlog is burned down and the remaining hours (a.k.a. remaining effort) march toward zero.

In contrast to the burn-down chart is its close cousin the burn-up chart. The advantage of the burn-up chart, the so-called inverted chart, is that it is a true value accumulation chart. Value accumulation starts at zero, meaning that no value has been attained—and ends when the last backlog object is delivered and *done*.

The WIP Chart

When the team begins work on a specific story or use case from the backlog, the sequence of work steps and work status of each entity is maintained on a WIP chart or table.[11]

WIP Chart Characteristics

There are multiple ways to build and maintain a WIP chart or table, but all versions share these characteristics:

- Each backlog item that is work in process is uniquely identified.
- Each backlog item includes a story, use case, or specification.
- There is a defined and stationary sequence of steps for a backlog item to traverse from beginning to end.
- All items may not follow the same sequence; thus, the sequence may depend on the nature of the entity and its development needs.
- There may be a timeline associated with the sequence, but usually not. Usually, the time metrics are:
    - ◆ Time of entry into a particular sequence step
    - ◆ Time accumulated at a sequence step
    - ◆ Time of exit from a sequence step
- Items can be abandoned at any step; held at any step for some external condition to be satisfied; moved to the next step when the step criteria is satisfied; and retired at the end of the sequence.

WIP Chart Example

Figure 10.3 shows a WIP chart. In the Kanban methodology, the WIP chart is the Kanban board. There are several points to note from Figure 10.3 that are explained below in the section on management actions.

Management Actions

There are several management actions attendant to the WIP chart:

- **WIP limit:** Only so many balls can be in the air at one time, so the number of backlog items that can be started and kept in a WIP status is limited. There are practical considerations, but often a WIP limit is a matter of project or team policy, rendered according to experience.
- **Criteria for advancement:** Moving from one step to another is sometimes moving from one workstation to another, and that next workstation may be remote or virtual. Thus, a WIP item should be *promoted* from one step to the next only according to some criteria determined for each step.
- **Feedback:** WIP processes should not be open loop, meaning backlog items are started down the WIP sequence with no feedback. This is especially so if the workstations are virtual or remote. Often systems or process without feedback are not stable and prone to chaotic or unpredicted performance. At the very least, feedback is needed in order to manage WIP limit, and to correct errors before they propagate further.

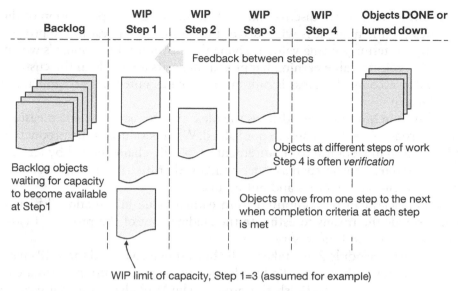

| Backlog | WIP Step 1 | WIP Step 2 | WIP Step 3 | WIP Step 4 | Objects DONE or burned down |

Feedback between steps

Objects at different steps of work
Step 4 is often *verification*

Backlog objects waiting for capacity to become available at Step1

Objects move from one step to the next when completion criteria at each step is met

WIP limit of capacity, Step 1=3 (assumed for example)

Work in process (WIP) dashboard to support Kanban process shows objects at various steps of work

Figure 10.3 Work in process

- **Verification:** When an item is *done* and to be retired, some verification of functionality and/or performance is required. The test script, use case, story, and specification are all applicable to verification.
- *Linkage to burn-down chart:* When an item is *done*, the hours remaining are deleted from the burn-down backlog; a revised estimate of the WIP and the un-started backlog is made and transferred to the burn-down chart.

Module 2—Discussion for Critical Thinking

In many ways, the burn-down chart and WIP chart, in concert with the projects synchronizing milestones, can take the place of project task-level schedules. Does this fact give you pause? Is it apparent that you can run the project off of a spreadsheet rather than a scheduling tool?

Summary and Takeaway

The theme of this chapter is that agile projects earn value by delivering value incrementally, periodically, affordably, and according to the priority of the customer.

From Module 1, we discuss and explain that value is a perception of the business; in the main, it is what drives the business to invest in the project. In simplest terms, earning value is giving the customer their money's worth. In agile projects, value earning happens as deposits are made in the customer's value account. Progress is only measurable as outcomes accumulate in production.

Also from Module 1, we discuss the ideas that for earned-value measurements, requirements per se, are not valued. What is valued is the production of the team in response to requirements, typically characterized by an outcome-oriented metric, such as story points. Other metrics are usable so long as they focus on outcomes and not inputs.

Efficiencies can be computed from earned-value information. Efficiencies provide the means to estimate the landing spot of the project. If close enough, no action is necessary.

And, from Module 2, we take up the burn-down chart and the WIP chart. The burn-down chart is applied to the task of keeping a current estimate of the hours remaining to finish the project. The WIP chart is a tool used to regulate the flow and sequence of work in process.

Appendix

First Example: Cost-of-Value (Earned Value) Example

Business Case

The $100K Gizmo Business Case: $100K is to be invested in the product development of a Gizmo, due to be completed incrementally in three releases contained within one planning horizon.

Planning narrative:

- Within one planning horizon, three releases—Releases 1, 2, and 3—are planned for $25K, $25K, and $50K worth of features and functions at milestones M1, M2, and M3, respectively.
- Collectively, these dollars and dates are called the performance measurement baseline (PMB, or project plan).
- The project begins at Milestone 0 (M0), and ends at M3.

Example Milestone Results

M1 Results:

- *Project management* reports that the intended backlog features and functions due at M1 were delivered and put into production—that is, *done.*

- *Cost accounting* reports that $35K has been spent, $10K more than the $25K that was planned.
- *Project administration* reports investment efficiency, in terms of *cost-of-value efficiency*—dollar of value per dollar of cost—is below expectation. CoV efficiency at M1 is calculated from two factors: (1) Cost = $35K and (2) Value released at M1: $25K. Calculated efficiency: 25/35 = 71%

Release 1 results at Milestone 1		
Scorecard	**Metric**	**Commentary or measurement**
Project management	*done*	All backlog *done*
Cost accounting	Actual cost	$35K actual, $25K budget
Project administration	CoV efficiency	Efficiency: budget/actual, or 25/35 = 71% (dollar of value per dollar of cost)

Team members reflect on lessons learned at M1; efforts are made to improve CoV.

The project team works onward to M2. At M2 the project plan scorecard is examined again:

M2 Results:

Release 2 results at Milestone 2		
Scorecard	**Metric**	**Commentary or measurement**
Project management	*done*	All backlog *done*
Cost accounting	Actual cost	$25K actual, $25K budget
Project administration	CoV efficiency	25/25 = 100%

M3 Results:

Release 3 results at Milestone 3		
Scorecard	**Metric**	**Commentary or measurement**
Project management	*done*	All backlog *done*
Cost accounting	Actual cost	$45K actual, $50K budget
Project administration	CoV efficiency	50/45 = 111%

Overall Project Results

For the three releases in aggregate in the one planning horizon:

Total results at end of horizon at M3		
Scorecard	**Metric**	**Commentary or measurement**
Project management	*done*	All backlog *done*
Cost accounting	Actual cost	$35K + 25 +45 = $105K actual, $100K budget
Project administration	CoV efficiency	100/105 = 95%

Second Example: Burn-down Chart (Remaining Hours, Value Earned) Example

Business Case

The Gizmo Product Business Case: Resources are to be invested in a product development of a Gizmo, due to be completed incrementally in three releases within one planning horizon.

Planning narrative:

- Within one planning horizon, three releases—Releases 1, 2, and 3—are planned, having backlogs of 25, 25, and 50 stories at milestones M1, M2, and M3, respectively
- Collectively, these stories and their resource hours are called the performance measurement baseline (PMB, or project plan):
  - ◆ 400 hours required to achieve M1
  - ◆ 450 hours required to achieve M2
  - ◆ 600 hours required to achieve M3
  - ◆ 1450 total hours estimated to clear the backlog for all three releases
- The project begins at M0 and ends at M3.

The following tables at each milestone show the evolving project management narrative and metric results.

Example Milestone Results

M0 Plan:
   At M0, no work has been done; the project is ready to start.

PMB at M0, beginning of project		
Scorecard	**Metric**	**Commentary or measurement**
Project management	Stories remaining (not *done*)	100 stories remaining, 100% not done
Cost accounting	Actual hours consumed	0 hours of 1450 consumed
Project administration	CoV efficiency Estimated hours remaining	Plan/Actual, % efficiency 1450 hours remaining

M1 Results: (as an example)

- *Project management* reports that the intended backlog features and functions due at M1 were delivered and put into production—that is, *25 stories are burned down* and *done*.
- *Cost accounting* reports that 450 hours were burned, 50 more than the 400 planned.
- *Project administration* reports investment efficiency, in terms of *cost-of-value efficiency*—hours of value per actual hours—is below expectation: value released at M1: 400; cost 450 hours. Calculated efficiency: 400/450 = 89%.

M1 Retrospective:

At M1 retrospective, a reestimate is made of the hours remaining as part of the retrospective of the release at M1, and as part of the backlog planning for Release 2 at M2. The reestimate takes into account technical debt from Release 1 as well as an adjustment in throughput for Release 2 based on the experience of Release 1.

Reestimate at M1 after Release 1 retrospective		
Scorecard	**Metric**	**Commentary or measurement**
Technical debt from Release 1	Technical tasks requiring resource hours	100 hours estimated for debt tasks
Throughput adjustment for Releases 2 and 3	Adjust for 89% efficiency	(450+600)/0.89 = 1180
Hours remaining	Debt + remaining stories for Releases 2 and 3	100 + 1180 = 1280 hours remaining

M2 Results: (as an example)

M2 Results		
Scorecard	**Metric**	**Commentary or measurement**
Project management	Stories remaining (not *done*)	No Release 2 stories remaining; all *done*, and all tech *done*
Cost accounting	Actual hours consumed	575 hours consumed
Project administration	CoV efficiency Estimated hours remaining	(450 + 100)/575 = 96% efficiency To be determined at M2 retrospective

M2 Retrospective:

It is learned from the product owner that:

- Ten of 50 stories are to be dropped from Release 3, accounting for 200 of 600 hours being dropped

- Five new stories are to be added at a cost of 150 hours

It is learned from project management that there remains 140 hours of technical debt from Release 2 that must be completed in Release 3

Reestimate at M2 after Release 2 retrospective		
Scorecard	**Metric**	**Commentary or measurement**
Technical debt from Release 2	Technical tasks requiring resource hours	140 hours estimated for debt tasks
Throughput adjustment for Release 3	Adjust for 96% efficiency for hours remaining to M3	(600 - 200 + 150)/.96 = 550/.96 = 573
Hours remaining	Debt + remaining stories for Release 3 – stories abandoned + stories added	140 + 573 = 713 hours remaining to M3

M3 Results at end of project:

M3 Results		
Scorecard	**Metric**	**Commentary or measurement**
Project management	Stories remaining (not *done*)	Release 3 stories and tech debt remaining; all *done*
Cost accounting	Actual hours consumed	700 hours actually consumed
Project administration	CoV efficiency Estimated hours remaining CoV entire project	(600 - 200 + 150 + 140) / 700 = 99% efficiency Zero hours remaining (1450 – 200 +150) / (450 + 575 + 700) = 81%

Chapter Endnotes

1. To simplify matters, the terms customer, end user, and business are used interchangeably on the basis that the business represents the customer interests with high fidelity.

The business includes the sponsors and stakeholders. Sponsors have a direct responsibility for the business case; stakeholders have a responsibility for the balanced scorecard.

Customers are beneficiaries of the project; customers can be internal and part of the business, or external. Users are functional experts. Users are part of the customer community, but many customers who set the value proposition are not users.

2. *Design Thinking* is a term of art. Many are accredited with its coinage— early on, by Herbert Simon writing in *The Sciences of the Artificial* in 1969, but

probably most prominently by David Kelley, founder of product design firm IDEO.

3. Goodpasture, *Managing Projects for Value*, 6.

4. "Free search" was one of the first large-scale free-value applications, but before that "free" was pioneered by the integrated "free browser" that put "for sale" browsers out of business.

5. The reader is reminded that this book integrates several agile concepts from different methodologies. A focus on output is ubiquitous. Velocity is an XP idea; a story point, also from XP, is one of several ways to dimension throughput, but it is the dimension used throughout the book.

6. Anderson, *Agile Management for Software Engineering*, 15-20.

7. Value and cost are really quite different. For instance, a manager might plan a certain cost to render a backlog into production, only to find that it's possible to reuse objects already developed. The manager can claim the planned value, but a much lower cost of value.

8. Earned schedule is a relatively new calculation in the earned-value space, having been brought to prominence in 2003 by Walter Lipke in a paper entitled "Schedule is Different" published by the Project Management Institute in their magazine entitled *The Measurable News*, Summer 2003: 31-34.

Rather than calculate schedule variance as the difference between the PV and EV at a point in time, earned schedule calculates the time difference between EV measured at a point in time—a point called the earned schedule (ES)—and the time on the project calendar when the EV should have been earned, a point called the actual time (AT).

9. The reasoning is as follows: a standard team with a fixed staff costs a certain number of dollars and is benchmarked to produce some number of story points. Cost can be accounted for in dollars or in the equivalent currency of story points. If additional staff is needed, then the staff cost is made proportional to some number of story points and added to the team's cost in story points, even though the throughput remains constant. If tools and other non-staff expenses are needed, their cost is made proportional to some equivalent number of story points and added to the actual cost. In effect, a relative cost is used in the scorecards. Knowing the actual dollars and keeping track of actual dollars is not necessary unless it is convenient. However, in the end, all units on the scorecard must be similarly dimensioned so that the mathematics are consistent.

10. And, of course, when we say "team," we could just as well say any organizational unit that is working on a backlog. Thus, the chart is useful at various levels of scale.

11. Per se, the WIP chart or table is not a sequence plan for the backlog at large, only for the sequence of work steps for an entity on which work has begun.

11

Scaling Up and Contracting

Agile methods are scalable; within limitations, agile methods are amenable to the advantages of contracts and virtual teams.

We must not, in trying to think about how we can make a big difference, ignore the small daily differences we can make which, over time, add up to big differences that we often cannot foresee.

Marian Wright Edelman

Agile methods started out as a great way for small teams to manage their affairs and get quality work done. In fact, the Agile Manifesto and the Agile Principles seem optimum in just that way. But success on a small scale makes one wonder if agile methods can scale up to larger projects requiring multiple teams, virtual teams, or even contracted teams. Within limitations, the answer is yes.

Module 1: Scale Amplifies Every Problem
Scale means large reach, breadth, and extent

Module 1—Objectives
- Discuss and explain the effects of scale on the customer, on communications, and on other project objectives and relationships
- Discuss and explain scaling down—getting to smaller

Big Picture Issues

All software projects are uncertain in scope and complex in their structure—that is the nature of dealing with intangibles. With a system of intangibles, it is hard to imagine all the scope, even scope on a small scale—but it is even harder to imagine how all the scope elements really work in context, because there are so many interrelationships, and because imagination itself is not bounded or managed. Even though not all complex systems are large-scale systems, all large-scale systems are complex. Scale means large reach, breadth, and extent, typically addressing a broad customer community with a cacophony of input about how things should work.

A summary of the macro issues of complexity and architecture that confront large-scale endeavors is given in Table 11.1.

Large-scale efforts cause tensions between teams. Teams are no longer independent; they must cooperate in networks and honor dependencies from team to team. Teams are required to yield some autonomy for the larger objective. The material in Table 11.2 summarizes these points and shows the general mitigations and extensions that are peculiar to agile methods.

Table 11.1   Big picture issues—complexity and architecture

Issue	Mitigation	Agile mitigation
Complex systems span hardware, software, and their integration.	Implement work specialization and division of labor[1]	• Identify professionals with varied work specialties and put them on the same team, seeking redundancy and synergy in the same team • Redundancy means teams need not work in assembly-line fashion with handoffs among members • Synergy is the leading indicator of cooperative and collective work
No one can keep the whole system in mind	Document top-level architecture	• Add an architect role to the project and teams • Diagram, or otherwise use models, to document system architecture
Complexity has many points of influence and control, some of which self-conflict	Disallow certain system states and chaos responses	• System engineer for safety and stability • Maintain a rhythm of red-green-refactor to prove working designs and maintain high levels of quality • Teams must honor sequencing and regression testing • Rebuild the system often, daily if possible

[1]Division of labor is perhaps the oldest mitigation. Adam Smith saw the need to have work specialties, a division of labor so to speak, in order to get any but the simplest work done well with high quality, something that he wrote about in his 18th-century book *The Wealth of Nations*.

Table 11.2 Big picture issues—teams, customers, and business

Issue	Mitigation	Agile mitigation
Cost is very sensitive to the N^2 effect[1]	Relentlessly remove arbitrary complexity	• Manage the N^2 effect as part of the budget–cost gap on the project balance sheet • Make architecture maximally cohesive but minimally coupled to reduce friction in large systems • Automate tests to quickly evaluate design at least every day for unnecessary redundancy and complexity that drives cost and inefficiencies
Team-level optimizations conflict with bigger picture	Architect from the top down to minimize constraints Place incentives on enterprise optimization	• Reevaluate architecture after every release; make corrections and adjustments for the next release • Include architect in the team-of-teams
Customer and business priorities conflict with technical priorities	Prioritize technical feasibility and logical sequencing ahead of customer needs	• Embed customers in development teams to improve information exchange and build trust in the development process • Manage priorities by a team-of-teams facilitated by the project manager and architect • Escalate priority unresolved disputes to the sponsor or governance council
Customer and business constituencies are large and self-conflicting with no anointed leader	Seek top-level executive ownership of the customer and business community	• Set up coaching and mentorship for customers and business embedded in teams • Set up team-of-teams for customers and business to communicate and coordinate

[1] N^2 effect refers to the exponential increase in the number of communication paths as the number, N, of communicators increases.

Customer Scale

Very likely, the first hurdle to be overcome is defining the customer community.

- **Large-scale projects inevitably reach many disparate constituents:** Trying to find focus and a common purpose among them is hard enough; finding a group of product masters that can accurately and effectively represent all of the customer, user, market, and sales issues is harder— often hampered by the functional manager's real inability to commit resources to the project for the duration.

- **Mitigations for customer scale are situational:** The executive team often must intervene to establish priorities. It is rare that day-to-day business key performance indicators are relieved to make way for the project, only adding to the conflicts between providing good people to the project and retaining good people in the business.

As gaps are opened by assignment of staff to the project, it is inevitable that someone must take a risk, much like the effort to bridge the gap on the project balance sheet. There is no formula, no prescription. Each organization must make its own choices. However, agile methods are not effective without close customer attention; without customer integration on the teams, priorities and adaption are more likely to be technically driven, raising the specter of a technical project rather than a business project.

The N^2 Effect

Scale amplifies complexity exponentially; the simplest software systems are, by nature, complex, so large-scale software is extremely complex.[1] This phenomenon is known as the N^2 effect—sometimes written N2. The N^2 effect is named for the mathematical formula that describes how the number of interaction possibilities increases by nearly the square of the number of system components. Scale makes even small things seem larger and more complex; systems, networks, organizations, and environments are hard to imagine and keep in mind.

The N^2 effect brings the difference between detail complexity and system complexity into the picture. Detail complexity is about individual objects and effects. It may be possible for a customer or a developer to keep in mind many objects and object details, such as colors, buttons, fonts, fields, authorities, names, and so on. However, system complexity is about how these objects interact, and interact differently according to a myriad of conditions that change with user intervention and system inputs.[2]

System complexity is much more difficult to imagine, much less keep up with. Therefore, even small increases in detail complexity lead to N^2 larger-system complexity. Thus, the need for simplicity—that is, the simplest complexity possible—is quite real since it is a high-leverage parameter on development cost, schedule, and post-release support. Figure 11.1 illustrates the interconnectivity phenomenon; Figure 11.2 shows how close the approximation is for N larger than 20.

Among correspondents, there are N × (N — 1) potential communication paths to exchange and acknowledge information, and to interface procedures

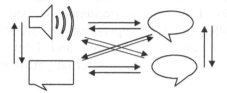

As shown above 12 = 4 × 3

Figure 11.1   The N^2 effect

For large N, the approximation of N × (N – 1) is N^2 as shown below in the curves for each that nearly overlay each other

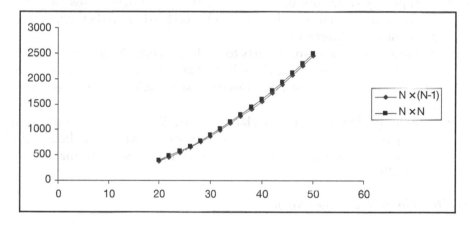

Figure 11.2 N^2 for large N

Getting to Smaller

Critics note that neither the Agile Manifesto nor the Agile Principles address personal and organizational discipline, product and support architecture, or proven engineering practices, which are all necessary to do serious work on an enterprise scale. To be sure, there are elements of truth in what they say.[3] Critics often charge that small team methods do not work well in the context of contracts; or when there is no co-located environment; or when there is no face-to-face contact and communication; or when teams are required to honor dependencies with other teams and projects. But there are mitigations for each of those charges.

The trick is to translate scale into something that appears smaller and more manageable. In all too many situations, the friction of all the moving parts overwhelms the opportunity. This very phenomenon motivates deconstructing the system into smaller, nearly independent increments, exposing internal functions that might have been obscured, and defining object interfaces that are more easily manipulated than internal pathways and procedures.

Decompose into Smaller Units

The proven mitigation for working with systems of large scale is to break them down into smaller units, to encapsulate or abstract the unit details to the smallest number of interface points, and then to rejoin the units at their interfaces. Issues that need to be addressed are:

- **Complexity is disguised:** The larger perspective may be lost, and the interactions of smaller-scale objects may be hard to predict, when they are rejoined or integrated.
- **There are now many small parts to be developed:** The number of parts could be quite large, even though they are individually simpler, more understandable, and less risky. Decomposition adds to detail complexity.
- **The N^2 problem at the interfaces grows:** With a larger number of small parts, there are many more interfaces to address—although the interfaces are simpler, more understandable, and easier to manage individually.

Scaling Up and Scaling Down

Scaling up and scaling down do not usually follow the same path, cost the same amount, or present the same issues. In physical systems, one version of the phenomenon is called hysteresis. It is caused by time lags between input and output.[4] In management systems, there are effects of bias, resistance to change, and sensitivities to loss of prestige or position. In large-scale systems, there are issues of architecture and dependency, in which an object or function may not be made smaller simply because of its place in the architecture.

Scale-by-contract

One way to achieve scale is by contracting for additional staff, expanded capacity, or unique capabilities, thus, scale-by-contract has to be considered by project managers. But contracting has its own special problems. Contracts, for instance, are adversarial by nature in their party-to-party relationships.

Trusting and being adversarial are opposite sides of the coin. To increase one is to reduce the other, but almost always, contracts increase the adversity.

The typical project contract is invariably high ceremony, low trust, expensive, and untimely to administer—all in contrast to the objectives of agile. Contracts invariably add to overhead and dilute lean practices, for reasons such as:

- Meetings must be scheduled
- Agenda and content must be prepared
- Parties must be brought together from disparate locations
- Homework is to be done before coming together
- Surprises are hard to avoid; surprises dilute trust and add to the adversarial environment

Contracts require documentation. Documentation substitutes for personal real-time discussion, debate, and decision. It is hard to apply the agile idea of *just enough* when writing documents. Documentation tilts toward plan-driven; documentation requires that some things be thought through in advance and not left to just-in-time.

Module 1—Discussion for Critical Thinking

Person-to-person real-time embedded participation is the cornerstone of all agile teams. It seems counterintuitive to substitute remote relationships for a real-time environment, especially if in a time zone half way around the world. Good documentation will be needed to carry communications beyond the boundaries of face-to-face. Do these things mean that agile methods are incompatible not only with contracts but also with virtual teams?

Module 2: Networks Enable Large Scale

Networks—effective coupling of myriad scope and communications

Module 2—Objectives

- Discuss and explain management networks as a means to address scale

Communicating in the Large-scale Network

In prior chapters there was material that addressed scaling practices of multiple teams working together on the same project. Table 11.3 gathers those ideas together.

Table 11.3   Summary of team scaling practices

Team scaling practice	Commentary
Multiple work streams	• Each work stream addresses some aspect of the project scope • Work streams can be dedicated to infrastructure, technology, product development, post-production support readiness, training, supply chain, project management, and others
Network of teams	• A network couples the activities of multiple teams to produce a collective outcome • Networks are employed when the productivity of one team is inadequate to satisfy the value proposition in a timely fashion • There may be teams that are somewhat more specialized than the multifunctional performance units
Team-of-teams	• The team-of-teams is the group responsible for coordinating and communicating activities among the teams on a daily basis • It may be necessary to form a steering committee to coordinate between work groups
Network buffer	• Buffers are periods of time for which no activity is scheduled • Buffers absorb unknown and unplanned events and activities • Buffers are the times that can be used for the schedule overrun of a team that needs a bit more time to complete its iteration • Buffer time is typically managed as a project resource by the project manager.

Documents Support Networks

Although the Agile Manifesto states a preference for person-to-person communication over documentation, the manifesto doesn't declare that documentation is unnecessary. The simple fact is that with a large number of teams, multiple work streams, and a large number of participants, the person-to-person dialogue necessary to communicate and distribute all the information about the system quickly becomes impractical.

Accuracy, timeliness, and completeness are all put in harm's way with scale. To mitigate these effects, documentation becomes more of a necessity. Indeed, documentation can satisfy many project agendas simultaneously. Jim Highsmith, one of the original 17 authors from the Manifesto Group, writes that this documentation:

- Supports collaboration and communication
- Enhances knowledge transfer
- Preserves historical information
- Assists ongoing product enhancement
- Fulfills regulatory and legal requirements[5]

High-scale projects require documentation for team operations. Examples of operational documents are architecture, product design, and test scripts and scenarios. Electronic templates are lean tools used to gather the minimum information elements (MIE). Document management systems that regulate access, versions, and privileges are effective and lean for keeping a library according to the conventions of the project that dictate which information elements can be simply comments in software code and which are to be committed to written documentation.[6]

Whiteboards and War Rooms

Much of the literature on agile methods expounds on the whiteboard and the virtues of story cards written on index cards.[7] As temporary expedients for personal group settings, there is probably no better method, but results and conclusions need more permanence. Most teams do not retain the index story cards; except for the test script—there is no documentation of the requirement at the story level.

Yet, when working in networks, portability of information must be considered. Physical war rooms, whiteboards, and index cards are for local use and consumption. In networks, electronic scorecards and dashboards are the preferred means to communicate widely, accurately, and with timeliness about information that is temporal, time sensitive, or of general interest.

Work Dependencies in the Network

Working successfully in a network requires honoring the dependencies between the teams. Honoring dependencies means respecting everyone's time, finishing iterations as scheduled, and delivering scope as planned to avoid idle time until work can be sequenced for completion. The identification and coordination of these dependencies is the agenda of the team-of-teams.

Networks impose limitations on customers and users working on development teams. Customers and users working in a network give up some latitude to reset priorities and to introduce new requirements because the priorities of other teams must be considered. Optimization at the team level gives way to optimization at the network level.

Networks for Management

Networks facilitate a large number of people working on the same project. Networks have these attributes for structure and control:

- Nodes, where work gets done, having points of entry and exit for communications—typically a team, but a node could be a person in a virtual team

- Pathways and means to bind together nodes in a common community; and means to carry communication between nodes, regulated by protocols—some formal and some informal and unspoken
- Administrative tools to keep the network going; implement redundancy and workarounds for outages; and provide security, privacy, and access control

Networks are more agile than ever before: adaptive, informally lean, and operationally efficient. Recent societal changes account for many of the ways networks apply in the project context:

- Widespread access and adoption of instant messaging and wireless connectivity has given unprecedented pace and democracy to communications.
- The cultural acceptance of informality in business relationships has flattened the operating model and made it acceptable to skip an echelon when communicating. Flatness encourages lateral relationships; lateral relationships speed communications and transfer information more accurately.

The web and electronic networking have raised expectations that information should be readily available and easily accessed, used, and applied, and that feedback response should be nearly instantaneous. In system terms, there is now an expectation that the loop should close; action begets acknowledgment and follow-up in the network.

Workflow

Most projects will want to introduce a workflow process to regulate activity and to communicate the MIE for various actions. For example, feedback from users during acceptance testing is commonly gathered, analyzed, archived, and regulated by the workflow. Templates provide a way for users to enter the MIE; formatted information in templates is routed via a governance process, as discussed elsewhere in this book.

Tactical information in the team network is provided by a number of artifacts:

- Templates for architectural, technical, and functional designs and configuration data
- Project backlog, release backlog, and the team's iteration backlog
- Progress charts consisting of the Scrum burn-down list—a list of items completed and yet to be completed—or the XP burn-up list, a similar idea

- Trend charts of progress and accumulated value calculations
- Other scorecards and dashboards

Module 2—Discussion for Critical Thinking

How would you scale a war room, which is very much about visualization of the solution and real-time collaboration? Would you dispense with the concept altogether and substitute some other practice that is more attuned to the time delays and communication restrictions, or would you look for a tool that would extend the war room virtually?

Module 3: Virtual Teams Expand Throughput

Adding capacity and capability by emulating a real team

Module 3—Objectives

- Discuss and explain how virtual teams add capacity to a project
- Examine factors that influence management and performance of virtual teams

Emulating a Real Team

A virtual team is one whose members are not all co-located. Indeed, the members may not be, and often are not, in the same organization, business unit, or time zone. Virtual teams are characterized by having membership with different environments and culture; membership that works at different times and locations; and membership that may have differing views of priorities and imperatives. Nevertheless, virtual teams are a way to expand the throughput of the network by incorporating members that cannot otherwise be present together.

Communicating among Virtual Teams

Virtual teams often begin by emulating the behavior and circumstances of real teams. The first thought is the character of communications.

- Real teams can handle a much greater N^2 communication intensity because much of person-to-person communication is nonverbal.
- Nonverbal is a very high-bandwidth channel that is capable of communicating a large-information message instantly, although the message is often highly encoded and subject to inaccurate decoding.

- Verbal communications are more easily digested if the context is understood simply by being present. It is much easier to sort out the cacophony of discussion if face and voice and context are put together.

Consequently, when planning for virtual teams, bear in mind these factors:

- That virtual teams do not have the luxury of infinite bandwidth
- Their more restricted channels tend to have less richness, lower throughput, and throughput that moves more slowly
- There is a natural tendency to filter messages and only communicate the least complicated message

Electronic communications is the most available countermeasure. Everything from a constantly open conference line, to instant messaging, video linkages, webinars, and a common dashboard that operates like a social networking wall are effective.

The impact of less communication on velocity is not intuitive. Some teams relish the hubbub of real-time communications, and others do not. Some miss the osmosis of casual communication as a way to keep on top of things, and some prefer more regimented approaches.

Assigning Work to Virtual Teams

The release and then the iteration planning meetings are the agile mechanisms for assigning work. All members of the teams attend. The same applies to a virtual team. The operational difference is that the whiteboard and index cards are replaced by an electronic whiteboard shared by a webinar application and an audiovisual conference.

Assigning work to virtual teams should follow this simple rule: partition work according to natural boundaries that minimize and simplify interfaces. To that end, a quotation by Albert Einstein is instructive: "Make everything as simple as possible, but not simpler." By this he advised that arbitrary complexity holds no value and may even contribute to inefficient and ineffective solutions. But oversimplification is also hazardous. Effective solutions are impossible to build from the too-small parts.

Tracking Progress and Identifying Problems

Two agile practices for tracking progress and identifying problems are earn-burn charts and trending graphs developed from the earn-burn data. Other progress-and-problem trackers are testing scorecards, pipeline scorecards,[8] and daily stand-up meetings.

The daily stand-up meeting is affected by the communications that are unique to virtual teams. The less-efficient electronic channels may have to be compensated by extending the time box of the daily stand-up meeting. Nevertheless, the usual rules that require everyone to speak, and that limit those speeches to two minutes, are still applicable.

Commitment and Accountability

Agile practices demand total commitment and accountability, both for personal and for team achievements; no less is expected of virtual teams.

Incentives and Rewards

It is obvious on the face that celebrations are more possible and more effective with co-located teams. In the virtual space, rewards are more personal and made specific to the situation—especially if virtual team members are physically challenged. In some situations, local functional managers take over some of the project manager and team leader responsibilities to ensure proper recognition.

Module 3—Discussion for Critical Thinking

The use of virtual teams in a management network is quite ordinary in the software business, but, sometimes virtual teams work too slowly. What would you do to increase the pace and throughput, if you were asked to accelerate the schedule on a large-scale project?

Module 4: Agile-by-contract Enables Scale

Yes, you can buy capacity and capability by contracting scope to others

Module 4—Objectives

- Discuss and explain the many factors that bear on the usefulness of contracts in agile projects

Contract Objectives

In one sense, every agile project operates under the auspices of a contract because the business case is a contract in all but legal form. As it happens in all bilateral agreements, there are times when the sponsor-project relationship becomes challenging, the vision is not clear enough, or the gap on the project balance sheet widens unfavorably.

The challenge becomes greater with the decision to contract with a provider—now the relationship is expanded to sponsor-project-provider. At each juncture, there is the possibility for misunderstanding, obfuscation—deliberately or unwittingly—and misalignment of aims and means.

Why contract? There are several reasons, all of which are forms of risk mitigation and resource management:

- **Capability:** To gain access to people with skills and methods that are otherwise unavailable to the project
- **Feasibility:** To acquire deliverables from a lower risk source
- **Capacity:** To temporarily increase production when the need for long-term capacity does not yet exist

Contracting is motivated by a business calculation that a contract is more beneficial than to do it yourself—there is a cost and there is a benefit, each to be calculated in light of risks. In order for the contract to pay off, the cost and benefit estimates must be realistic about the supplier's capacity and capability, and about the project's capability to convey needs and wants effectively to the supplier.

Much can go awry. It is risky business to communicate through a contract channel about fluid and unknown requirements. It is also risky to assume the contractor can do a good job in the agile environment, or a better job than the project can do for itself. In short, there is nothing firm and fixed about a contract for technology work on complex undertakings. Be on guard to not make a risky proposition worse by contracting inappropriately. Here are important points to grasp:

Contract Points to Consider
• A contract in any form is a risk management tool for transfer of risk • Every transfer of risk comes at a price—requiring cost and benefit calculations • Every contract requires exchanges of information between parties of dissimilar context—culture, accepted practices, management biases, and perhaps language

	Five elements of a contract
A project management tip	It is generally understood that the following five elements need to be in place, either orally or in writing, before there is a legal and enforceable contract: 1. There must be a true offer to do business by the project. 2. There must be a corresponding acceptance of the offer. 3. There must be a specified consideration for the work to be performed. Consideration does not need to be in terms of dollars. 4. The supplier must have the capacity to perform as represented in their acceptance offer. 5. The statement of work must be for a legal activity; it is improper to contract for illegal activities.

Contracts through the Risk Management Lens

Risk is managed by both parties to the contract. Each follows a similar process:

- Identify risks
- Estimate and rank risks by impact
- Estimate and rank risks by likelihood
- Direct mitigation to the high-impact-with-high-likelihood risks first

A contract is another form of the project balance sheet:

- There is a business side
- There is a project side
- There is a gap between expectations and affordability on the one hand, and capability and capacity to meet expectations profitably on the other.

The gap is called risk.

With only top-level visionary requirements specified, there is no scope specification that is actionable without customer or end-user interpretation. Consequently, there can be no detailed estimate of cost, schedule, or even of the methods and tools that might be required. Any contract that is written has to account for these risks and establish risk premiums accordingly.

Contracting in any form cannot eliminate project risk; contracting can only make project risk more manageable. There are choices:

- The project manager may choose to retain some or most of the cost risk and only transfer the performance risk

- The project manager may choose to transfer both cost and performance risk

The risk premiums will be different according to choice—the more risk retained in the project, the lower the risk premium will be.

Even so, the project may not get what it expects. As an example, in a so-called fixed-price arrangement, the contractor may fail to perform, leaving the project with a schedule problem at the very least. The contractor may run into unforeseen feasibility problems, experience business failures elsewhere that affect the project, or be impacted by external threats, such as changes in regulations or acts of God.

Contracting Concepts for Cost and Results

Two concepts that underlie all contracted arrangements are shown in Table 11.4. One concept is around effort and results—the idea of completion as different from a best effort. The second concept is around cost responsibility—the idea of fixed price as different from cost reimbursable. Concepts of effort and results can be mixed and matched with different forms of cost responsibility to reduce risk and reward achievement.

Contracted Incentives and Rewards

Incentives and rewards motivate contractor teams just as they do with internal project teams. The common convention is first to apply incentives based on cost performance, and then based on value-added achievements. Some common arrangements are shown in Table 11.5 in the appendix. Also in the appendix to this chapter, Figure 11.3 illustrates sharing between the project and the contractor.

Contracting Relationships

Contracts establish relationships and provide the means and methods to transfer knowledge, data, and priorities. In return, the project benefits from the contractor's work, and the contractor benefits from the business relationship.

Contractors Have Values, Practices, and Methodology

Qualified contractors bring compatible methods and practice to the relationship; if contractors did not do this, they would not be selected as a provider. Qualified contractors also have their own values, and these may be

Table 11.4 Contracting concepts

Contracting concept	Commentary
Completion vs. best effort	• When pledging *completion*, the contractor commits to a finished product; typically the price is "fixed." • When pledging *best effort*, the contractor commits to making a good faith attempt to fulfill all the requirements with quality work, but makes no commitment to a finished product. Work continues as long as the contractor is paid for progress. • *Best effort* is the better choice when feasibility is unproven, requirements are incomplete, or the strategic direction is uncertain.
Fixed price vs. cost reimbursable	• Fixed-price contracts require the contractor to deliver a completed product at a price, including the risk premium, negotiated and agreed-to before work begins. • Fixed-price contracts are *completion* contracts. • Fixed-price contracts are the most lean to administer. • Fixed-price contracts transfer all the cost risk to the supplier for which the project is charged a relatively high risk premium. • Cost-reimbursable or cost-plus contracts pay the contractor's cost, usually at the invoice amount, and also pay a fee calculated separately from cost. • Cost-reimbursable contracts transfer very little of the project's cost risk to the contractor and require only a contractor's "best effort" toward completing the work. • The risk premium is very low, even to the point of no premium at all. • Cost-reimbursable contracts are not completion contracts. • Cost-reimbursable contracts are not as lean as fixed-price contracts; more administration and exchange of business data is necessary to be successful with cost-reimbursable contracts.
Time and materials (T&M)	• T&M is used to buy labor, typically by the hour, at a fixed price per hour. Expenses, tools, and supplies are usually reimbursed at cost. • There is no commitment to completion or even best effort. The contractor takes no project responsibility except to supply qualified people. • A risk premium is built into the hourly rate to cover the high cost of recruiting to fill turn-over.

different from the project. If one objective is to normalize values between the contractor and the project, some caution is advised: contracts are a poor vehicle to transfer values and culture (the things believed in and thought to be the right things to do).

Nevertheless, commitment and accountability are two values that really need to jump across to the contractor. Fortunately, contractors often mimic what they observe, seeking to minimize differences by absorbing their best customers' style of work to some degree. And of course, there is the carrot and stick: incentives and penalties are two means to get attention and drive behavior.

Some caution, however: W. Edwards Deming famously eschewed all slogans, exhortations, quantitative goals, and incentives. Since Deming, research has shown that incentives or penalties can affect behavior. But for either incentives or penalties to be effective, some conditions must be in place:

- Consequences must be obvious
- There must be widespread knowledge and understanding of the possibilities
- Effects must be felt immediately and be relevant
- Outcomes must meet social norms for fairness and reasonableness

Agile with Fixed-price Contracts

Firm-fixed-price (FFP) completion contracts are inappropriate for contracting agile projects.

- FFP completion requires an agreement on a price firmly decided up front for a set of unchanging deliverables; scope must be stable for a fixed-price determination.
- Conditions for FFP are not present in an agile project.

Even though FFP, as commonly applied in traditional methodology, is inappropriate, there are alternatives that are effective for agile contracts. One workable strategy is *fixed-price work orders*. In such a contract, the project first establishes a framework and then contracts for one iteration at a time, each such contract being a work order. To reduce administration and make such contracts timely, steps such as these are followed:

- A framework is created to provide basic contract services for the work orders
- The project team selects from the backlog for the contractor to evaluate and price
- Requirements—or backlog constituents—are frozen during the work order execution
- The work order contains *space* for velocity errors and for debt that may accumulate
- The project specifies a time box for the duration of the work order
- The contractor is paid a fixed price upon work-order completion

For a work-order scenario to be practical, the agile concept of the embedded user must be addressed in context of the contracted situation:

1. One possibility is to send a user from the project organization to the contractor for the duration of the time box. If the contractor is nearby, this arrangement may work well.
2. Another approach is to set up a dashboard and other access that provides an electronic emulation of being onsite.
3. Another possibility is to preload the work order with an acceptance test scenario coordinated with the user in advance. The scenario is written by the project team users; of course, it is written in advance of any coding by the contractor. The test scenario becomes a part of the work-order scope and a form of requirement specification.

Any of these approaches creates tension with the contractor. Caution is needed—the traditional rules of fixed-price contracting are that the project cannot be intrusive; the project is given only the very minimum oversight of the contractor's activity. There is no privilege to direct or advise the contractor's approach or methods. Further, there must be respect for the terms of the contract, or there could be chaos. The scope of the work order is fixed by negotiation; the user is on hand to interpret needs but not to change scope.

Incentive contracts are a possibility for those situations where customer interpretations, priorities, and urgency are understood to a degree that would allow for the reasonable estimation of a price range, bounded by a target price and a ceiling price. The range should be generous so that the impacts of numerous points of guidance from the user can be absorbed. To construct an incentive contract, there are two prices to agree on:

1. *Target price*: The target price is the optimistic price based on everything going well. The contractor's profit is greater at the target price than it is at the ceiling price.
2. *Ceiling price*: The ceiling is the most pessimistic price and allows for missed requirements and other risks to materialize and to be included. The contractor's profit is minimal or even nonexistent if the work is delivered at or above the ceiling price.

The project and the contractor share the cost between the target and ceiling, with the project typically taking 70 to 80 percent of the risk. At the ceiling price, the contractor assumes 100 percent of the risk for any further cost.

Cost Reimbursable Contracts for Agile Projects

Cost reimbursable contracts are designed specifically for the agile project situation. The rules of engagement expect and allow intrusion, redirection, and interpretation of requirements. Insofar as such actions increase cost, that increase is passed along to the project without risk to the contractor.

However, there is no completion commitment. Performance risk is transferred from project to contract. All cost risk is retained by the project in the cost reimbursable fixed-fee arrangement; some cost sharing can occur in an incentive fee structure. In all forms of cost reimbursable contracts, there is little impetus for the contractor to control costs, although an incentive fee can boost cost control.

In the simplest cost reimbursable form, a fixed fee is paid based on the contractor's expected cost of capital and a reasonable return on equity. However, as actual cost goes up or down from the original estimate, the fee does not. The fee is fixed once agreed to.

Incentive fees and award fees are very applicable to cost reimbursable contracts. Incentive fees are cost-sharing arrangements, with the project usually accepting the larger share. Award fees are parameter-based fees. A scorecard, not unlike the balanced scorecard, is agreed to at the inception of the contract. At periodic points of evaluation, a fee is awarded based on the scores attained. In the agile situation, the award period is typically one planning wave. The scorecard can be for functional, technical, or managerial parameters:

- Quality of features and functions as perceived by the customer
- Quality of the unit development as measured by the pass rate of unit and integration tests
- Responsiveness and accuracy of updating scorecards, dashboards, and other media to forestall surprises

Agile Time and Materials Contracts

T&M contracts are the way to buy labor by the hour, usually by hiring independent contractors. Once a contracted developer is embedded in a team, the team's cohesion is of primary importance.

	Work orders versus T&M contracts
A project management tip	• Work orders transfer more risk than does T&M • T&M simply solves a staffing problem • Work orders bring additional staff, a management team, and a commitment to completion with accountability

Module 4—Discussion for Critical Thinking

You want to contract for an agile project development, but you want to avoid the usual adversarial tensions in a contract situation. What would you do to accomplish your objective?

Summary and Takeaway

The theme of this chapter is that agile methods are scalable; and within limitations, amenable to the advantages of contracts and virtual teams.

From Module 1, we learn that scale amplifies every project problem, and may create problems that are unique to the scale. For agile practitioners to scale up requires some to give up on the autonomy and independence of the performance unit. We learn that scale brings the N^2 communication problem into the management frame, and that if we want to reduce scale, the path back to smaller may be different.

From Modules 2 and 3, we learn that several scale-up techniques are applicable:

- **Networks:** To ramp productivity in order to meet business objectives in a timely fashion, multiple teams are required. To be effective, teams work in networks, forming relationships and exchanging information.
- **Virtual teams:** To add staff from disparate locations that cannot be co-located for one reason or another, virtual teams are a solution. Virtual teams must overcome the disadvantage of not being co-located; they require accurate and timely communication, a dedication to overcoming cultural differences, and assignment of work according to rational decomposition of requirements.
- **Contracts:** Contracts can be used to address risks of capacity, capability, and feasibility. Contracts transfer risk out of the project and into other hands. However, contract situations have all the issues of virtual teams, plus the overlay of the contract structure. Fixed-price contracting is inappropriate for agile projects. T&M or completion work orders—either fixed-price incentive or cost reimbursable—are workable contract frameworks.

Properly applied, scaling techniques do make it possible to extend agile methods beyond simple projects.

Chapter Appendix
Incentive Contracts

Table 11.5 Incentive contracts

Incentive program	Commentary
Fixed price incentive	• The contractor is given an incentive to perform within a price range rather than perform to a specific price point. • In the range between the target and the ceiling price, the project and the contractor share the price risk. • Outside the range, either higher than ceiling or lower than target, the contractor assumes all risk. • There is a lower risk premium built into the price, so the target price is typically lower than a fixed-price contract with a fixed-price point.
Award fee contract	• The contractor's fee is based on achievements on a number of parameters negotiated in advance before work begins, something like a balanced scorecard. • An award fee is typically applied to cost reimbursable contracts, but can be an additional fee on fixed-price contracts.
Cost reimbursable fixed fee (CRFF) and Cost reimbursable incentive fee (CRIF)	• CRFF: The fee is fixed, but the cost is reimbursable. The idea is that fee and cost are separable. • The fee is negotiated in advance as a fixed amount, paid regardless of the cost performance of the contractor. • Since the contractor bears no cost risk, there is no risk premium built-in. • The fee is modest and usually based on a reasonable return on capital employed, an economic value add argument. • CRIF: Fixed fee incentive shares improved cost performance with the contractor. Based on a sharing ratio, each dollar of cost savings is shared with the contractor.

Fixed-price Incentive Contract Example

A fixed-price incentive contract is a risk-sharing cost-sharing arrangement over a range of contractor cost between the target and the ceiling price

Agile iterations can be contracted with fixed price incentive contracts

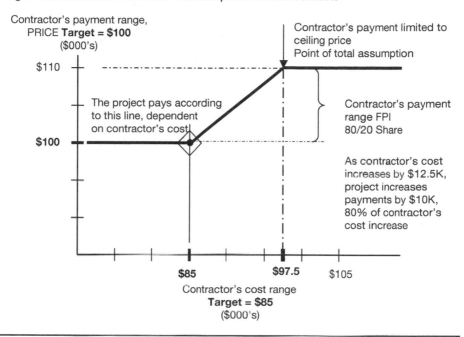

Figure 11.3 Fixed-price incentive contract

Chapter endnotes

1. Interaction between components grows by approximately the square of the number of devices interacting, $N \times (N - 1)$. For large N, this formula is very close to N^2. This phenomenon explains why making teams larger becomes counterproductive after a point. A similar concept applies to any components that communicate, whether a software object or a subsystem.

2. Anderson, *Agile Management for Software Engineering*, 15.

3. Schawber, *Agile Project Management with Scrum*, 119-132, 147.

4. See: http://en.wikipedia.org/wiki/Hysteresis

5. Highsmith, *Agile Project Management: Creating Innovative Products*, 12.

6. McConnell, *Code Complete*, Chapter 19, 453-492.

7. Beck, with Andres, *Extreme Programming Explained*, 95.

8. *Pipelines* and *pipelining* are terms that describe the use of a scorecard to capture data that seems to flow by. See Goodpasture, *Pipelining your Project*, 37-43.

12

Transitioning to Agile

Perhaps there is one true way to do agile—the way that works best for each team.

Mike Cohn[1]

Our theme for this chapter is that the true way to do agile is the way that works best for the team, the project, the portfolio, and for the business. There is no absolute best way, and there is no absolute set of practices. As we described in Chapter 1, many of the agile methodologies are incomplete or not as well defined as their traditional counterparts. So, to what are you transitioning? That's for each project office to decide.

In a manner of speaking, this entire book is about transition, about getting agile working in an enterprise environment and business context. With that said, there are some topics specifically on the point of transitioning from traditional methodology; those topics are what we will cover in this chapter.

Module 1: Business Leadership Transition

Lead with the problem, or lead with the answer

Module 1—Objectives

- Examine the necessary attributes of transition leadership
- Discuss and explain how the grand bargain can work in transition
- Examine transition factors that affect the business scorecard

Leadership and Leadership Style

It is all but axiomatic that big changes are more likely successful when led from the top—though in the case of changing project methodologies, it is probably best that the *top* is a functional leader with a technical understanding of the methodology. So, perhaps the very first transition idea is to recruit that transition leader if he or she is not already the agile leader.

Agile Transition Leader

Some attributes required of the agile transition leader include:

- Has the respect of, and influence with, the business management who sponsor and invest in projects
- Is willing to try a variety of agile practices with an expectation that they won't all work *right out of the box*; some tuning and experimentation will be required at some cost to the organization
- Has the capability and willingness to fund training, tools, and environment for agile practices
- Has a proven ability to work collaboratively with the business and with the customer/user community
- Embraces leadership as an activity, less so a *thing*, with a take-action orientation

What duties or actions are expected of the transitional leader? We can say with certainty these will be on the agenda:

- Set strategic direction for the action teams that will experiment with practices
- Evaluate and then establish cultural values that may be different from the traditional culture—especially the so-called shift in dominance (discussed in prior chapters)
- Resolve conflicts among the practitioners, and between the practitioners and the business managers as transition projects are carried forward (again, dominance may become an issue and a conflict)
- Bestow protection and security since there will be some failures and inefficiencies as practices are learned, modified, or even abandoned
- Restore and maintain order when there are arguments, especially in the *storming* phase of team development

Transition Leadership Style

There are two major leadership styles that can work effectively for the transition leader:[2]

1. *Lead with the answer:* "I've got the answers to our issues; we're going to do this or that, so follow me!" You might expect such a leadership style of a transition leader who has internalized the Agile Manifesto and absorbed the lessons of the Agile Principles. Apart from self-assurance and confidence in the strategic outcome—which a lead-with-the-answer person would have—this style of leadership can be very technocratic, bordering on management detail rather than leadership vision. Indeed, some might even say too much management; too much hands-on.

2. *Lead with the problem:* "We have some issues to resolve to make this a better business, so let's all work together and contribute to a transition to something better." Such a style exudes self-security, insofar as the leader is comfortable not having all the answers; and such a style is enabled by a willingness to cast a wide net for ideas. Some hold that leadership is often most innovative when driving for multicultural and multidisciplined participation.

Even though the transition leader may lead with the answer or with the problem, there are still going to be these situations that will be faced in any transition project, requiring some nuance of style:[3]

1. A need to be directive and compelling, leaving nothing to chance
2. An opportunity to be delegating and trusting, leaving all the tactical decisions to the teams
3. Something in between, where direction is mixed in some proportion with delegation

The choice among those three is made according to circumstances and the willingness, capacity, and capability of *followers*. Per se, there's nothing uniquely agile or transitional about these styles, but the circumstances of transitioning to agile will bring one or the other more into play.

	Long-range outcome
A project management tip	With any style, the long-range outcome could be either transactional or transformative for the business: • Transactional: agile methods are used where necessary or where they can be effective, but the default is and continues to be traditional methods • Transformative: the methodology of choice becomes agile; the traditional methodology is all but in the rear view mirror

Leading without Authority

Leading without authority comes up in the agile context quite often. Leading without authority does not mean committee leadership; it doesn't mean the laws of dominance have been repealed. Indeed, someone without portfolio may well dominate the discussion, may be a *great man or woman*, and may go for bold, even without the corner office.

And, in the case of transitioning to agile, leadership needs may draw forward a natural leader. If position, authority, and responsibility are not in alignment, a natural yet *informal* leader presses forward.

Consider the possibilities of *no authority*:

- Without the constraints of authority, presumably there can be more latitude for creative deviance from the norms. Unfettered from a broader array of concerns and responsibilities, the informal leader can focus on a single issue or a selected set of limited issues.
- The leader without the formal position of authority is also usually on the frontline where he or she can absorb the detailed experiences of stakeholders.
- And perhaps most importantly, that informal leader has the latitude to make himself the poster child of the issue.

The Grand Bargain

In Chapter 4 we took up the *grand bargain*—the idea that there is a trade to be made with the business by the project.

The Grand Bargain
Wherein for the latitude to be tactically emergent and iterative, the project promises to deliver best value in accord with strategic intent.

If such a grand bargain is accepted as a part of transitioning to agile, then that may usher in something transformative:

- The sponsor has control of the strategy
- The customer has control of many of the tactics
- The project has control of the practices and detailed design

The grand bargain relies heavily on trust and safety. A trusting environment is usually a safe environment; safety, like trust, is a cultural characteristic.

Safety is the idea that someone will not be pilloried for a contrasting or opposing idea to the mainstream, that they will not be drummed out of the team, and that they can speak truth to power without fear of some kind of retribution.

Trust and safety are matters of culture. Since the agile transition may go against the grain in some circumstances, practitioners will look to leaders to establish the cultural parameters and then regulate by persuasion and enforcement the limits of the behaviors acceptable within that culture.

	Culture and virtual teams
A project management tip	Culture is hard to port across the virtual space; thus, most beginning agile projects call for co-location as one of the important enablers of uniformly held values that are the framework of culture.

Business Case and Scorecard

A lot of what makes up the business objectives on the business scorecard is predicated on a predictable outcome of business-oriented projects. What is to be said then about scope creep as an impact to business objectives? Is agile a move away from scope creep, or not?

Scope Creep

With the agile transition, we want to shift the conversation—

- From: a detailed specification of scope, or any change to which gets the label of creep
- To: a conversation about managing the expected changes such that the essential business value is retained

In theory, agile handles scope creep by defining it away:

- The customer/user gets to pick from the backlog those things that are most important, urgent, or needed
- If there's not enough money, they have to put something back
- As the project progresses, they get to change their mind about what is taken from the backlog, but their shopping budget is fixed

Thus, changes are traded among the backlog such that the overall cost and schedule are not affected, yet the predicted business outcomes are unaffected—change without creep!

So, even if not technically creeping, the scope is still changing. The issue at hand is then: what is the sponsor's reaction to the customer/user's selection, as it is initially, and as it evolves? The sponsor's vision may not be implemented in full or in the sponsor's order of priority. But, agile presumes that fidelity to the customer/user's needs trumps fidelity to the sponsor's vision.

Other People's Money

However, when it's the sponsor's money, the sponsor may feel that their priorities have been unduly discounted and unnecessarily trumped. After all, no serious project is approved without a business case. There is a narrative, a vision, and a corresponding business expectation. Thus, money speaks; the sponsor always has a vote on all strategic aspects of the project—including, are we *done?*

There's no fixed answer to the customer-sponsor tension since the sponsor's personality, the business case, the project charter, and the relationship to the customer/user all play a part in sorting out what the developers do. These are all issues to be tested and practiced during a transition project.

Module 1—Discussion for Critical Thinking

The grand bargain may work well for pilot projects where it's understood that there will be risk to the business case, but what could be done to institutionalize such a bargain as the everyday working model?

Module 2: Customer Relationship Transition

Committed, collaborative, engaged, and present when needed

Module 2—Objectives

- Examine a number of factors around customer commitment that may be present in transition
- Examine the likely need for training of a business customer who joins the team as the business product representative

Commitment

Built into the agile psyche is the idea that the customer/user so cares about the project and its outcomes that they are willing to dedicate resources to its success. Consequently, the agile project plan not only presumes customer/user commitment, but commitment over the long haul—whatever it takes.

And so those ideas bring these transition issues to the fore, to be examined in this module:

- The customer/user or product owner is simply too busy to commit to an embedded and long-term relationship, which is not necessarily required in traditional methods
- Managing a close-knit customer commitment and relationship, especially an embedded customer, does not come for free

Their Participation

Clearly the following is not good, as recounted to the author:

> *"On projects that were not successful, the product owner was simply too busy. The project deteriorated into a development project where design decisions were made by the team without direct consultation with the product owner."*

But *too busy* may not be the only issue:

- There's no culture (norms of behavior) to guide participation
- The customer/user may not be accustomed to the pace of the project; what is sustainable to the developers may not be sustainable by the customer/user
- The customer/user may not have *permission* to represent all the clients of the product or service outcomes; thus participation is constrained by external factors
- There may be a contract between the project and the customer/user that describes the dos and don'ts, limits of authority, and escalation protocols

Among these factors, permission and constraints may be the most vexing and difficult to overcome.

And then there are *product owner ghosts*, a term coined by blogger Mike Griffiths.[4] They don't show up, or hardly ever show up, or you can't find them when you need them—yet in the background they have influence, sometimes moving the project in mysterious ways. You may not see ghosts during a transition phase since the product owners are likely to be fully committed, but they may show up later.

Other participation maladies to be aware of long term, though again you may not face these during transition, are:[5]

- Flip flop on important issues, or withdraw support unexpectedly
- Fail to communicate effectively, perhaps out of shyness, or boredom, or simply a personal modus operandi
- Pass the baton too often, thereby losing continuity, and failing to leave behind institutional knowledge

Transitioning to Stories and Use Cases

Usually, the impact is felt when fashioning the backlog. The traditional method of structured *shalls* and *wills*, is replaced with conversations about stories, and use cases.

Now, when does such a conversation take place? Really it should be at the beginning, before architecture rules it out. But how do we bring about such a conversation? In large projects you are often not talking directly with users but with user surrogates—their representatives—and perhaps from afar, not only geographically, but organizationally. For example, in military or public sector projects, it's not uncommon to be more than once removed if an acquisition organization contracts for the deliverables and then provides them to a training operation, which then deploys them to an operating element.

The solution, to be practiced during transition, is to set up some transition protocols to gather the requirements. In the beginning, in a pilot situation, these are often in the form of scripted scenarios, passed along and up and down the customer/user hierarchy. These are still conversational in tone, perhaps in the form of storyboards and white papers, but amenable to parsing into a database. These become the back log.

An electronic database is capable of being much more than just a repository of sticky notes or story cards. A database can provide services not otherwise available, but these may be quite different than their counterparts in the traditional methodologies because of the somewhat unstructured and conversational nature of stories, thus requiring some thought during transition about how these circumstances will be handled:

- Persistence of the story over a long period of time, thus mitigating lost and mutilated cards
- Search on key words for *birds of a feather* stories or use cases
- Search for redundant or duplicate stories
- Linking of technical and functional debt to a larger story context
- Validation and verification services

A project management tip	From database to backlog
	At the time of the build of the iteration backlog, selected stories are printed onto cards if that is useful. But in a fully distributed project with everybody working remotely, the war room has to be virtual, thus electronic.

Your Management

It may be presumptuous to say there is to be a project task called customer management; usually it's the other way around, with customers speaking of managing their providers or contractors. From a transition perspective, your first agile project may well be your customer's first agile project.

Frankly, many are not prepared by experience, or equipped with tools and protocols, or culturally attuned to the participation required by agile. If in a public sector, or in a private sector contract arrangement, the contract vehicle may prohibit or impede participation.

Even with committed participation, the idea of being in charge of the candy store may be overwhelming. Thus, some thought, some project management energy, and some project management resources will have to be diverted toward the overhead of customer management in the following ways:

- Define and document protocols for participation and escalation
- Define and explain expectations for how the embedded customer will be the ambassador and representative of the business at large
- Provide training for the jobs expected of the customer, such as story or use case development; backlog review; change approvals; user testing and validation; interpretation of requirements for developers; and others specific to the project
- Assist the customer with understanding technical and functional trades that will influence the backlog
- Assist the customer with risk management
- Assist the customer with reporting to business management to include reporting any scorecard metrics

Product Owner at Scale

In the enterprise context, the customer/user or product owner may not be a person so much as it's an organization, committee, working group, or council. Such organizational overlays recognize that no single person is capable of adequately representing user needs that encompass the entire operational and support environment—for example:

- User training and rollout or deployment to operating units
- Supply chain considerations for resupply, maintenance, and user support
- Service support for fixes, field repairs and patches, changes, and upgrades

When the business or public sector agency has a global reach, the product owner-at-scale is all the more complicated by geography, cultural and language differences, regulatory differences, and user preferences. One example told to the author is a Product Owners Council, made up of several voting members representing the users in the global markets, all of the business groups, and the software services organization. The voting members are responsible for translating their constituent user requirements into user stories for review by the council.

Transitioning to such a council which has unaccustomed hands-on influence of the backlog, the quality proposition, and the satisfaction of the business case worldwide is no small matter. Obviously, the smart play is to start small and expand the council's scope, guided by experience and feedback.

	Global deployment
A project management tip	One could imagine that when global deployment was in progress, the council, committee, or working group would make sure that all user stories that enabled the country teams to go-live would be prioritized ahead of just functional requirements, including some less critical defects or debt.

Training for the Job

Some training is required. You might have expected such; a good project-embedded customer is not strictly off-the-shelf, as it were. Actually, there's training and there's coaching. The former is actually teaching a new customer/user or product owner the various steps for each task expected of them—many of these tasks may have already been discussed, but others are project specific.

Some investment in materials and job design will be required, with all, for the most part, being reusable. Again though situationally dependent, these materials could be deliverables of a transition project. This could be so if a savvy and experienced product owner is recruited to the transition, one who can work effectively without benefit of formal materials. In effect, we are talking about a product owner who can tolerate the uncertainty of trying something for the first time.

Of course, going forward, you will want to profile the optimum trainee—given that profiling is acceptable in your culture. Certainly on everyone's list of desired characteristics is someone who is receptive to new ideas, capable and willing to absorb training, and is eager to be coached from the perspective of a leadership style somewhat near S4, or delegating.[6]

Other traits on a training profile would be:

- Geographically available to the team; a virtual product owner is possible, but not in the transition phase
- Willing to accept responsibility and capable of driving for results
- Continuously available in the sense of not rotating the job with a colleague, though agile values redundancy
- Recognized and respected in the domain of the product or service—in other words, the product owner shouldn't be an outsider to the customer/user group that is being represented
- Carries some authority along with the responsibility, though the reader is referred to the material on *leading without authority*
- Sufficiently versed in interpersonal communications so that both collaboration and communications are natural

Module 2—Discussion for Critical Thinking

We say it's presumptuous to think of managing the customer, but is it? Shouldn't anyone joining a project team, especially in a near full-time embedded situation, expect to be subject to the project management?

Module 3: Project Management Transition

There's a role for project management in agile methodologies

Module 3—Objectives

- Discuss and explain many transition factors that influence transitioning to agile project management

Project Design

When you boil down a lot of what has been written about agile, there are two ideas that seem to get repeated:

1. Agile is liberating for developers
2. Agile is threatening to managers

Each of these is a consequence of what we call *project design*. For developers—to include all those in the so-called construction cycle of design, development, test, and integration—agile means less project management overhead, more emphasis on lean practices, and quick cycles of *fail early, or succeed*. Of course, less overhead is often taken to mean less planning and documentation, fewer project office measurements and metrics, and lighter process control. There is no doubt that the Agile Manifesto plays directly to this theme of less overhead and more quality throughput.

For the manager, agile-for-the-first-time plays into a bias which has the formal name *prospect theory*,[7] but less formally says: *we greatly fear losing what we've got more than we value the upside to change*. Thus, there is a tendency to overstate the risk of losing something we value, and to understate the benefit of a change to our status quo.

What risk? I heard this idea in a public forum: project managers should embrace agile because it would do away with project management as we know it. And, wouldn't such a lean project be the best thing for the business? Frankly, there was no race to the door to implement agile by the project managers in that forum.

Of course, as these chapters have shown, there will be changes, and so an understanding of the natural bias that we all have toward losing what we have is to be honored. We'll discuss some elements of project design that should mitigate some concerns.

System Engineering and Scale

When we're talking about system engineering, we're generally talking about *the big three ideas for system engineering*:

1. Requirements
2. Architecture
3. Validation

There's certainly nothing incompatible with the Agile Principles or the Agile Manifesto among those three.

> Let it be said: We're from System Engineering, and we're here to help...

Really? What can system engineering do for the Agile project? The answers are found in the following discussion of requirements, architecture, validation, stage gates, and peer reviews.

	System engineering and project design
A project management tip	• System engineering is often tied directly to the project office as a matter of project design, usually reporting to the project's chief technologist or the project manager. • We could substitute *portfolio* for *project*, since system engineering is often found at the portfolio management level.

Requirements: It's true that system engineers are more accustomed to structured analysis, decomposition, and lots of *shalls* and *wills*, than the conversational informality of stories and use cases. Much of structured analysis is not present in most—but not all—agile methods, except perhaps in the more complex and larger-scale projects that engage with agile modeling.[8] Nonetheless, the engineer's motivation to engage with the requirements and backlog development—to develop not only a narrative from the many disparate stories, use cases, and statements, but also to fashion an architecture that supports the whole collection of backlog—fits the agile need nicely.

Architecture: A close cousin to requirements is architecture—presentation, structure, interfaces, large-scale design, and interrelationships. The important activities of architecture—apart from presentation and appearance—are:

- Allocating requirements to the major system constituents
- Defining the constituent relationships
- Adjudicating conflicts that would compromise coupling, coherence, cohesion, redundancy, and diversification between and among constituents

---

Coupling, Coherence, Cohesion, Redundancy, and Diversification

Coupling: The ability to transfer an effect from one constituent to another. Loose coupling refers to having a good deal of loss in the transfer, such that only a small effect is felt. Tight coupling is the no-loss version. Loose coupling is good for isolating risks; tight coupling is good for conveying and demanding immediate responsiveness. Encapsulation loosens the coupling between iterations, objects, and dissimilar methodologies.

Coherence: The reinforcement of one activity by another, often brought about by phasing or timing one activity with respect to another. A lack of coherence can be destructive. Thus, the need to synchronize and time phase between encapsulated activities, and between traditional and agile methods in hybrid environments.

Cohesion: The ability of constituents to stick together, or not fly apart, under stress. Agile-produced objects, as well as traditionally-produced objects, are tested for stress.

> **Redundancy:** The availability of alternate means to accomplish an activity, though such alternates may not be exact duplicates and not produce a faithful rendering in all respects. Cross training team members is an example of creating redundancy.
> **Diversification:** Distributing the means for cause and effect such that errors and risk events that might impact one such cause does not impact all such causes. The overall outcome is less risky, since only a portion of the overall cause and effect environment is affected by an event, rather than the whole environment.

Validation: In other chapters we've spoken to the issue of validation and also verification. But why bring system engineers into the validation process? The reason is mostly to bring the big picture and largest scale to validate the architecture. Such attention to the big picture reassures the sponsor that the strategic intent of the business case is being honored, gets marketing fully on board, and if there is to be manufacturing or post-release support, then those organizations are represented in the validation as well.

Stage gates: Agile is not a gated methodology primarily because scope is viewed as emergent, and thus, the idea of predetermined gate criteria is inconsistent with progressive elaboration and emergence. But, agile does embrace structured releases. Either the system engineer or the project manager could put criteria around a release and use it as a gate for scope to be delivered.

Peer review: Peer review is not exclusively a system engineering function, but every system engineering shop conducts peer reviews of proposed deliverables. Peer review is a very powerful, inexpensive, and moderately easy practice to implement. Some teams call peer reviewing *red teaming*, and then there are other colors to denote teams at different maturities—red, then gold, etc.—recognizing that things improve with each review. To be efficient, a standing review team is needed so as to not invent the wheel with each review.

	Peer review authority
A project management tip	There should be protocols regarding whether the peer review has any power of veto or enforcement, and an appeal or escalation process/work flow.

Project Scorecard

Budget: In theory, agile is effectively *zero base* at every release, if not at every iteration. In theory, the sponsor can call the question and rebudget, reconstitute, or even stop the project at each release, if not at each iteration. This is a marked departure from traditional budgeting in which the project would have to be well along before an opportunity to zero base presents itself. But, in practice, zero base is usually a last resort to rescue a project in trouble. Most projects of any reasonable scale have so many related activities that the momentum to continue is hard to resist.

Variance vs. rebaseline: If the project has missed a date, that's a variance. The baseline is still the plan you are managing to—as long as you are trying to recover the schedule. However, common sense applies at all times. In most crucial situations there are two plans at all times:

1. The baseline plan—which is the agreement between the sponsor (business) and the project
2. The operating plan—which is the day-to-day plan derived from the baseline

As project manager, you maintain a strategy to merge or bring together the operating plan and the baseline so that, at the end of the day, the baseline is the plan of record—all variances of record are measured against the baseline.

Now, if the situation develops that the baseline is no longer valid—for example, approved changes that affect strategic intent—such that there is no practical way to merge the operating plan with the baseline, then rebaselining is appropriate.

- Record and archive all variances to the baseline
- Replan the project; this replan becomes the second baseline

At the project conclusion, sum the archive of variances from both baselines. These become the cumulative variances of record.

Change Management

Business case changes: If the customer/user or product owner recommends changes in requirements (not anticipated in the business case) and material to the business proposition—affecting cost of value—when does the reassessed business case occur? Agile provides two methodology opportunities:

1. The retrospective evaluation—leading to the next backlog
2. The release planning—leading to production releases to the business

Beyond these methodology opportunities, each business may have processes to handle business case changes that would overlay to the project methodologies.

Project plan changes: Should there be a project plan for agile? Yes, as we discussed elsewhere in the book, the project plan is the business case rewritten in project language, adding just enough to begin the project on the right course.

Can it be changed? Yes. Just think of the plan as a model. All models are temporary and lack all the detail. As the detail becomes evident, it may be worth the trouble to modify the plan, bringing the business into the change management process.

Agile Plans, or Not?
Think of this: the project manager is standing before an executive—who has all the money and influence—pitching a project and saying: "I've no written plan, no model for my actions, and no firm requirements for what I want to do, but trust me to get it done!" Would you fund this project, even if only a pilot, and even if only to prove a transition strategy?

Remote Working

In this book, remote working and virtual teams have been mentioned a number of times. From a transition point of view, there are several techniques that can be factored into a pilot project. The pilot team should establish a means for evaluation of their effectiveness in the agile context. These techniques may include:

- A private, one-on-one chat channel on Skype (or equivalent)
- Virtual document and artifact repositories in the cloud with document editing and collaboration services
- Virtual task boards (there are apps for this)
- Everyone on a call, even if local
- Everyone in a conference room at each location to limit phone connections
- Meeting notes distributed in advance
- Standard call times that bridge time zones
- Video conferences where possible
- Online desktop sharing, like WebEx or equivalent (there are many others)
- Chat text channels, like IM, or Office Chat, etc. (many others)
- Participating in a shared experience to build trust
- Visits to remote locations to get a face-to-face familiarity

- Established rules and protocols of behavior, and follow-through agreements

Environment Density

There's no real difference between the effects of co-location and density on either an agile or traditional project. We've discussed elsewhere the velocity fall-off from narrower channels given by virtual working. And the counterpoint is true also: policies that discourage density likely have an unintended consequence of inhibiting improved productivity.[9]

So, is there a transition factor here? Perhaps. It depends on whether or not the traditional project design is baseline virtual and remote—many are, because that's the way enterprise entities are quite often organized.

Certainly, the agile practitioners who met in Utah in 2001 were of a mind that agile methodologies work best with physical co-location and close-at-hand density. If possible, transition should be to that model.

- Project managers should expect to discount productivity for a distributed or virtual team
- If the ordinary situation is the distributed team, co-location presents an opportunity for a premium on productivity

Similar to productivity, observers have noted that innovation seems correlated to density: greater density begets more innovation. We see this phenomenon played out in geographically dense centers that emerge as the engines of innovation. But, we can also see this effect at the project level and the enterprise level, as well. It's no accident that there has been a recent trend to call the virtual workers home to the mothership. Steve Jobs was famous for putting the restrooms at Pixar in a very central place, so that there would be ample opportunity for people from all departments to run into each other and exchange ideas.

There have even been studies about how far apart to seat knowledge workers to optimize innovation by close collaboration. One such study outcome is the so-called *Allen curve*, named for its principal investigator, which predicts that innovation trails off exponentially beyond a certain *dislocation* or separation of people.[10]

The Power of Pairs
Complementing the Allen curve are some observations that are spot-on with agile: genius and innovation are really about pairs of people working together. It's not the lone genius, or the larger team of six.[11]

On the other hand, there are counterpoints:

- Introverted people need space—they have a rapid decrease in productivity in a crowd, if present for an extended time
- Extroverts are just the opposite—eschewing privacy, and being more productive when bouncing ideas off the crowd

---

Universal Advice Regarding Density and Co-location

The universal advice for those transitioning to agile is to also transition to the densest environment that is practical. Such also includes co-located war rooms and common meeting areas.

Risk Management

Perhaps the one element of risk management that is unique to agile, and thus worthy of a test run during transition, is the idea of fail-safe scheduling. There are two main contributors to fail-safe scheduling:

1. Scheduling for a sustainable pace (an Agile Principle)
2. Scheduling with slack for the unknown that may emerge

Sustainable Pace

The most influential contributor to a sustainable work pace is slack, built into the iteration. This is accomplished by not over-committing the team. As observed by Scott Ambler and other agile methodologists, a team should not be scheduled for more than 70% of the capacity of the team—as established by a velocity benchmark. The 30% *white space* is then available as a buffer to absorb overrun within the iteration—or if there is no overrun, to then work on the myriad of technical debt that collects in the backlog.

Scheduling for Slack

The other technique, borrowed from the critical chain idea in traditional critical path scheduling, is to insert empty iterations to serve as overflow buffers to absorb technical debt (unfinished small bits of scope or testing) and to allow for emergent testing needs not foreseen.

Sign-off and Approval

You might not think of sign-off and approval as a risk to be managed, but in the agile community this question comes up, setting up a risk situation: *should there be a release sign-off when applying Agile methods?*

Those who ask that question also ask: doesn't an imposed sign-off taint agile with bureaucracy?

Actually, yes, but it can be lean. Here's the set-up:

- Is it just going into the code base, or going into business production?
- If going into business production, is it just a bug fix or new functionality?
- If new functionality, is it user facing?
- If user facing, is it intuitive or is training and formal rollout needed?

There is risk attendant with each of these. How much risk is project dependent? Thus, there should be a sign-off process that will convey assurance to the business. And, the sign-off authority should be the one closest to the issues who can also take responsibility for the risk.

Pilots

For something as important as changing a methodology for projects of significant business value, there's almost no substitute for starting with a pilot project supported by a willing sponsor. To that end, there are many sources with advice for agile pilots which can more or less be summarized as follows:

- Pick a project that you know you can do technically at reasonable risk
- Pick a small project by enterprise standards, yet large enough that important transition ideas can be practiced
- Pick a project that has business appeal, will attract a supporting sponsor, and will be resourced adequately by the business
- Don't pick a project with an extreme schedule constraint; you'll need time to debug processes, tools, and environments
- Don't start with a virtual and remote team if you can avoid these issues

Those ideas are universally thought to be the right thing to do. Less agreed upon is how to go about picking the pilot team. There are two schools of thought:

1. Hand-pick the *A-team* which will most likely turn in a successful pilot project, whose team members are eager to try agile and work out the kinks, and will be good ambassadors to the business and to traditional developers for agile methods.
2. Pick a good team in the usual way, expecting some team members to be reluctant participants, but nonetheless cooperative. Take a risk that the pilot will not turn in good results the first time around.

The former is all about getting a good handle on agile practices in the context of a real project and thereby reassuring the business that agile is a good bet for a project methodology. Although the pilot per se may not be at any real risk, such a handpicked team may leave the question open as to whether or not the pilot results can be replicated by others, and whether or not the pilot success is scalable to enterprise levels.

The latter is more about testing the efficacy of agile, taking a risk on pilot success in order to more quickly get to the issue of scaling agile to enterprise levels.

The question as to which of these is the correct thing to do, is situationally dependent on each enterprise. Thus, there is no universally right answer—though for any specific situation, it should be possible to decide which of these is the best approach to try.

Culture

The Change Environment

Agile is a high-change environment, definitely more uncertain in many regards than a traditional project. About agile we can say:

- There are fewer rules
- Those rules that exist are subject to violation
- Processes are looser

Not all cultures or all individuals align well with such circumstances; some transition is required:

- **Low tolerance for change:** These individuals are not looking for change, nor loose process and few rules, but if these things come they have certain expectations of their leaders, starting with the establishment and maintenance of order, safety, and fairness. Insofar as change is required, even radical change can be accepted and tolerated as long as it comes with firm and confident leadership. Lots of problems can be tolerated when there is transparency, low corruption, and a sense of fair play. In other words, the little guy gets a fair shake.

On the other hand, in some cultures, agile is likely to blossom:

- **High tolerance for change:** These individuals are experimental and emergent in their thinking; they're more likely to welcome the leaner management that underwrites agile. Confusion—even a bit of chaos— provides fuel for innovation, a point well made by Nassim Taleb in his book about being antifragile.[12] Disruption and eccentric behavior is valued, or at least not eschewed. Indeed, for innovative change, particularly destructive innovation, the traditional filters that regulate must come off to permit rapid and out-of-the-box responses; you can't work change—or see enough context—through a straw, as it were.

Competencies

For a really long time, there has been talk about *core competencies*, those competencies that "*... are the collective learning in the organization, especially how to coordinate diverse production skills and integrate multiple streams of technologies.*"[13] It's understood that in an optimum business model, core competencies lead to core products and services—those products and services that are the very definition of the business and its strategic intent.

So it is that business and project context, which affect collective learning and the ability to coordinate and integrate diverse skills and technologies, often color the choices of what competencies are most important. And from competencies, businesses and projects build culture—beliefs, values, and behaviors that are, themselves, core. Thus, when considering a transition to agile, the fit of the Agile Manifesto and Agile Principles to the core competencies, products, services, and culture is up for evaluation.

For example, in a culture that highly values process, stability, and predictability, all the Agile Principles that support that mindset are highly valued: safety, barrier removal, and written values and principles. But looser, lighter, and leaner process and rules; self-organization; and more autonomous working may not fit at all. Indeed, the need for such may even smack as incompetent in the eyes of those who value traditional methods.

Overcoming such bias is a clear and present transition need.

A project management tip	Competency or incompetency?
	Competencies at variance with the culture may be received as incompetence—i.e., a culture where cowboys are not valued.

Volunteers as a Cultural Factor

Some agile projects are so agile that they attract and embrace volunteer workers.[14] Such could be a transition issue if the enterprise is traditionally not disposed toward volunteers.

Of course, some cultures welcome and support volunteers and volunteer projects. Volunteers may be different from paid staff in ways other than not collecting a paycheck, such as:

- Their training and willingness to follow directions
- Motivation, accountability, and commitment

In *Practical Project Management for Agile Nonprofits*, Karen R. J. White tells us about volunteers:

- They don't always show up, and they don't often give notice or reasons ... they just don't show.
- Virtual teams of volunteers are almost unthinkable. You've got to meet and greet in person.
- If they do show up, they may leave at odd moments, right in the middle of something important, but not important enough to trump their need to leave.
- They can be territorial; prone to settle into something they like to do; and sometimes hostile to help or direction.

But, if volunteers are working outside of their normal identity and comfort zone, they'll usually take direction readily, if they perceive it is value-added. They're really not committed strategically to the host organization—they don't get a paycheck, benefits, promotions, a corner office, or a place to hang out long term.

- But, volunteers can be very committed to organizational success for the project they are working on, putting in longer hours and working harder than the formal demands made by the project.
- There are obvious inefficiencies: the labor is cheap; there's more of it if you need it.
- The pressure to be lean is much relaxed. Consequently, the overhead may be a lot higher, and its impact may not be anticipated in the schedule.
- Benchmarks attained with paid staff are often way too optimistic (see the previous points about inefficiency, overhead, and commitment).

Volunteer teams bond just like any other; leaders emerge like they always do; and sometimes there's an issue of dominance to be settled. Be aware that volunteers are sensitive to being played for an advantage since they often do not have access to senior paid management and organizational escalation and appeal. And, volunteers can be very sensitive to being the teacher's pet, or not. Don't play favorites!

	Differences with distinction
A project management tip	• There's often an age difference, and an experience difference, that can be quite stunning: volunteers who were executives and senior technologists were *supervised* by 20-somethings. • The young supervisors need to be aware that age has a toll—the older generation may move a little slower, etc.

Module 3—Discussion for Critical Thinking

Among the many factors discussed that affect project management transitioning to agile methods, which have the most influence in your situation, and why?

Module 4: Portfolio Management Transition

If you're a portfolio manager, then some agility is required!

Module 4—Objectives

- Examine factors of scope management that are unique to agile transition
- Discuss team management in the context of portfolio management

Scope Management

Transitioning to a portfolio of agile projects brings up one really unique issue: managing effects of tactically emergent scope in each of the projects within the portfolio. The nature of the issue is this: the usual mission of the portfolio manager is to distribute scope among projects in a manner most beneficial to the business—but if scope is emergent, how is this done?

This is accomplished by using the usual tools we've discussed before: coupling, diversification, and redundancy. Desired attributes are coherence and cohesion throughout the portfolio. Factors that influence the scope distribution are often these:

- Natural lines or interfaces between units of architecture that make it beneficial to place each unit with an optimum project team
- Requirements for redundancy between one project and another for failsafe purposes and to absorb shocks of unforeseen external events

- Need to decouple certain units to contain or diversify risk by distributing the units to different projects
- Need to tap capacity and capability not available in one project

But if scope is tactically emergent, how is business benefit to be managed? For the portfolio manager, one or more of these objectives could be frustrated by emergent and tactically changing scope—even if each project is faithful to its strategic intent. Thus, from a transition perspective, experimentation with practices that influence the backlog in each project, with the objective to retain not only the intent but the effect of scope distribution, is something to be tried.

- Retain an architect at the portfolio management office to oversee the distribution of architecture units, and maintenance of these units within projects regarding strategic intent.
- Develop protocols to control changes that would impact redundancy.
- Deploy decoupling techniques like buffers and slack, encapsulation, stationary interfaces, and middle-layer communications.
- Approve the development of throw-away objects in order to prevent backlog freezes and lockouts due to missed milestones by dependent projects.

Team Management

Not unlike scope management, the portfolio manager has certain responsibilities and authorities regarding the effective working of project teams within the portfolio. For example, the portfolio manager can make decisions on matters such as these:

- **To co-locate or not:**
    - ◆ Co-located teams are tightly coupled with high density, which favors innovation and accurate, timely communications
    - ◆ Virtual teams are loosely coupled, but provide access to unique capabilities at an affordable cost
- **To manage release sequence:** Releases are sequenced among projects according to the portfolio business case, but also according to the ability of the business to absorb change
- **To establish safety and fairness among projects:** Disharmony is mitigated to optimize coherence and to minimize nonvalue, nonlean activities between projects

Inevitably, there will be tensions of accountability among teams, and between teams and the higher-level portfolio objectives:

- Projects are focused on project metrics of value earning, resource utilization, and hitting benchmarks
- Portfolios are focused on customer satisfaction and measures of business success by hitting strategic milestones with business deliverables.

	Managing tension
A project management tip	• There will be competition and disagreement among projects as each seeks local optimization for resource allocation and backlog construction • There will be business objectives that are optimum for the portfolio, but are compromising to projects with emergent and iterative scope

Module 4—Discussion for Critical Thinking

We posit that one tension to be managed is that between business objectives at the portfolio level and the demands of emergent scope at the project level. What practices would you employ to handle this tension?

Module 5: Agile Transition in the Public Sector

Public sector projects can be agile, even with more rules

Module 5—Objectives

- Examine the factors that influence success or not transitioning to agile in a public sector context

In Chapter 11, we discussed contracts; contracts are an enabling vehicle for contractors to do work in the public sector. Since contracting for agile is a work-in-progress for most public agencies, readers should look upon Chapter 11—insofar as it applies to public agencies—as a discussion of transition issues regarding contracts.

In this module, we'll look at transition issues in the public sector that differ from contracts.

Scope and Change Management

Public sector projects may have little public expectation. They are simply part of public administration. On the other hand, many public sector projects attract the attention of a widely diverse public following. These may run afoul of agile methods, and would have to be factored into any transition plan:

- The autonomy of the agile team to make even tactical backlog decisions may be constrained
- There will be pressure to maintain strategic intent very faithfully, and simultaneously control resource consumption
- Lean oversight may not be allowed by public oversight rules and statutes
- Tolerance for failure is very low (fail often, fail early is a hard sell to the public)
- Schedule delays are more tolerated than cost overruns (whereas agile is more focused on schedule than cost)
- Politics may trump project management or team choices and decisions
- Public accountability starts with plans

Agency Bias and Rules

Every public sector agency has its own biases and rules, to say nothing of business jargon, regardless of the larger public context of which it is a part. Whereas working for a public agency may be a core competency of a contractor unit, that competency comes with strings or modifiers:

- The ability of the contractor to speak the language and write in the style of the customer agency
- Trust among parties—developed by a successful track record (track record will port to other agencies, but trust will not)
- Familiarity and understanding of standards and standard documents of the customer agency
- Understanding of the biases of the customer agency

Consequently, and speaking the obvious, any plan for a transition pilot should be with an agency or a contractor with which the agency or contractor has a knowledgeable relationship.

On the other hand, many, if not most public agencies have put transitioning to agile in their strategic thinking, if not actually in their strategic plans. Thus, there are many opportunities to join with the public sector with agile methods. Even the standards committees and regulators are publishing more standards aimed at supporting the Agile Principles.

Cost of Value

Cost of value is often a matter of utility (value to the user, if not to others).

- Strategic intent is the first description of utility—what the outcome means to the customer/user and sponsor
- Mission success may trump all conventional project metrics—failure is not an option; success at whatever cost it takes
- Public budgets are sacrosanct, usually much more so than a project or agency milestone. But, with that said, every project has some objective regarding financial performance
- Return on investment (ROI) is somewhat, but not entirely meaningless in the public sector. Many fall back to the financial measure of return of benefits or cost-benefit analysis.

The issue is ageless: public benefits are often not monetarily quantifiable, in spite of bumper stickers like *you can measure anything*,[15] if for no other reason than causality is often very vague in public sector contexts. The environment is more wicked than not.[16]

Is It Worth It?
To complicate matters, the ROI, or NPV (net present value), or EVA (economic value add)[17] may all be unfavorable, but yet the benefit of the project, as envisioned in the narrative, is deemed essential to strategic business success. Thus, the project and then the post-project operational focus turns to minimizing the risk of negative project measurements while maximizing the return of benefits in the long term.

Module 5—Discussion for Critical Thinking

If your agency wants to be agile by methodology, but is traditional by doctrine and rules, what are possible remedies in order to get to agile?

Summary and Takeaway

Our theme for this chapter is that the true way to do agile is the way that works best for the team, the project, the portfolio, and for the business. This chapter covers some topics specifically on the point of transitioning from traditional methodology—the beginning of which is leadership in business management.

In Module 1, we posit that there is a grand bargain to be made between the business leadership and the project team—such that a promise of faithfulness to strategic intent by the project permits the business to give the project latitude to be tactically emergent.

Since agile is all about customer satisfaction, Module 2 is all about the customer relationship. There are two main points, each having to do with the likely unfamiliarity of the customer with their role in agile projects:

1. Commitment to be embedded and work directly with the team
2. Training required to bring the customer up to a degree of competence to work with the team

Project design is the topic of Module 3. The reader should take this module, along with the other chapters of this book, as a guide about how to design a project for best fit to the business, considering co-location, virtual teams and remote working, environment density, and other factors. But most importantly, any transition to agile should include a pilot project. Of course, we warn that a pilot may not scale well or predict routine results on other projects if the pilot team is a pick of the A-team.

Module 4 brings us to the portfolio—perhaps just as important as the project itself—since the emergent scope aspects of agile bear directly on scope distribution strategies in the portfolio. The portfolio manager has a variety of tools that can help manage scope distribution, and to some extent these same tools are applicable to team management as well. The distribution of teams among locations and projects will impact portfolio objectives; resulting in some transition issues regarding how to handle these in the enterprise context.

And last, but certainly not least—given the amount of money and number of projects—is transitioning in the public sector to include government projects, projects in nonprofits, and even volunteer projects. This model is meant to reinforce some of the ideas in the chapter on contracts which are also an important tool in the public sector project context.

Chapter Endnotes

1. See: http://www.mountaingoatsoftware.com/blog/the-one-true-way-to-be-agile, blog by Mike Cohn.
2. Some of these ideas are adapted from Heifetz, R. *Leadership Without Easy Answers*, Harvard College, Cambridge, MA, 1994, though the book was written well before agile methods were codified by the Agile Manifesto and the Agile Principles.

3. These three styles are loosely modeled on the four leadership styles of the Hersey-Blanchard model of situational leadership. See: en.wikipedia.org/wiki/Situational_leadership_theory. The complete Hersey-Blanchard model also has styles for followers; there is a mapping between leader and follower styles.

4. See Mike Griffiths's blog at http://www.leadinganswers.typepad.com

5. Derived from Mike Griffith's CASPER list: Contrary, absent, switching, passive, elusive, reclusive.

6. S4 is a reference to the Hersey-Blanchard situational leadership theory, previously discussed.

7. See an explanation of prospect theory at http://en.wikipedia.org/wiki/Prospect_theory

8. Some of the best material on agile modeling is found at ambysoft.com, the website of Scott Ambler.

9. This is the general message of this book: Avent, R. *The Gated City*.

10. See: en.wikipedia.org/wiki/Allen_curve

11. See: www.nytimes.com/2014/07/20/opinion/sunday/the-end-of-genius.html

12. Taleb, N. *Antifragile: Things That Gain from Disorder*, Random House, NY, 2012.

13. Prahalad, C.K. and Hamel, G. "The core competence of the organization," Harvard Business Review, May-June, 1990 at https://hbr.org/1990/05/the-core-competence-of-the-corporation

14. Volunteers are not interns, unpaid interns, part time, or contract workers. For this discussion they are skilled practitioners who choose to give their time to a project.

15. Douglas W. Hubbard wrote a book with a similar title: *How to Measure Anything: Finding the Value of Intangibles in Business*, John Wiley, NY, 2007.

16. Wicked refers to environments with circular cause-effect relationships with no obvious entry or exit. See http://en.wikipedia.org/wiki/Wicked_problem

17. NPV and EVA are measures of risk adjusted cash flows from a project outcome. Usually, the cash flow should be positive: investment less than benefits.

Appendix I: Methodologies

There is no point in being precise when you don't know what you are talking about.

John von Neumann

Practice details about each of the four methodologies featured in this book, Scrum, XP (Extreme Programming), The Crystal Family (Clear and Orange), and Kanban, are described in this appendix that is complementary to the methodology quick-read provided in Chapter 1.

Scrum

"... Scrum, a most perplexing and paradoxical process for managing complex projects."

Ken Schwaber

The Scrum Methodology is Management-centric

Scrum is first and foremost a management regime; it is a mind-shift from traditional project paradigms about how to organize work, apply talents, involve the customer intimately, and deliver quality to all the project beneficiaries. Scrum is a management framework on which many different practices can be hung and linked into a project process. Among the four methodologies, Scrum is most prescriptive about management concepts; it only suggests best technical practices.

Scrum is applicable beyond the software industry; indeed a variant started in industrial projects in Japan, as described in Chapter 1. However, in this book, Scrum is the software-centric methodology aligned with the Agile Manifesto.

The following points are the main ideas in Scrum; notice that many of these are also shared with all agile methods:

- Working product is the main measure of success and the main focus of team activity.
- The customer is represented by the product master; the product master is embedded in the team; other users and customers are always very close at hand to offer near-real-time user evaluation and feedback
- Product should evolve incrementally as influenced by customers
- Working lean under empirical control is critical for the speed and nimbleness required to be agile
- Small, co-located, self-organizing teams do the best work with the least invested effort
- Project managers add value by facilitating teamwork, clearing hurdles, and mitigating impediments to team productivity

The Original Scrum

Scrum did not start out as a software project management process. Indeed, Scrum is relevant and applicable to projects of all character. Recall from Chapter 1, the early industrial products work done by Hirotaka Takeuchi and Ikujiro Nonaka. They envisioned the rugby sports analogy for the project behaviors they observed: in Rugby Union, the Scrum is a formation of eight multifunctional teammates who *link together* in a common mission to gain possession of the ball and advance it to the goal:

- Getting to the goal is not handed-off from one squad to another
- Practices like kicking and passing are *not rigidly sequenced*—the tactics of the Scrum are situational and quite varied
- *Leadership comes from within the team*—although there are coaches who provide a framework to operate within, *the team is not centrally managed*
- The game dynamic starts over at each Scrum possession allowing for a near-real time assessment of strengths, weaknesses, opportunities, and threats

Table I.1, summarizes Takeuchi and Nonaka's ideas that are still very relevant to agile project thinking.

Continuing with the sports metaphor, the coach plays the role of Scrum master, and the fans play the role of product master. Other parallels with agile methods in general and Scrum specifically, include:

- **Time boxes:** The game is divided into quarters or halves that are rigidly managed by time, equivalent to the sprints. Certain repetitive activities are rigidly time-boxed, like the *time-outs.*

Table I.1 Scrum according to Takeuchi and Nonaka

Feature	Commentary
Built-in stability	• Management sets stretch goals and challenging requirements, but otherwise grants generous freedom and latitude to the implementation team
Self-organizing teams	• The team dynamic takes on the attributes of the entrepreneurial opportunity, setting its own norms and electing its own leaders • In Takeuchi's and Nonaka's words, the team is driven to a state of "zero information", operating much less on prior knowledge and much more on the collective wisdom of the team as augmented by the customer • A team has successfully arrived at self-organization when it can operate autonomously, cross-fertilize itself with knowledge from its participants, and set its own goals that may in some cases transcend those of management
Overlapping project phases	• Project phases are not rigidly sequenced in finish-to-start formations with gated entry and exit and handoffs from one staff to another • Rather, the team carries forward, much like the rugby Scrum, and overlaps are allowed and encouraged between phases
Multi-learning	• Learning occurs in multiple ways: members in close proximity learn about the markets and customers and business from the embedded users; members learn cross-functionally from each other
Subtle control	• Management lays a light hand, allowing self control while managing ambiguity, uncertainty, and roadblocks that might enable chaos • Measurements are made and reported but the overhead is subordinated to the objective of delivering value to the customer • Takeuchi and Nonaka list seven specific control mechanisms: 1. select the right people, 2. encourage suppliers to mimic the team behavior, 3. tolerate mistakes, 4. reward and incent performance, 5. encourage listening, 6. create an open work environment, and 7. manage the rhythm and velocity of the activity from one phase to the next
Organizational transfer of learning	• Embrace knowledge transfer outside the team to the enterprise as a whole to create more of a reservoir of institutional knowledge and permanence of investment

- **Milestones:** The game itself is driven by a milestone at the end—in effect, the release schedule.
- **Adaptive outcomes:** Although there is a goal and a strategy to win, the outcome, particularly the score, is not predictable with any certainty in spite of considerable resource commitment.
- **Game plan:** The game plan is the business plan architecture of the team's mission. Beyond the game plan, tactics are just-in-time and developed on the field by the team.

Contemporary Scrum Methodology

Scrum, as it is popularly known, is an adaptation of Takeuchi-Nonaka specifically for the software industry. The leaders most associated with it are Ken Schwaber and Jeff Sutherland, but there are many others who did early work and continue to contribute to the Scrum community. The main features of Scrum are given in Tables I.2, I.3, and I.4. Most Scrum practices are common to all agile methods. The Scrum methodology is clean and simple, reflecting the strong emphasis on a light-touch central management and much faith in the development team.

Figure I.1 illustrates the basic Scrum sprint.

Table I.2   Scrum human factors

Human Factor	Commentary
Teams	• Work on Scrum projects is done by people on teams of small size, up to about 5-10, perhaps up to 15 participants • Teams are self-organized • Teams are multi-disciplinary, and include more than the software sciences • Teams complete iterations without handoffs
Product master	• Products are sponsored by a product master who is responsible for the product vision and business requirements • Product is the surrogate for all the project's business outcomes
Scrum master	• Teams are mentored and facilitated by a Scrum master who is the Scrum project manager • The Scrum master is responsible for clearing the way and breaking down all the internal and external barriers, providing the subtle touch described by Takeuchi-Nonaka • When the team cannot resolve issues, the Scrum master provides management

Table I.3   Scrum practices

Practice	Commentary
Product backlog Sprint backlog	• Backlog is the list of priority-weighted requirements awaiting implementation • Requirements from the product backlog are allocated to sprints and become sprint backlogs • The product backlog is continuously reevaluated at the conclusion of each sprint • Unsatisfied requirements are re-prioritized back into the product backlog.
User stories	• User stories are fleshed out and more detailed by face-to-face conversations with developers during the course of the development • In this sense, detailed requirements are just-in-time input for the development process • During the sprint, requirements are considered fixed
Sprint	• A sprint is 30 days on the calendar during which the team works on a fixed unit of scope that has been assigned to the sprint
Time-boxing	• Time-boxing is a practice whereby a given activity is limited to a pre-scribed time • Scope is variable in a time box
Daily stand-up meeting	• The team assembles each day for a short stand-up meeting, typically "time-boxed" to 15 minutes • Each team member speaks • The Scrum master facilitates • Outside stakeholders are not invited • Solutions are not discussed • The main topic is the daily work objective and any barriers to success
Refactoring	• Refactoring is a design and development practice • Refactoring means changing internal design to improve quality and conform to standards without changing external performance and properties • Refactoring is a practice that enables a quick-pace project with flow and rhythm

Table I.4   The Scrum methodology

Method step	Commentary
0. A project is envisioned	0. A project is chartered to meet a need, execute business strategy with the intended purpose of achieving a business goal.
	• The goal encompasses a vision of the product, a community of users and stakeholders who will benefit, an investment plan, milestones, and a benefit plan
1. Requirements and user stories are collected into a product backlog	1. Requirements for the project outcomes, whether a product or a process, are gathered in the form of "user stories" and prioritized by the product master.
	• There is an expectation that the unallocated backlog will change over the course of the project
2. Sprint planning meetings map the backlog to sprint windows	2. One or more sprint planning meetings map the backlog of customer and end-user requirements to a fixed-duration sprint.
	• These meetings have the effect of loading the teams with their workload for a specific sprint
	• The product master and the embedded users on the sprint teams have full knowledge of the backlog allocation
	• Unlike plan-centered methodologies, specific outcomes are predicted and forecast at the sprint level and not at the project level
	• All outcomes conform to the product vision described in the business plan
3. The development sprint is executed	3. The first allocation of the backlog to the first development sprint is most important.
	• It is expected the backlog and user stories will be modified as the sprints deliver functionality and users become more aware of what they need and want
4. A close-out or lessons-learned meeting	4. Feedback and a retrospective look at the sprint execution in near-real time to the completion of the sprint is necessary to correct faults going into the next sprint.
5. Releases to production	5. The outcome of a sprint may or may not go to production.
	• As the backlog allocation is made, release-to-production plans are developed

Scrum is a methodology centered on daily activity, loosely managed by the Scrum master, in which the team executes development of a set of user stories every 30 days and puts them into production

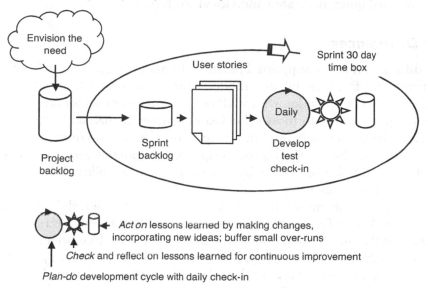

Figure I.1 Scrum methodology

Extreme Programming (XP)

> *"XP is my attempt to reconcile humanity and productivity in my own practice of software development and share that reconciliation."*
>
> *Kent Beck*

Extreme Programming Is Disciplined

In applying this methodology, project managers who are experienced in more traditional methods should draw some reassurance from the fact that many of the practices will be familiar. However, there are some that are *extreme* by comparison to traditional methods, for example, test-driven development (TDD).

Refactoring, already introduced in the discussion about Scrum, is a practice that Beck now includes in *incremental design*. Of course, forms of incremental design have been around for decades in various forms, even in hardware development. Incremental design in agile methods includes evolution from increment to increment, following customer priorities rather than a *big design up front*.

Pair programming is an extreme practice that is somewhat counterintuitive to the programmer productivity ideas developed in the 1980s—ideas that stressed quiet, dedicated, individual workspace.

XP Differences

XP differs a bit in the supported practices from other agile methods, and its methodology is a little bit unorthodox, starting as it does from a test perspective. This concept, known to XP proponents as *test-driven development*, sounds quite strange to those schooled in structured analysis. In structured analysis, design begins by accumulating a complete requirements specification. But TDD begins with a test script that documents a requirement in the form of a test, and verifies by test failure that capability does not exist already in the product base.

Beck is assuredly the intellectual catalyst behind XP, although he has had a lot of help: Martin Fowler, Ward Cunningham, and Ron Jefferies were all compatriots at the first XP application at Chrysler and have since been advocates for the methodology. First to apply the methodology on an enterprise project, Beck's team more or less set the rules and practices. Beck provided a good overview of XP with his 1999 book *Extreme Programming Explained—Embrace Change*.[1] After five years of experience applying XP, he then did a significant redo of values, principles, and practices in 2005, with a second edition.

XP Values and Principles

The five values, given in Table I.5, are not prescriptive in a how-to sense, but rather set a mental framework for the endeavor. All agile methods put great stress on the individuality and humanity of the participants; Beck gives emphasis to the social change required by XP and the importance of the human factor in his XP values.[2]

Table I.5   XP values

Value	Explanation
Communication	"…Important for creating a sense of team"
Simplicity	Unwitting and unnecessary complexity is a hazard. Simplify to improve quality. However, the simplest design may still be complex.
Feedback	Information about defects is used to improve the process
Courage	"…effective action in the face of fear"
Respect	Caring about the people and the project
Others	Chosen by the team and the project

The 14 XP principles, given in Table I.6, are a treatise on many environmental and procedural effects that teams will encounter.[3] XP principles provide guidance to practitioners, that they can apply according to circumstances.

XP is, in the end, a methodology. Practices are embedded in a process. The process envisions frequent production releases. Each release is composed of a number of time-boxed iterations, similar in scope and purpose to the sprint described in the Scrum method. Each iteration is scoped to produce some part of the requirements. The XP requirements are gathered as part of listening and interviewing that is done by the development teams during release planning. Requirements are first documented as higher-level scenarios, then dissected into user stories, and then turned into test scripts. The scripts are the initial design step in the iteration, which is somewhat discomfiting to the traditionally trained. Another uncomfortable idea is that, in its most pure form, at least as exercised on a small scale, there is no methodology requirement for a system design that transcends the various releases. However, in this book, we frame all projects with architecture.

There are 24 practices, divided into a group of 13 most important (primary) and then a group of 11 corollary (secondary) practices, as given in Tables I.7 and I.8.[4]

Table I.6 XP principles

Principle	Commentary
Humanity	Providing safety, accomplishment, belonging, growth, and intimacy
Economics	"Somebody has to pay for all this"
Mutual benefit	"The most important XP principle…"
Self-similarity	Re-use good design
Improvement	Everything can be improved with diligent action
Diversity	Multifunctional skills on teams to reduce risk
Reflection	Think about how and why work is being done the way it is
Flow	Maintain a project rhythm and avoid periods of inaction and no production
Opportunity	Appreciate change as driver for innovation
Redundancy	Avoid disaster with more than one way to solve the problem
Failure	"If you are having trouble succeeding, fail;" failure imparts knowledge
Quality	"Quality is not a control variable"
Baby steps	Break down complex things into manageable pieces
Accepted responsibility	"Responsibility cannot be assigned; it can only be accepted"

Table I.7 XP practices—primary

Practice	Commentary
Sit together	Co-locate everyone
Whole team	Include all the necessary technical and business skills in the team
Informative workspace	Use visuals to communicate continuously
Energized work	Do not work to burn-out; maintain a sustainable pace
Pair programming	Program in teams, sitting together
Stories	Plan using stories that are units of customer functionality
Weekly cycle	Plan a week in detail
Quarterly cycle	Plan ahead by quarters
Slack	Build buffers into the schedule
Ten-minute build	Design for short, numerous builds
Continuous integration	Maintain the product base rigorously so that everyone is working with the latest design
Test-first programming	Test-driven design
Incremental design	Design a little bit of the system everyday

Table I.8 XP practices—secondary

Practice	Commentary
Real customer involvement	The customer should be committed to team participation
Incremental deployment	Product is deployed on a pace governed by the customer's ability to absorb change; parallel legacy operations may be required
Team continuity	Teams stay together so long as they are effective
Shrinking teams	Teams shrink as productivity improves so that velocity remains constant
Root cause analysis	Always get to the bottom of problems; use Ohno's "five why's" process to drill down
Shared code	Anyone can work on any of the code and improve the system
Code and tests	Code, test scripts, and test conditions are the permanent artifacts of the project
	Code and test scripts help bridge the gap among disparate developers on virtual teams
Single code base	Integrity of the design is maintain by keeping one gold copy; test and development copies are temporary expedients
Daily deployment	New design is integrated daily; add to production daily if the customer can absorb change rapidly
Negotiated scope contract	Work orders are contracted in short sequences where parameters can be stabilized
Pay per use	The benefit stream is monetized system use

XP Process

There are two overriding process ideas in XP: (1) gain efficiency by being ruthless about disciplined practices and design simplicity and (2) deliver customer value by building product incrementally according to the customer's priorities of importance and urgency. The first development cycle begins by designing the simplest object that is likely to be successfully coded. Thereafter, more complex objects are coded.

	Architecture and XP
A project management tip	Experienced project managers and system engineers who apply XP to larger-scale development projects ordinarily create architecture and identify the critical success factors regarding feature, function, and performance.

Table I.9 summarizes the XP process; note that it is very similar to Scrum in terms of the process steps as shown in Figure I.1.

Crystal

Computers must support the way in which people naturally and comfortably work … I care about whether the team is thriving, and whether the software is being delivered. Keeping the people trained and the process light are keys to both.

Alistair Cockburn

The Crystal Methodology Is Human Powered

The Crystal methodologies are called *people-powered*. The central theme is: people drive methodologies and are responsible for outcomes—not management artifacts like documents and metrics. So, Crystal advocates the minimization of documentation and other overhead, and a maximization of, and dependency on, human interaction. And, in a definite contrast with XP, Crystal assumes that people do not and will not adhere rigidly to a set of rules; the methodology is deliberately tolerant of variant behaviors. In fact, it is assumed that people sometimes act irrationally, unpredictably, and fail to maintain a constant productivity. People, in other words, are not entirely linear and thus, planning must take such into account. Each team is empowered to set its own minimum standards of behavior and accountability.

Table I.9   XP process

Process Step	Commentary
0. A project is envisioned	0. A project is chartered to meet a need, execute business strategy with the intended purpose of achieving a business goal. • The goal encompasses a vision of the product, a community of users and stakeholders who will benefit, an investment plan, milestones, and a benefit plan
1. Requirements gathered and evaluated	1. Requirements for the project outcomes, whether a product or a process, are gathered in the form of "user stories" and prioritized by the product master. • There is an expectation that the unallocated backlog will change over the course of the project
2. Release planning meetings	2. One or more release planning meetings map the backlog of customer and end-user requirements to a fixed-duration release
3. Development iterations	3. The first allocation of the backlog to the first development iteration is most important. • It is expected the backlog and user stories will be modified as the iterations deliver functionality and users become more aware of what they need and want
4. Spike and iteration	4. Refactor for quality and correct serious defects
5. Close-out and lessons learned	5. Feedback and a retrospective look at the iteration execution in near-real time to the completion of the iteration is necessary to correct faults going into the next iteration
6. Releases to production	6. The outcome of an iteration may or may not go to production. As the backlog allocation is made, release-to-production plans are developed

Crystal Beginnings

Cockburn began promoting his ideas even before his participation in the group-of-17 meeting in Utah in 2001. From the outset, Cockburn advocated small, highly interactive teams but was quick to say that one size does not fit all. He conceived Crystal as a group of methodologies distinguished by team size, project complexity, and practice details. To keep it all straight, Cockburn labeled each with a distinctive color, beginning with *Clear*. The principal book on the topic was published in 2005: *Crystal Clear: A Human-powered Methodology.*[5]

Clear is the color given by Cockburn to the smallest team size for the simplest projects—a team of six to nine. The optimum situation is engaged people, working face-to-face with generous interaction. Cockburn accepts that people are fallible, not good at repetitive tasks that require high discipline, and are usually unable to meet demands for the same, uniform quality time after time. Frankly, if Cockburn has an argument with XP, it is on this point: as a methodology, in his opinion, XP is too demanding about discipline and sticking with the rules, even though a beneficial side effect of XP's disciplined behavior is less required documentation.

Dr. Cockburn posits that from one person to the next, performance expectations must allow for some variance, maybe even unpredictability. Cockburn calls this the *nonlinear* attribute of human behavior.[6] He rejects the plan-driven project development lifecycle (PD-PDLC) planning premise that people can be plugged into roles, like components into sockets, with an expectation that they will perform day in and day out according to the planning model, just so long as they meet the requisites of the role specification. He argues that plans that forecast outcomes according to the performance of role models are bound to end up badly.

Nonlinear Behavior
Nonlinear behavior simply means that the output of a process or activity is not uniformly proportional to input, and the output may even reverse itself, even if the input direction remains unchanged. Linear behavior is just the opposite—linear systems obey the rule that *output follows input proportionately and directionally; at zero input, the output may be zero or some other bias value.*

The Crystal Body of Knowledge

Like the other agile methods we will discuss, Crystal has its own body of knowledge. At the top level are seven principles. Although authored in a Crystal context, these principles are applicable to all agile methodologies, and if read in a value-added sense, they really apply to all project methodologies. Most have their roots in prior quality movements, but they provide a nice grouping that is easy to internalize. The main ideas are in Table I.10.[7]

Implementation strategies support the Crystal Family as given in Table I.11.[8]

Crystal embraces a number of day-to-day techniques, many of which are adapted from other methodologies. They are applied at the discretion of the team as situations arise. Cockburn makes the point that if somebody has a good idea, then put it to work. It's all part of methodology shaping—the first technique on Table I.12.

Table I.10   Crystal principles

Principle	Commentary
Frequent delivery	Put product into production as often as the customer can accept it
Osmotic communication	Communicate by word, gesture, and by general association; listen to what is going on around
Reflective improvement	Always look back to seek improvements
Personal safety	Do not attack people; only attack problems
Focus	Do not multiplex between problems
Easy access to subject matter experts	Make experts available quickly and easily
Technical environment	Make the technical environment effective for supporting project objectives

Table I.11   Crystal strategies

Strategy	Commentary
Explore 360	Look at the envisioned need from many perspectives
Early victory	Do something simple to get into production and reinforce a "can do" attitude
Walking skeleton	Build an end-to-end functionality that works and can be used to build more functionality incrementally; gives the customer an early first look
Incremental re-architecture	Be prepared to reexamine the architecture after every release
Information radiators	Radiators are dashboards, whiteboards, newsletters, and other media distribution
	The principle is be open with team communications; make it easy to find and use information, and easy to maintain

The strategies and techniques given in Tables I.11 and I.12 fit into a process. Table I.13 provides an overview of the Crystal Clear process steps.

Kanban

"A ... process-management system that tells what to produce, when to produce it, and how much to produce."

Wikipedia[9]

Kanban, as used in software development and as grouped with agile methodologies, is a workflow practice, not really a complete methodology.

Table I.12 Crystal techniques

Technique	Commentary
Methodology shaping	Shape the project methodology for unique aspects of each project
Reflection workshop	Use a workshop to thoroughly examine lessons learned
Blitz planning	Rapid fire, just-in-time planning, using a planning game or other quick means to plan; see planning poker detail in Chapter 7
Delphi estimating	Apply estimates from many independent experts; see Chapter 7
Daily stand-up	Time-boxed meeting, as in Scrum, to hear daily plans of team members
Essential interaction design	Share the design experience with users, customers, and sponsors
Process miniature	Run a benchmark of the team process with a scaled down process for quick turn around of benchmark numbers
Burn charts	See Figure I.2 at the end of this chapter for an example of a control chart for tracking objects planned, started, and completed
Side-by-side programming	See XP's pair programming

Table 1.13 Crystal clear process

Process Step	Commentary
The project	• The project has three major components: the charter, the deliveries (one or more), and the wrap-up and close-out.
The delivery	• The delivery consists of one or more iterations, the actual go-live event (actually, a process with an event or milestone at the end), and then time for reflection.
The iteration	• The iteration is led-off by a planning activity; then there are day-to-day activities consisting of the daily stand-up, design episodes, code and unit test, integration into the code base, and then reflection and celebration.
The episode	• The design episode is the actual design activity. • Requirements from the backlog, as assigned by the plan to the iteration, are committed to the design with tools like the UML use case and CRC* cards. • The actual design is allowed to be refactored so objects are started quickly by coding an outline based upon the CRC data and the use case.

Process Shift in Dominance and Allegiance

The word *Kanban*[10] is taken from the Japanese production management process in which there are a series of sequential steps in a process, and at each step there are raw materials or partial product—a.k.a. inventory—to do the task. Important to all Kanban systems is that inventory needed to do a particular task or at a particular process step is managed at a minimum level. Enough inventory is available or provided *just-in-time*, such that excess inventory does not get stored at work stations.

Readers who are familiar with the Theory of Constraints (TOC)[11] will immediately recognize the influence of that theory on the Kanban process. The TOC teaches that optimum production occurs when *just enough* inventory passes through the overall system, such that the tightest constraint with the least throughput is operated at maximum capacity. Piling up inventory before a constraint is unnecessary and not lean.

However, the point of Kanban is not really to manage inventory per se, but to put demands on inventory based on the need to *pull* an outcome through the process steps to meet a customer need. Thus, Kanban, like all of agile, shifts the management dominance from a forecast of resource consumption (plan-driven up front) to outcome dominance. And, with this shift of input to output dominance, there is a shift of allegiance from a forecast to a customer need.

Elements of Workflow

Most workflow systems have common elements among them, and agile Kanban is no different:

- A prescribed process of ordered steps
- A means to manage, control, or constrain the new work that enters the process stream
- A means to sequence, order, or prioritize new work
- Criteria to move from step to step
- Inventory that moves from step to step, and/or is provided at the step

Elements of Agile Kanban

Kanban is an effective workflow tool for small teams, because it lends itself well to visualization and direct interaction with work in progress (WIP). In general, agile Kanban is set up this way:

- There is a backlog as discussed in the main body of this book
- There are one or more processes that are defined in advance that are applied to the backlog in some ordered sequence—each process having some number of steps
- An item of backlog enters a process at a certain step; it is worked upon; and then it is *promoted* to the next step in the process—this is WIP

- An estimate of *remaining effort* is made for each WIP item; this estimate drives a burn-down chart—the burn-down chart is managed as described in the main body of this book
- A control system regulates the WIP to a specific *WIP limit*, such that the overall system is not overwhelmed

Visualization of the WIP situation is made possible by a Kanban board. Physically, a Kanban board looks much like a pipeline board of traditional methodologies. Stories or requirements or work items are written on cards, notations, sticky notes, or some other artifact. Cards are placed on the board at each step for each WIP item. The cards are moved along from step to step as each step is finished.

- Initially, all cards are in the backlog, and none are WIP
- Finally, all cards make it to *done* and none are in WIP
- In between, some cards will be in backlog, some in WIP, and some *done*

Not Time-boxed

Those familiar with pipeline systems recognize that maintenance of a smooth flow is a main objective. Any barrier to flow causes inventory to back up before the barrier. We see this in all manner of flow systems—including hydraulic, auto traffic, and electromagnetic propagation. Such barriers often cause reflection of incident energy or inventory; these reflections often interfere with, may be destructive to, or cause errors in new inventory coming down the pipeline. Again, we see this as waves in hydraulic systems, rolling traffic jams, and standing waves or multipath interference in electromagnetic systems.

For these reasons, Agile Kanban is not time-boxed. Smooth flow is paramount. WIP limit is carefully managed until the backlog is burned down. A smooth flow is lean, since unusable energy, reflected by a constraint, is not expended; a smooth flow is more error free, reducing rework, and enhancing lean production. A smooth flow is predictable, or more predictable, than a flow with reflections that may be chaotic. Nonetheless, everything may not flow as smoothly as intended. Small tasks may be put aside; refactoring may be deferred; or some backlog deferred. Much of this we call debt. As debt is collected in the backlog, it too, becomes potential WIP.

Managing Releases

Generally a release is managed by managing the backlog that, when *done*, becomes the release package. Just like in time-boxed methodologies, as the backlog is progressively done, is integrated, and tested according to customer demand and enterprise policy and protocols, so it is in Kanban—which becomes the driver for the release process.

Whereas in time-boxed methodologies, empty iterations can be planned to guard the release date with a buffer that can absorb unforeseen eventualities, there are no natural buffers in a Kanban system. Thus, the project manager plans buffers somewhat in critical chain style,[12] to ensure faithfulness to the release milestone.

Summary and Takeaway Points

All four methods described in this appendix are practical agile methods with an established track record. Scrum is perhaps easiest to apply; XP is the most disciplined and should be the most predictable. The Crystal Family is best at accepting that people are fallible and methods must be shaped to the circumstances; and Kanban takes the best principles from production management and applies them to the development process.

Each of these methods is supported by passionate proponents, thought leaders in the industry, and myriad others who have written and blogged extensively. See the many references in this book of other material that amplify many points.

Appendix Endnotes

1. Beck, K. with Andres, C. *Extreme Programming Explained*, Addison-Wesley, Boston, 1999.

2. Beck, K. with Andres, C. (2005), op. cit. Chapter 4.

3. Beck, K. with Andres, C. (2005), op. cit. Chapter 5.

4. Beck, K. with Andres, C. (2005), op. cit. Chapters 7 and 9.

5. Cockburn, A., *Crystal Clear: A Human-powered Methodology for Small Teams*, Addison-Wesley, Boston, 2005.

6. For more on Cockburn's ideas, see his article presented at the 4th International Multiconference on Systems, Cybernetics and Informatics, Orlando, Florida, June, 2000, Cockburn, A., Characterizing People as First Order Nonlinear Components, 1999.

7. Cockburn, A. *Crystal Clear: A Human-powered Methodology for Small Teams*, Addison-Wesley, Boston, 2005, 19-39.

8. Cockburn, A. (2005) op. cit., 46-55.

9. See: http://en.wikipedia.org/wiki/Kanban_(development)

10. Kanban roughly translates to billboard or signboard you can see, but has come to mean card or even signal in the sense that when inventory gets down

to a minimum level and exposes the Kanban card, such exposure is the signal to suppliers to refresh inventory. Thus, inventory is not managed to a forecast at the work-station level, but is supplied to the work station according to actual demand.

11. Goldratt, E., *The Goal: A Process of Ongoing Improvement*, North River Press, 1992.

12. Goldratt, E., *The Critical Chain: A Business Novel*, North River Press, 1997.

Burn charts, whether burn-down or burn-up, show earned value progress against plan for developing objects for production

Effort to go is the difference between the operating plan and the effort burned for the object for the week

When R-G-RF [red – green – refactor] is in status RF, the object is considered complete

Object	Assigned to	Complexity	Baseline effort	Iteration week	Operating plan effort	Effort burned	Effort to go	Planned R-G-RF	Actual R-G-RF	Variance R-G-RF
1	AB	10	40	1	45	40	5	G	G	No
2	BC	25	100	1	100	100	0	R	R	No
3	RF	25	100	1	100	100	0	R	R	No
4	JG	5	20	1	25	25	0	RF	RF	No
5	RH	10	40	1	45	40	5	G	G	No
1	AB	10	40	2	40		40	RF		
2	BC	25	100	2	100		100	R		
3	RF	25	100	2	100		100	R		
6	JG	5	20	2	20		20	RF		
5	RH	10	40	2	40		40	G		
7	AB	10	40	3	40		40	RF		
2	BC	25	100	3	100		100	R		
3	RF	25	100	3	100		100	R		
8	JG	5	20	3	20		20	RF		
9	RH	10	40	3	40		40	G		
7	AB	10	40	4	40		40	RF		
2	BC	25	100	4	100		100	RF		
3	RF	25	100	4	100		100	RF		
10	JG	5	20	4	20		20	RF		
9	RH	10	40	4	40		40	RF		
			1200		1215	305	910			

Figure I.2   Burn charts

Appendix II: Glossary

The following glossary defines the terms used in this book.

Item	Definition
Adaptive	A response to circumstances that changes behavior or outcome; feedback enables adapting to circumstances. Adaptive situations are often emergent in character. See emergent.
Agile methods and practices	Methodologies that are more situational-driven, less centrally managed and more self-managed, with an emphasis on near-continuous responsiveness to customer need. The focus is on the quality of the result, even if the result is not very predictable at the outset and not according to plan. Example: XP (Extreme Programming).
Blitz planning	Rapid fire, just-in-time planning using a planning game or other quick means to plan.
Burn charts	Burn charts are a plot of what has been done and what is left to do. Burn refers to effort, and *burned* is often associated with completed or done. Burn-up or down refers to working up or down a list of things to do, or a surrogate or stand-in for things completed and things left to do.
Business	The organization or enterprise that hosts the project. The business may be a governmental unit, nonprofit, or a business unit within a larger enterprise. Organization, enterprise, and business are used interchangeably.

Calendar	A system for fixing the beginning, end, and duration of absolute units of time in relation to a year, week, or month.
Chaos	A system concept that characterizes the sensitivity of system responses to system stimulus. Systems that have big and unpredictable or unforecasted responses to relatively minor stimulus are chaotic or near chaos.
Charge-back rate	Charge-back rate is the rate/unit of time that the individual is charged to the paying organization. The rate may be the base salary, or the salary lifted by a factor for benefits, or it could be a rate that includes a lift for both benefits and overhead. In some organizations, and particularly if contracted, the charge-back rate may be a *standard cost*. Standard cost is a fixed rate by labor or job category, regardless of the person's paid-out compensation; in some cases, the standard cost is greater than the actual compensation, and other times, not. Other practices may use a rolling average of actual compensation as the charge-back rate. Standard cost is sometimes computed as a rolling average.
CMM (I)	Capability Maturity Model—Integration was developed by Carnegie Mellon University. It integrates software and system engineering with product integration in a set of recommended practices loosely framed in a methodology. CMM (I) is a service mark of Carnegie Mellon University.
COCOMO	COCOMO is an acronym taken from the phrase COnstructive COst MOdel, emphasizing the model's focus on the construction phase of the project. COCOMO II is a follow-on model to the original COCOMO 81 developed by Dr. Barry Boehm and his associates in 1981.
Complexity	Complexity is quality described by how many ways units can interact, a measure of how many unique states a system can be in, and how many responses one stimulus causes.
Containment	A concept that seeks to prevent defect *creep* from one code base.
Contractor	Provider, supplier, and contractor are used interchangeably to denote the entity that is doing the work governed by a contract. The project is the entity that does the contracting with the provider.

Cost-of-value	Synonymous with budget; synonymous with planned value (PV).
CRC cards	Class-responsibility-collaborator is a model of an object that specifies a class name, such as *Order*, one or more responsibilities, such as *Knows Item*, and collaborators, such as *Inventory Item*.
Critical path	The critical path is the longest connected path through the network.
Customer	The people and organization that are the principal beneficiaries of the project. End-users, or users, are customers with detailed functional knowledge. Customers may be external or internal to the organization.
Debt	Units of work, typically small in scope, that are left over from an iteration or release. Debt is prioritized in the project backlog and allocated to iteration backlogs to be completed. Debt may be technical, as in tests not completed, or functional, as in a function or feature left out or not completed.
Defined process control	Defined process control is a concept from manufacturing, promoted strongly by the work of W. Edwards Deming and others in the post World War II era. It presumes definable error limits that are acceptable in the finished product, means to measure, and means to correct.
DoD	U.S. Department of Defense.
EIA	Electronics Industry Association.
Emergent	A characteristic of systems where the interaction of simple rules and parts creates very complex systems and responses—output. Emergent systems have output based upon agents and agent processes interacting in seemingly unpredictable ways, adapting to circumstances, but bounded by rules set down by governance.
Entropy	For software system purposes, a measure of capacity or capability that is unusable.

Epic	The top-level business story or theme from which all use cases and user stories are developed.
Episode	The actual design activity within an iteration. Episode is a Crystal term.
Finish-to-start	Finish-to-start is a scheduling precedence taken from the Precedence Diagramming Method (PDM). It means that the finishing activity of a task must be completed before the starting activity of the successor task can begin.
Gantt chart	The Gantt chart is a bar chart with individual bars representing activities. The length of the bar is the schedule duration for that activity. The overall timeline of the project can be computed by summing the non-overlapping bar segments. Dependencies between bars are not usually shown.
IEC	International Electro-technical Convention.
IEEE	Institute of Electrical and Electronics Engineers.
Information radiators	Radiators are dashboards, whiteboards, newsletters, and other media distribution.
Investment	Money put up by the business to fund a project. Investment is the money on the business side of the project balance sheet; funding demand is the project estimate that corresponds to investment. Investment and demand may not be equal.
ISO	International Standards Organization.
JAD	Joint application design, a practice whereby users and developers sit together for a design session. JAD sessions can be part of an agile iteration.
Knowledge area	A body of knowledge about how to do tasks, or activities, that has a common association. Example: risk management.
Method or practice	A means of doing a specific activity within a knowledge area. Generally speaking, there are inputs which drive actionable steps, thereby producing outcomes. Example: Monte Carlo simulation of schedule outcome.
Methodology	Activities linked to produce an outcome, with the specific methods or practices of each activity identified. In effect, a methodology is a lifecycle of the project (a PDLC as we have described elsewhere). Example: Crystal Clear.

N^2	The number of unique communication paths between N individuals is given by the formula $N \times (N - 1)$. When N is large, this formula is effectively N^2.
Nontraditional methodologies	See agile methods.
Operating model	Operating model is a synonym for the organization chart of the project. Operating model also stands for the roles, responsibilities, and relationships of individuals in the project operation, even if not full-time or administratively assigned.
Osmotic communication	Osmotic communications refers to communications by osmosis: absorbing information in your immediate vicinity, whether directly or indirectly intended for you.
Pipeline	Pipelines and pipelining are terms that describe the use of a scorecard to capture data that seems to flow by.
PMI	Project Management Institute, a professional association for project managers.
Practice standard	An agreed upon way of doing a practice, where the agreement is managed by a standards body (organization) with credentials in the standards community. Example ISO/IEC 12207 practice standard for software engineering.
Process	Like a methodology, activities linked to produce an outcome, although the methods may not be specified. Example: project initiating process.
Process miniature	A benchmark of the team process with a scaled-down process for quick turnaround of benchmark numbers.
Product	The intended outcome or deliverables of a project that is useful to a customer and fits the customer's idea of quality in the large sense: feature, function, effective in application, efficient to use, environmentally compatible, and economically operable and supportable throughout a useful lifespan. Product may be tangible or intangible, and it may be a process, system, application, or product for internal or external customers.

Product base	The current *gold copy* of the product that is in production. The gold copy is the standard to which all other copies are compared. Increments of new product are added to the product base at each release.
Providers	See Contractor.
PSP	Personal Software Process is a service mark of Carnegie Mellon University.
Pull	A *lean* methods concept whereby external ideas from the customer community are pulled into the design rather than relying on developer whim to push new ideas out.
RAD	Rapid Application Design, a prototyping methodology for quick-reaction design and coding.
RAM	Resource Assignment Matrix, a matrix presentation of the operating model and the work breakdown.
RUP	Rational Unified Process, a set of practices from IBM/ Rational.
Self-organizing	A team has successfully arrived at self-organization when it can operate autonomously, cross-fertilize itself with knowledge from its participants, and set its own goals that may, in some cases, transcend those of management.
Six Sigma	Six Sigma is a quality management process in which a problem analysis protocol is followed by solutions that implement error control within approximately 3.4 defects allowable outside control limits in a million opportunities. Errors are sensed and corrective information is fed back to bring the process within the Six Sigma boundaries.
SOA	Service Oriented Architecture.
Stakeholder	Primarily a business unit or individual that is in the supply chain, or provides some resources to the project, but has no specific commitment to project success. In other words, involved but not committed.
Story point	A story point as a quantity of effort to develop one unit of product with minimum relative complexity; in effect, *a story point results in a unit of outcome.*
Supplier	See Contractor.

Team	A team is a social structure wherein all members individually and mutually work collaboratively for the achievement of a common goal only attainable by committed, collective contribution of all members.
Timeline	A timeline is measured in units of time, but has no reference to a calendar. When a timeline is affixed to a calendar, it becomes a schedule.
Time box	A time box is a prescribed length of time for a set of multifunctional activities. Scope is modified to fit the time box, not the other way around. The daily stand-up meeting is done with a time box. Each development iteration and planning wave is time-boxed.
TPM	Technical performance measures envision periodic measurements of technical achievement, comparison of achievements to benchmarks, and then actions to mitigate variances.
Traditional methodologies	Methodologies that are planned-out at the outset and managed centrally according to the plan to produce outcomes. The emphasis is on predictable results according to the specifications of the plan (a PD-PDLC as we have described elsewhere). Example: waterfall.
TSP	Team Software Process is a service mark of Carnegie Mellon University.
UML	Unified Modeling Language, a text and diagrammatic language for specifying the interaction of actors and systems.
Uncertainty	Uncertainty is risk without knowledge of an unfavorable event or neutralizing mitigation.
Universal Modeling Language	See UML.
Use case	A text or diagrammatic specification within the UML that specifies a specific operational scenario involving actors and systems.
User	See Customer.
Velocity	Applied generally to all agile methods, velocity is an XP term that is a measure of throughput: objects actually put into production.

Walking skeleton	The construction of a tiny, end-to-end functionality that works and can be used to build more functionality incrementally; gives the customer an early first look.
Waterfall	Another name for traditional methods, though misleading, because most traditional methods have feedback from step to step.
	Waterfall is the name given to a sequential project plan that roughly steps along from gathering requirements, to designing the solution, to developing and testing the solution, and then delivering the outcomes.
	It gets its name from the appearance on charts of a series of cascading steps.
	To improve the waterfall sequencing, an iteration back to prior steps was added in the 1970s.
WBS	Work breakdown structure, a means to depict how project deliverables are related and organized.
Wicked	A problem description whereby the problem is described by the solution; typically, there are so many competing and circular dependencies that no up-front problem statement is possible.

Index

Note: Page numbers followed by "*f*", "*n*", and "*t*" refer to figures, notes, and tables respectively.